THE PRINCIPAL AS
PROFESSIONAL DEVELOPMENT
LEADER

THE PRINCIPAL AS PROFESSIONAL DEVELOPMENT LEADER

Phyllis H. Lindstrom • Marsha Speck

CORWIN PRESS
A Sage Publications Company
Thousand Oaks, California

For information:

Corwin Press
A Sage Publications Company
2455 Teller Road
Thousand Oaks, California 91320
www.corwinpress.com

Sage Publications Ltd.
1 Oliver's Yard
55 City Road
London EC1Y 1SP
United Kingdom

Sage Publications India Pvt. Ltd.
B-42, Panchsheel Enclave
Post Box 4109
New Delhi 110 017 India

Printed in the United States of America

Library of Congress Cataloging-in-Publication Data

Lindstrom, Phyllis H.

The principal as professional development leader : building capacity for improving student achievement/by Phyllis H. Lindstrom and Marsha Speck.
      p. cm.
Includes bibliographical references (p.) and index.
ISBN 0-7619-3907-5 — ISBN 0-7619-3908-3 (pbk.)
    1. School principals—United States. 2. School personnel management—United States. 3. Teachers—In-service training—United States. 4. School improvement programs—United States. I. Speck, Marsha. II. Title.
LB2831.92.L53 2004
371.2′012—dc222

                                                2003022790

This book is printed on acid-free paper.

03   04   05   06   10   9   8   7   6   5   4   3   2   1

Acquisitions Editor:	Rachel Livsey
Editorial Assistant:	Phyllis Cappello
Production Editor:	Kristen Gibson
Copy Editor:	Carla Freeman
Typesetter:	C&M Digitals (P) Ltd.
Indexer:	David Luljak
Proofreader:	Ruth Saavedra
Cover Designer:	Tracy E. Miller

Contents

Foreword

It warms my heart to have the privilege of writing a foreword for a book titled *The Principal as Professional Development Leader,* particularly a book that will prove as useful to its readers as this one. For many years, I told anyone who would listen that it was critically important that principals view themselves as staff developers. But even some of the most talented principals would resist my claim, and I eventually understood that they do so because they could not see themselves as skillful presenters, trainers, or consultants—the responsibilities most commonly associated with being a "staff developer."

As a result, I began to draw a distinction between staff development leaders and staff development providers. *The National Staff Development Council's Staff Development Code of Ethics* makes this distinction:

> Many individuals who make important decisions about staff development have not traditionally viewed themselves as "staff developers." To help clarify the various staff development responsibilities assumed by school board members, teachers, administrators, and other school employees, this Code of Ethics divides these responsibilities into two categories: staff development leader and staff development provider.
>
> Staff development leaders are individuals within a school, school district, university, state education agency, or other educational organization who plan, implement, coordinate, and/or evaluate staff development efforts. They include but are not limited to directors of staff development, superintendents, school board members, principals, curriculum coordinators, and teacher leaders.
>
> Staff development providers use their knowledge and skills to promote adult learning or to help groups and organizations perform more effectively. They include trainers, facilitators, consultants, mentors, and instructional and leadership coaches.

The *Staff Development Code of Ethics* offers a number of principles that I am pleased to say Phyllis Lindstrom and Marsha Speck have emphasized in their book:

- Staff development leaders are committed to achieving school and district goals, particularly those addressing high levels of learning and performance for all students and staff members.
- Staff development leaders select staff development content and processes that are research based and proven in practice after examining various types of information about student and educator learning needs.
- Staff development leaders continuously improve their work through the ongoing evaluation of staff development's effectiveness in achieving school system and school student learning goals.
- Staff development leaders continuously improve their knowledge and skills.

The Staff Development Code of Ethics provides a broad and important context from which *The Principal as Professional Development Leader* can be viewed. First, they both recognize that school leadership is a moral endeavor. "Behavior that is regarded as ethical," the *Code of Ethics* says, "is described as beneficial to everyone involved, truthful and accurate, and based on a commitment to doing one's duty, keeping promises, and not causing harm." Lindstrom and Speck express it this way: ". . . America needs well-informed principals to focus on ensuring high-quality educational experiences for all students. This means improving the instruction in every classroom. It is no longer a luxury to conduct professional development in our schools."

Second, the *Code* and *The Principal as Professional Development Leader* make it clear that leaders matter and that the actions of individuals can have a profound effect on their organizations, particularly as mediated by the relationships and cultures they establish. "High-quality professional development," Lindstrom and Speck write, "is a means to help reculture the school and improvement practice. The principal as professional development leader must understand deeply how changes take place in the structure and culture of the school organization and create a culture that understands and values high-quality professional development."

Third, both the *Code* and this book recognize that, as Lindstrom and Speck explain it, "Professional development is a lifelong, collaborative learning process that nourishes the growth of individuals, teams, and the school through a daily job-embedded, learner-centered focused approach." That learning begins when leaders understand that it is important that they embody the changes they seek in others and then continue to grow alongside teachers and students.

A number of phrases that Lindstrom and Speck use in their book resonate with me—*shared leadership, professional learning community,* and *job-embedded learning* are but a few. Likewise, their view that effective principals serve as builders, designers, implementers, and reflective leaders is in tune with what I also regard as essential leadership responsibilities. School leaders who give this book the sustained attention it deserves will be rewarded for their effort, as will the teachers and students for whom they work.

—Dennis Sparks
Executive Director
National Staff Development Council

Preface

All school principals are keenly aware that their schedules are fairly unforgiving and accountability expectations are high. There is no "down time" during the day or, for that matter, during the school year. The typical school resonates with a constant buzz of activity. First and foremost is the goal of improving student learning. Every principal wants to know how to use time better to achieve improved instruction rather than just add more to the schedule. Unfortunately, professional development is often viewed as an "add-on," and the idea of the principal as the professional development leader can be daunting. "I cannot be all things to all people," lamented a principal recently. Yet it is clear from recent educational research that site-based, job-embedded professional development that becomes an integrated part of the daily work within the school can better serve the learning process of the adults and thus actually improve student learning. This last point is extremely important, especially in providing high-quality teachers for every classroom. There is absolutely no reason to consistently engage in any adult learning at a school if it does not successfully target improving the educational opportunities for students. *The Principal as Professional Development Leader* has been crafted as a book for busy principals and other school leaders that provides insights, models, strategies, skills, and tools to help build the capacity of professional learning within the school in order to close the achievement gap and improve learning for all students. This book offers a road map for the journey.

With the pace of change in schools and society, the need for continuous, high-quality, and aligned professional development is critical. Today's principal and teachers, faced with demands of students, parents, and the community to provide quality education for all students, must be professionally prepared, not at one point of time, but continually professionally prepared. Without the sound practices of quality professional development understood by the principal, schools cannot effectively change. Professional development means a lifelong, collaborative learning process that nourishes the growth of individuals, teams, and the school through a daily job-embedded, learner-centered approach. It emerges from and meets the learning needs of participants as well as clearly focuses on improving student learning. Professional development is not something that is done to individuals or faculties on a periodic basis as new mandates or educational fads appear. It is an ongoing renewal process that permeates the professional learning community culture. It becomes a part of the complex nature of a successful school environment.

Given the demands of high expectations and increased accountability, a principal's understanding of professional development is a critical leverage point for sustained change and improved student achievement. It is our intent with this book to help principals understand their role as professional development leaders to enable collaborative sustained learning for teachers and other staff that directly affects student learning. This book simplifies and focuses the work of the principal as professional development leader by providing scenarios, processes, context, and content that principals can use in planning, implementing, and evaluating long-term professional development for their schools. As former school principals, we believe that this book specifically provides principals the tools and the procedures needed to help teachers and staff grow professionally.

With this background, we invite you to an overview of the book. The *Principal's Scenarios* that begin each chapter are intended to ground the reader in the reality of the work. The *Focused Questions* will provoke deeper thought about the chapter topic to focus the reading and learning to the reader's specific context. Research and best practices are provided so that the reader has a clear foundation regarding professional development and examples of what works in schools.

Chapter 1, "What It Means to be a Professional Development Leader," provides an overview of our professional development model as well and the importance of the principal as a professional development leader within the school. The chapter focuses on the roles of the principal as professional development leader and the impact on the school culture. Professional development is viewed as the key lever for creating the change necessary to close the student achievement gap. A model is presented as a lens for understanding the framework of the book, including the principal's role and critical components for high-quality professional development.

Chapter 2, "Builder: Building the Capacity of the Professional Learning Community," specifically provides guidance for understanding the school culture and targeting goals for professional development. Readers will be able to compare their schools to a research-based, high-quality professional development model using a rubric. Tools are provided to help the reader prepare a long-range professional development plan, including assessing the need, considering data, and understanding individual differences.

Chapter 3, "Designer: Developing Focus, Plans, and Resources," advances the model to the planning stage and includes critical strategies that can be used as alternatives to the traditional inservice. The National Staff Development Council Standards are introduced. Examples of "inside knowledge" and "outside knowledge" are provided.

Chapter 4, "Implementer: Taking Action," emphasizes the conditions, supports, and various models, strategies, and tools that can be used by a principal or other school leaders to take the necessary action that will lead to improved professional practices and student achievement. "Implementation" represents all the professional development planning put into action through a systematic process.

Chapter 5, "Reflective Leader: Evaluating Results," explains the final section of the model and gives credibility to the cycle of inquiry, continuous reflection on practice, and evaluation of progress. Principals are also encouraged to reflect on their own learning.

Chapter 6, "The Principal as Change Agent: The Challenge for the Future," serves as a summary to the book and a call to action for leadership and learning. A journey map is provided to assist principals and other school leaders in focusing on their own work and the steps to take to integrate high-quality professional development into the daily work and professional learning of the school.

Resources: The final section of the book provides the principal with additional readings, resources, and Web sites as a means of exploring and expanding the possibilities of professional learning.

We invite you to begin, and continue, the principal's journey as a professional development leader.

Acknowledgments

No book is created in isolation. We gratefully acknowledge our colleagues, mentors, friends, and families. Without their support, this work could not have been completed.

To our colleagues at San José State University—Dean Susan Meyers, Barbara Gottesman, Marty Krovetz, Gilberto Arriaza, Jim Ritchie, Noni Reis, and Gerry Chartrand—we appreciate your encouragement and the lively educational discussions. We are grateful to our practitioner colleagues, Mike Welch, Pat Stelwagon, Caroll Knipe, and Jeannie Steeg for their wonderful insights. Every learner has mentors, and we would like to thank Frank Smith, Ann Lieberman, and Marty Krovetz for being ours. In addition, we would like to express our appreciation for all the leaders in the field of educational professional development, such as Dennis Sparks, Stephanie Hirsh, Ann Lieberman, Lynne Miller, Tom Guskey, Rick DuFour, Bruce Joyce, Beverly Showers, Judith Warren Little, Caroll Knipe, and Richard Elmore.

Thank you to Rachel Livsey, our editor, and the Corwin Press staff. Rachel's thoughtful editorial comments and support throughout the process helped tremendously. We are appreciative of Corwin's expertise and diligence in making this book possible. We were fortunate to have strong reviewers and owe sincere gratitude to each for their thoughtful critiques and insights that strengthened the content of this book: Dennis Sparks, William A. Sommers, Becky Cooke, Caroll Knipe, Marian Reimann, Flo Hill-Winstead, Bobbie Eddins, Eva Long, and Daryl Eason.

Finally, to our friends and family who have been patient and tolerant with us, we are deeply indebted. We are especially grateful to Bob Lindstrom and Sue Webber for their encouragement and support of our professional work and writing; without them, we could not have completed this timely work.

We welcome your comments regarding *The Principal as Professional Development Leader*. Please e-mail us: Phyllis H. Lindstrom email: plindstrom72@hotmail.com or Marsha Speck email: mslvtennis @aol.com.

About the Authors

Phyllis H. Lindstrom is a leader in school improvement issues and has a strong interest in developing collaborative leadership in schools. She is an associate professor of Educational Leadership at San José State University. In addition, her long career in K–12 education includes teacher, principal, director, and assistant superintendent. She serves on the board of directors of Futures in Education, an alternative education secondary school district in California. Through her research with secondary schools that sustain success, she understands the importance of collaboration and shared leadership. The focus of her recent work has been professional development as the lever of school improvement and improved student learning. She earned an EdD from Teachers College, Columbia University, an MA from United States International University, and a BA from California State University, Long Beach.

Phyllis enjoys visits with her grandsons, boating, traveling and reading. She can be reached at San José State University, One Washington Square, San Jose, CA 95192-0072 or via e-mail at plindstrom72@hot mail.com.

Marsha Speck is a leader in school reform, educational leadership and professional development issues. Her professional interests include building leadership capacity among teachers, administrators, and the community to improve schooling and achievement for all students and developing school-university partnerships that model these practices. She is currently Professor of Educational Leadership at San José State University. Marsha is the Director of the Urban High School Leadership Program, which is an innovative leadership development program linked as a partnership with regional school districts for teacher leaders and administrators to rethink the American high school and how it meets the needs of students and the community. She has diverse experiences as a teacher, high school principal, assistant superintendent of instruction, and professor, where she has worked collaboratively on school change efforts. She believes in a continued partnership linkage between the university and the school community, which is exemplified in her work. Creating school learning communities has been a central focus of her work with schools. She has published widely, including *Why Can't We Get It Right? Professional Development for Our Schools* (Corwin best seller); *The Essential Questions and Practices in Professional Development; The Principalship: Building a Learning Community* (for Prentice Hall); and *The Handbook for Implementing Year-Round Education in the High School* (for the National Association for Year-Round Education). Currently, Marsha is the president of the National Association for Year-Round Education and serves on the Leadership Council of the Association for Supervision and Curriculum Development. San José State University recognized her as a Teacher Scholar (1996–1997) in recognition of contributions toward promoting the scholarship of teaching, especially in education leadership. Her Fulbright Scholarship includes study in India, Nigeria, and Israel. She received a BA from the University of California, Davis; an MA from California State University, Stanislaus; and an EdD from the University of the Pacific.

Traveling, tennis, and reading are a few of Marsha's passions when she is not working on leadership issues. She can be reached at San José State University, One Washington Square, San Jose, CA 95192-0072 or via e-mail at mslvtennis@aol.com.

Dedication

We dedicate this book to all principals, other site leaders, and school staff who make a difference for students on a daily basis.

CHAPTER ONE

What It Means to Be a Professional Development Leader

Learning and leadership are inextricably intertwined.

—John F. Kennedy

Focused Questions

What does "principal as professional development leader" mean?

What is the meaning of "high quality professional development?"

What "focused questions" does a principal need as a professional development leader?

What are the critical roles for the principal as professional development leader and the impact on improved student learning?

Principal's Scenario

Juanita Sanchez, principal of Chavez School, is driving back from the district office August kickoff meeting for the new school year. As she drives, she thinks of all the dilemmas, demands, and challenges that face her as principal this year from the district, teachers, students, parents, and school community. As she arrives at the school parking lot, she can't help but reflect on the last school year and the lost days of summer when she was going to get so much done. The district office meeting inspired her, but she thinks, now the real work starts here at her own school! She decides to walk around the school, visit a few classrooms and check out the building and grounds before returning to her office.

As she enters the hallways of the school, she asks herself, "What is the most important thing I could do as principal to help raise student achievement and support my teachers in this effort?" Also, "How can I help teachers increase their success with each student, thus improving classroom and schoolwide achievement?" Before the busy demands of the school year starts, Juanita really wants to get focused by dealing with the district office mandates, schoolwide goals, and individual needs of her teachers, students, and school community. She stops and imagines the classrooms, hallways, and school grounds with teachers and students who are well prepared and achieving at high standards rather than being the lowest-performing school in the district. Out loud, she asks, "How do we get there?" Just as the words come out of her mouth, a veteran teacher pops out of his classroom and sees Juanita.

Mike: Juanita, what do you mean how do we get there? You look concerned. Is there something the matter?

Juanita: (surprised, but glad to see Mike): I've just returned from the district office kickoff meeting, and the list is endless of what needs to be done. I was just picturing the school as high achieving and asking how to achieve it this year.

Mike: Well, we've got a good start with our leadership team, but I think we are missing a process that lasts more than a few weeks, month, or a year. We know what we want. We just need to determine clearly how we will do it rather than keep changing with every new demand and confusing our teachers and parents.

Juanita: What do you mean by "process"?

Mike: It seems to me we need a process that helps us as teachers at Chavez better meet the student needs.

Juanita: You know, you just sparked something that I believe deeply about after all the past practices and research I've experienced. First, I know I can't do it all. I need teachers, parents, and the school community support. Second, professional development matters most to support teachers, and I don't mean the old "sit and get" inservices. Mike, you're right, a sustained professional development process, which meets the needs for increasing student learning and achievement, is the critical piece. We need to sharpen our focus to do this.

Mike: Wow! I thought I was just fixing my classroom up for the start of school. Now I think the leadership team and staff should discuss a professional development process that empowers us to design what learning needs we have based on our student and school achievement needs. Maybe this will really sustain the change we've always been talking about.

Juanita: Yes and we're going to do it together because I know if teachers continue to learn, grow, and succeed, student achievement will soar. We can't keep doing the same things in the same way because we know what we've gotten. Learning, grappling, practicing, and reflecting on our own growth as professionals and as a school will make the difference. This year and each day forward, we're going to work together to focus our learning efforts. Thanks for sharing your thoughts and hearing my wondering out loud.

Mike: We'll see, and I hope for best! Let me know how we can help! Professional development, huh! I wonder what Janet, as the teacher's union rep, will say about this? How do we know what really works in professional development?

Juanita: The leadership team will get a call today to set up a meeting to discuss the professional development process, and I want you to share your insights. We need to get an early start so we can share and get input from the faculty at our first-of-the-year meeting. I'm excited. Now I'd like to see what you've been doing to your room, and thanks again, a principal needs to share.

INTRODUCTION

Will schools change to meet the critical goal of our society for well-educated, productive citizens? If so, America needs well-informed principals to focus on ensuring high-quality educational experiences for all students. This means improving the instruction in every classroom. It is no longer a luxury to conduct professional development in our schools. Professional development is an essential and job-embedded component of any school improvement effort. It is a key leverage point for sustainable change in our schools, and it should be a way of life within every school. For high-quality professional development to occur at the site, the principal has a critical leadership role.

Teacher knowledge and its correlation to continued professional growth are the most significant factors relating to student success (Darling-Hammond, 1997). Elmore (2002c) says that the "Achilles' heel" of education today is the great variability between classrooms within a school. As the instructional leaders, principals are compelled to provide the type of support necessary to address that variability. In addition, more and more teachers are entering the classrooms under-prepared for the realities of providing quality education in today's world. Barth (1990) reinforces this with the statement that "nothing within a school has more impact on students in terms of skills development, self-confidence, or classroom behaviors than the personal and professional growth of their teachers" (p. 49). The professional learning of teachers is a central factor in determining the quality of teaching (Sparks, 2002). If principals expect to close the achievement gap for students, then principals must have a deeper understanding of what it takes to improve teaching and learning.

According to DuFour (2003), effective leaders take action. They do not wait for everything to fall into place, because they truly understand that the learning that occurs in a "professional learning community" happens during the course of the action. This book is designed to assist principals in taking appropriate action to implement and sustain effective schoolwide professional development.

Recently, the National Staff Development Council (NSDC) revised its standards for professional development (2001). Based on the premises that improved learning for all students is the goal and that the main difference between learning and not learning is the quality of the teaching (Barth, 1990; Darling-Hammond, 1997; Sparks, 2002), these standards provide the floor upon which a solid professional development program can be built. The 12 standards are divided into the categories of context, process, and content. The NSDC standards are embedded throughout this book for principals to deepen their understanding of their meaning and use. Chapter 2 will provide a more complete view of the NSDC standards.

> **What does "principal as professional development leader" mean?**

For principals to best develop the vision of quality education for all students, they must have a clear understanding, as well as the skills and abilities, to help lead professional development efforts within their schools. Educational researchers view professional development as the *key leverage point* for providing opportunities for continuously improved educational practices by teachers and staff to obtain higher student achievement (Darling-Hammond, 1997; David & Shields, 2001; Elmore, 2002a; Lieberman, 1995a; Sparks & Hirsh, 1997). School improvement happens when a school develops a professional learning community that focuses on standards, achievement, student work, and changing teaching practices. According to Fullan (1999), a principal and school trying to improve must think of professional development as a cornerstone strategy.

Professional development creates the change necessary to continually improve the teachers' practices that will close the achievement gap. This chapter will provide the overview as well as the meaning to the importance of the principal as a professional development leader within the school. The principal-as-professional-development-leader model presents a lens for understanding the framework of the book (see Figure 1.1).

As the model shows, the principal must have a *clear focus on improving student learning and achievement.* To reach this goal, continuous professional development within the school provides the *context,*

Figure 1.1   Principal as Professional Development Leader: Building Capacity for Improving Student Achievement

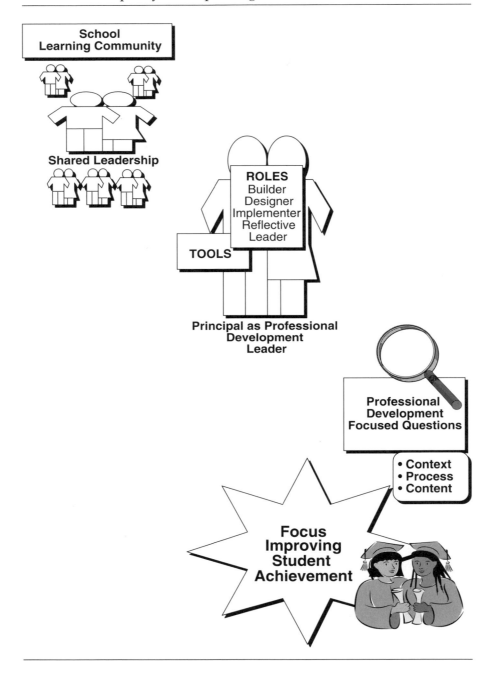

Figure 1.2   Shared Leadership—School Learning Community

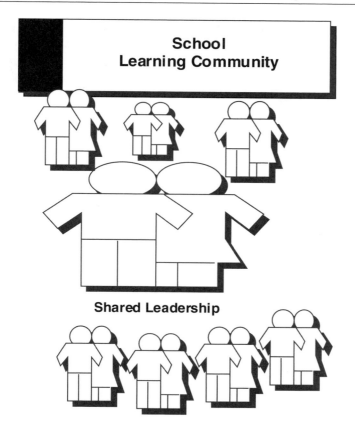

process, and content that helps create the changes in teacher classroom practices and school culture. Principals must possess the ability to ask themselves *focused questions* to guide their thinking and responses that help keep professional development on track. The school learning community, through *shared leadership* and ownership with the principal, sets the direction and carries out the professional development work (see Figure 1.2). The principal is not the sole leader of professional development, since it is imperative that leadership be shared within the school learning community. As Lambert (2002) puts it, "The days of the principal as the lone instructional leader are over. We no longer believe that one administrator can serve as the instructional leader for an entire school without the substantial participation of other educators" (p. 37).

SHARED LEADERSHIP

Shared leadership is a key component of a professional learning community. Having everyone involved in the work of the school not only creates team thinking but also provides the forum for the best thinkers to consider the intractable issues of education. It turns the lonely "I" into the productive "We." The task of the principal as professional development leader is to make this professional learning community happen as a shared school community undertaking. The premise of this book is that leadership and professional development are the work of everyone in the school, with the principal assuming the shared leadership roles of *Builder, Designer, Implementer,* and *Reflective Leader* to create the professional development frames that make a difference in student achievement. A variety of *tools* are available that a principal and school can use to implement powerful professional development experiences and build capacity. Chapter 2 further explores how to build a professional learning community. The old model of one-person leadership leaves out the tremendous talents of teachers and does not have the sustainability if the principal leaves (Lambert, 2002).

More than a decade ago, Barth encouraged principals to cast aside the notion of principals as the authority and "knower" and to become learners alongside the teachers and students. His term for this type of principal is the "Lead Learner" (Barth, 1990, 2001). Learning together creates a community that is dedicated to sharing and discovering what works well.

Sharing leadership is a challenge for many principals. For example, in one school, a teacher attending a principal-led faculty meeting, shortly after returning from a week's stint as a reader and scorer of a national exam, listened while the principal explained that there would be changes to the national test but that there was no information available regarding the changes. The teacher proceeded to tell the staff what the new changes would be, since they were provided at the scoring session. The principal became visibly annoyed, and the teacher, embarrassed, quickly stopped sharing her expert knowledge. Later, she wondered why it was so difficult for this principal to allow anyone else to be an expert. As this scenario demonstrates, shared leadership must be a part of the school culture to be inclusive and effective. In schools that have built a learning community, everyone acknowledges the need to learn together, and that means everyone can participate as the "teacher" or the "learner" on one topic or another. If the meeting agenda was too packed to continue with the discussion of the changes in the national exam, the principal could have acknowledged the teacher's expertise and recent experience as scorer of the exam and scheduled the discussion for another time.

Elmore (2000) describes this complex nature of instructional practice as requiring people to operate in networks of shared and complementary expertise rather than in hierarchies that have a clearly defined division of labor. Professional knowledge and practice get stretched across roles rather than being inherent in one role or another. By placing the responsibility of professional development within the school through a shared leadership model, more ownership is developed, and action is taken to improve areas of concern and build on achievements. Developing the professional capacity within the school means collaborative leadership and shared professional work. It is this kind of ongoing investment in the professional development of teachers and leaders that provides sustainable school improvement.

In addition to the shared responsibility to professional development, educators are responsible for their own learning. The individual and the school community of learners need to take action to keep themselves professionally current to meet the needs of the ever-changing diverse student population. This fundamental belief holds that as a school learning community, we are responsible for directing our learning as collaborative colleagues. Darling-Hammond (1997) states:

> When all is said and done, what matters most for students' learning are the commitments and capacities of their teachers. Teaching for understanding cannot be produced solely by spending more money or by requiring that schools use specific texts or curriculum packages, and it cannot be driven by mandating new tests, even better ones. Although things like standards, funding, and management are essential supports, the sine qua non of education is whether teachers know how to make complex subjects accessible to diverse learners and whether they can work in partnership with parents and other educators to support children's development. If only a few teachers have this capacity, most schools will never be able to produce better education for the full range of students who attend them. Widespread success depends on the development of a professional base of knowledge along with a commitment to the success of all students (pp. 293–294).

The traditional view of professional development is prescribed inservice with individual expectations. In a learning community, everyone is responsible for his or her own learning as well as that of colleagues. In this book, we have used terms such as *collaboration* and *collegial.* We attempt to define terms within the context of the text; however, these two terms seem to capture different meanings for different people, so we wish to address them. Common definitions of collaboration in schools are "working together" and "teamwork." The term collegial is a bit more difficult to define. We support Warren Little's effort to describe collegiality in schools through a list of behaviors:

Adults talk about practice

Adults observe each other

Adults engage together in work on curriculum

Adults teach each other what they know about teaching, learning and leading.

(cited in Barth, 1990, p. 31)

> What is the meaning of
> high-quality professional development?

REDEFINING THE MEANING OF PROFESSIONAL DEVELOPMENT

What does the term *professional development* mean? Professional development is a lifelong, collaborative learning process that nourishes the growth of individuals, teams, and the school through a daily, job-embedded, learner-centered, focused approach. It emerges from and meets the learning needs of participants as well as clearly focuses on improving student learning. Professional development is not something that is done to individuals or faculties on a periodic basis as new mandates or educational fads appear. It is an ongoing sustainable process (see Figure 1.3) that builds collaboration, generates and shares professional knowledge, uses current research, and informs the daily work of teachers and leaders (Darling-Hammond,

Figure 1.3   Professional Development Cycle

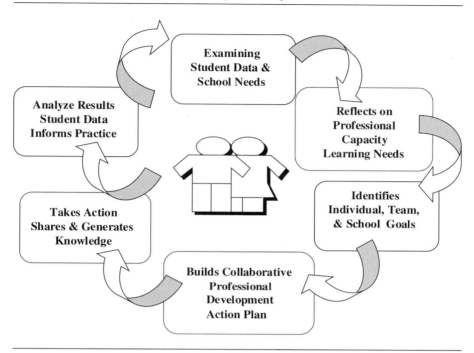

1997; Elmore, 2002a; Stigler & Hiebert, 1999). This emphasis on continuous improvement of professional practices is vital to a true understanding of professional development in our schools by principals. Professional development becomes an integrated part of the daily work within the school. It is not seen as an add-on or a mandated requirement, but rather as professional practice of honing knowledge to better serve the learning process of both adults and students. It is an ongoing renewal process that permeates the professional learning community culture.

Improved student achievement will occur with well-informed, highly qualified teachers using effective strategies. We can no longer afford to maintain the status quo and should heed the old adage that "if you keep doing the same thing in the same ways, you get the same results." The principal must understand the critical role professional development plays in bringing about change in instructional practice. The power of professional development is a critical leverage point for sustained change that will provide the means to produce the expected results of improved student achievement.

IMPORTANCE OF HIGH-QUALITY PROFESSIONAL DEVELOPMENT

Elmore (2002b) provides us with an important insight about the structures of schools and why professional learning is not clearly conceived by educators when he states:

> People who work in schools do not pay attention to the connection between how they organize and manage themselves and how they take care of their own and their students' learning. The structure and resources of the organization are like wallpaper—after living with the same wallpaper for a certain number of years, people cease to see it.
>
> In the present political and social environment of schooling, this lack of attention is dangerous and irresponsible. Schools are under pressure for increased accountability for student learning, and too many educators cannot account for the basic elements of their organization and how these elements affect the learning that teachers and students engage in. Further, most educators would argue that they need more resources to do the work they are being asked to do under these new accountability systems. But why give more resources to an organization whose leaders cannot explain how they are using the resources that they already have? (pp. 22–23)

Professional development typically is used to carry out a school reform agenda. Yet despite the considerable resources that most schools devote to professional development (6 to 10 days per year is not unusual), teachers and administrators alike generally have negative opinions of professional development practices. Most educators view professional development as an ad hoc, disconnected series of one-time activities that have little or no impact on improving student learning or the school culture in general.

High-quality professional development is a means to help reculture the school and improve practice. A principal as a professional development leader must understand deeply how changes take place in the structure and culture of the school organization and create a culture that understands and values high-quality professional development. It is hard work to redirect schools toward a common vision of high expectations for all students, strengthen academic curricula, tailor instruction to students' interests and life experiences, and carry

Figure 1.4   High-Quality Professional Development Key Components

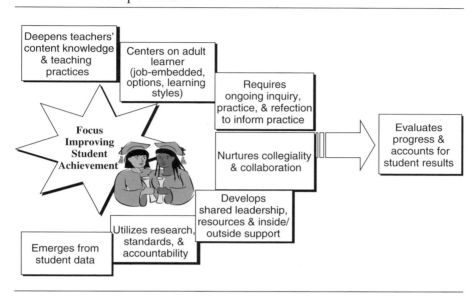

out multiple assessment measures of students' progress. This book is designed to provide tools for dealing with these issues. Chapter 2 specifically provides guidance for the change process and reculturing the school.

High-quality professional development should contain nine key components if it is to make a focused and sustained difference in altering the culture and structures of the school to provide a process for continuous improvement (see Figure 1.4).

HIGH-QUALITY PROFESSIONAL DEVELOPMENT COMPONENTS

- Focuses on learning and sustaining improved student learning
- Emerges from student data and the need to improve student results
- Nurtures collegiality and collaboration among teachers, other staff, and principal
- Develops shared leadership, resources, and inside/outside support

- Utilizes research with a foundation in standards and accountability
- Deepens teachers' content knowledge and teaching practices
- Centers on the adult learner through job-embedded work, options, and learning styles
- Requires ongoing inquiry, practice, and reflection to inform practice
- Evaluates progress and accounts for student learning by examining results (Elmore, 2002a; Guskey, 2000; Sparks, 2002; Sparks & Hirsh, 1997; Speck & Knipe, 2001)

The primary goal of a leader for professional development is to focus on and sustain a well-conceived plan for school improvement that reflects these key components. The outcome for this plan is improved student learning, and improved teacher learning can achieve that. Each key component will be addressed here briefly as an overview and will be treated more thoroughly in specific chapters.

Focuses on Learning and Sustaining Improved Student Learning

Professional development is clearly about the learning and improvements in teaching techniques, strategies, and understanding of content that occur after preservice training. Learning is always occurring and is a self-renewing process for the learner. It is the nature of humans. Unfortunately, learning can involve faulty assumption, poor habits, lack of current knowledge, and other undesirable traits that may need to be addressed in a comprehensive, cohesive, and aligned plan. A focus on student learning identifies the needs and direction for the plan. The mantra for school improvement is "How will what we are doing affect student achievement?"

Emerges From Student Data and the Need to Improve Student Results

As teachers, the principal, and the school community analyze schoolwide and individual classroom data, specific areas of concern are identified. Through inquiry into student work and results, there emerges targeted need areas. The experience of examining results and learning together creates a collegial commitment to professional development that is relevant and contextual (Lieberman & Miller, 1999).

Nurtures Collegiality and Collaboration Among Teachers, Other Staff, and the Principal

Professional development must be founded on a sense of collegiality and collaboration among teachers, other staff, and the principal, which becomes the essence of the school culture. A collaborative culture nurtures collegial work and supports an atmosphere of sharing professional knowledge and grappling with tough student achievement and learning issues. Isolation within a single classroom does not work. The richness of colleagues inquiring into practice, trying new strategies (practicing, modeling, coaching each other, and reflecting on practice), and examining results exemplifies the real meaning of continuing to develop as a professional. Professional development is not done to individuals or groups. It is collaboratively created out of engaging colleagues around real learning issues that exist within their classrooms and school. The goals and direction for professional development emerge from colleagues recognizing the needs and issues. The culture of collegiality and collaboration gives each teacher and principal the ongoing support needed as changes in teaching practices and content take place (Barth, 1990; Elmore, 2002b; Little, 1993). Professional teachers act as true colleagues who collaboratively meet, share, inquire, research, practice, and reflect on teaching and learning. Out of the intensive work a principal and teachers do as collaborative colleagues, a new form of professionalism emerges that clearly links leading and learning.

Develops Shared Leadership, Resources, and Inside/Outside Support

Shared leadership in professional development allows a broader understanding, ownership, and continuous focus on the critical issues that need to be addressed. Without shared leadership, professional growth plans are fragmented and episodic with little focus or direction. Principals can help schools focus their efforts by using appropriate resources and inside/outside support. These are powerful means to help carry out professional development plans. Looking inside as well as outside of the school for support, including research, expertise, and best practices, helps nourish and infuse the professional growth opportunities.

Utilizes Research With a Foundation in Standards and Accountability

Professional development can no longer be based on what educators think might work but is not substantiated by research. A research-based plan of action grounded in the standards provides a foundation for credible professional work. Accountability for actions and results brings meaning to the continuous improvement efforts. If professional development is to be of value, then it must demonstrate clear achievements of outcomes (Guskey, 2000). Research-based professional development bridges the gap between standards and achievement (Elmore, 2002a). Recent federal legislation enacting the No Child Left Behind initiative (2001) mandates this kind of professional development.

Deepens Teachers' Content Knowledge and Teaching Practices

Deepening teachers' understanding of specific content knowledge enables teachers to know their subject matter well and provides opportunities to improve instructional and assessment strategies. Using professional development with content-specific knowledge gives teachers rich experiences in what they are teaching as well as integrating the strategies of how they deliver the content. If teachers do not know their content area well, they lack the ability to create learning experiences for students that meet high standards and expectations for learning (Darling-Hammond, 1997).

Centers on Adult Learner Through Job-Embedded Work, Options, and Learning Styles

Professional development efforts have moved away from district-provided, general informational workshops to job-embedded, local-context learning opportunities where options and understanding about the learner and learning style are evident. What is required at each school site to improve student learning must be centered on what the teacher needs to know and be able to do. This learner-centered practice engages teachers in grappling with their daily practice and offers teachers options based on their own learning needs and styles of learning (Sparks, 2002). Honoring the developmental levels and experiences of teachers as they tackle specific classroom and subject matter learning issues gives meaning to ongoing job-embedded daily professional growth (Speck & Knipe, 2001).

Requires Ongoing Inquiry, Practice, and Reflection to Inform Practice

Ongoing inquiry, practice, and reflection to inform practice are critical if professional growth is to be sustained and integrated into daily classroom practices that make a difference for student achievement. A cycle of inquiry into practice by examining student work and results data creates a school culture that continuously reflects on practice (Center for Research on the Context of Teaching, 2002; Sagor, 2000). It is this ability to study, act, and inform practice that provides ongoing focus on the critical teaching and learning issues. Professional development is seen as a daily facet of teachers' real work rather than presented as an episodic, one-time event that is soon forgotten and rarely affects the learning within the school (Elmore, 2002a; Sparks, 2002). By its nature, inquiry into practice is focused on striving for continuous improvement and the means to reach that goal.

Evaluates Progress and Accounts for Student Learning by Examining Results

Evaluation of professional development as a means of making progress toward improved student achievement results is essential. Knowing whether the professional growth that is taking place is worthy of the efforts is a critical aspect of accountability. Evaluating professional development points to what needs to be done or changed (Guskey, 2000). Continuing to do professional development activities that do not generate improved student learning is ineffective. An evaluation process must be in place. The crucial questions here are What is making a difference in student achievement? How do we know? How does this evaluation process inform our current practices and cycle of improvement?

A principal needs to keep these critical components of high-quality professional development clearly in mind when sharing leadership and the development of professional learning plans. Table 1.1 provides a quick checklist a principal can use for developing, implementing, and reviewing a professional development plan.

Next, if we are to have high-quality professional development, principals must look at the questions they ask.

Table 1.1   Principal's Checklist of High-Quality Professional
Development Components

High-Quality Professional Development Components
Principal's Checklist
for
Planning Professional Development

- Focuses on learning and sustaining improved student learning
- Emerges from student data and the needs to improve student results
- Nurtures collegiality and collaboration among teachers, other staff, and principal
- Develops shared leadership, resources, and inside/outside support
- Utilizes research with a foundation in standards and accountability
- Deepens teachers' content knowledge and teaching practices
- Centers on adult learner through job-embedded work, options, and learning styles
- Requires ongoing inquiry, practice, and reflection to inform practice
- Evaluates progress and accounts for student learning by examining results

PAUSE

What "Focused Questions" does
a principal need as a professional development leader?

FOCUSED QUESTIONS FOR THE PRINCIPAL AS PROFESSIONAL DEVELOPMENT LEADER

Emerson once said, "The ancestor of every action is a thought." A pilot uses a checklist prior to every flight, no matter how long or short, to address the important elements of a complex machine. The metaphoric checklists for individuals and organizations are the guiding questions that are asked to focus thoughts, attention, and action. These have been referred to as "Habits of Mind" (Costa & Kallick, 2000; Meier, 1995) or "mental models" (Senge, 1990). In this book, the mental exercise of asking questions to guide thinking and decisions is referred to as "Focused Questions."

Meier's 1995 book, *The Power of Their Ideas: Lessons for America From a Small School in Harlem*, described the development of Central

Park East Secondary School (CPESS). Based on the work of John Dewey, the staff of CPESS decided that the sign of an educated person is reflected by the quality of questions he or she asks. The "habits" were framed as intellectual questions. Then the staff set about developing strategies for in-depth practice of the five questions as a critical part of every student's education. The CPESS Habits of Mind are not just about asking questions, but are more about focused probing and considering the answers. The specific words of the questions may vary, but they are centered on evidence (How do you know?), viewpoint (Who said it?), connections (What causes what?), supposition (How might things have been different?), and if it matters (Who cares?).

It is the premise of this book that the principal as a professional development leader must have "Focused Questions" that frame his or her thinking about professional development. These Focused Questions are tools for each of the roles the leader plays and guide the professional development work (see Figure 1.5). The questions are discussed under each of the roles and will be highlighted in each appropriate chapter (Chapter 2, Builder; Chapter 3, Designer; Chapter 4, Implementer; Chapter 5, Reflective Leader).

Principals who continually utilize these questions keep the focus on the learning goal by posing the important questions and facilitating the professional dialogue, learning, action, and reflection that bring about increased student achievement. The Focused Questions serve as an anchor to hold fast to what is truly important for professional growth. This book provides the principal with the research, experiences, examples, and tools to put the Focused Questions into action that make a difference for teacher learning and student achievement. We invite you to begin the journey of learning as we introduce the roles!

PAUSE

What are the critical roles for the principal
as professional development leader and the impact
on improved student learning?

ROLES AS PROFESSIONAL DEVELOPMENT LEADER

The principal and other site leaders must fully understand the impact they have on the organization and individuals. Certain roles can lead to organizational culture changes that create a professional learning community. To carry out this task, the principal has various roles

Figure 1.5   Focused Questions: Principal as Professional
                 Development Leader

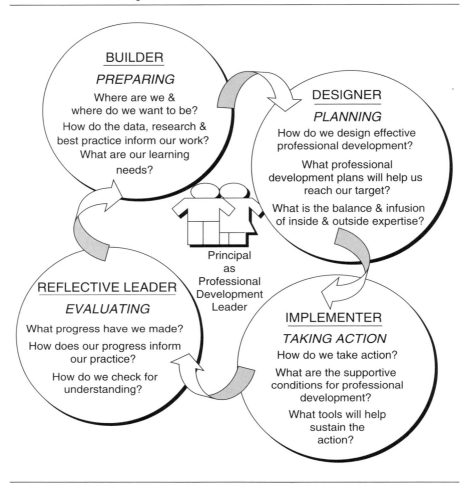

to play in partnership with the school community. The roles of the
principal as a professional development leader are as follows:

- Builder: Preparing the capacity of the professional learning
  community
- Designer: Planning professional development
- Implementer: Taking action
- Reflective Leader: Evaluating results

It is the premise of this book that the principal needs to understand each role to build professional learning within the school. A

Figure 1.6 Roles of Principal as Professional Development Leader

ROLES
Builder
Designer
Implementer
Reflective Leader

brief overview of each of these roles will be shared here (see Figure 1.6), and an in-depth discussion will take place in each of the following chapters (Chapter 2, Builder; Chapter 3, Designer; Chapter 4, Implementer; Chapter 5, Reflective Leader).

Builder: Preparing the Capacity of the Professional Learning Community (PLC)

The preparation role for the principal is as builder of a professional learning community. To carry out this role, the principal should focus on these preparation questions as he or she works with the teachers and the school community.

Builder—Preparing: Focused Questions
Where are we and where do we want to be?
How do the data, research, and best practice inform our work?
What are our learning needs?

Like many important things, "The Vision" can get lost in the hectic day-to-day pace of the principalship. A conscious revisiting is necessary to make the school vision a part of the normal everyday workings of the school. Educators can find themselves often side-tracked by multiple demands and daily crises even when the school vision is written and in hand. The principal has to help the school learning community come to terms with vision and answer the question: *Where are we and where do we want to be?*

For many years, experts have been touting the importance of having a vision for the organization. In the 1985 seminal book about successful business leaders by Bennis and Nanus, *Leaders: The Strategies for Taking Charge,* the first of four strategies for leadership is "Attention Through Vision." Bennis and Nanus argue that "vision is the creating of focus" (p. 28) and that "[a] vision is a target that beckons" (p. 89). Coming on the heels of the effective school research (Coleman, Hoffer, & Kilgore, 1982; Corcoran & Wilson, 1986; Edmonds, 1979; Lightfoot, 1983; Rutter, 1983) that began to define factors leading to excellence in schools, the knowledge that successful leaders used the concept of vision to keep the organization moving forward was simple yet earthshaking. Schools across the country were required to adopt written vision statements as part of school improvement plans.

A shared vision stems from each member of the organization examining his or her own beliefs and assumptions. Only then can the members address the vision for the school. Too often, this step is overlooked, and the vision statements become hollow recitations of slogans or developed by one person rather than clear statements of deeply held beliefs of the organization. Professional development that helps develop shared vision models the process of developing a learning culture within the school.

In schools where the vision exemplifies an agreed-upon future based on attaining excellence, site leaders can continually point to that focus in day-to-day activities. As one former principal stated recently, "No matter what, the staff knows I will ask this question; How does this help us reach our vision?" The goal is for every staff member to ask this question, too.

In creating a collaborative learning community, it is not unusual to uncover thoughts and beliefs that were previously unstated. Assumptions such as "If it weren't for the all the English learners in my classroom, my students' scores would be good" or "Certain students will never be able to learn Algebra" or "The parents don't care about their children's education because they never did well in school themselves" must be challenged. The greatest strength any principal can have is an unwavering passion for all students being held to high standards. The principal sets the tone for continually challenging assumptions and then leading the charge to find a way to change what is happening. The questions the principal continually asks include: *How do the data, research and best practice inform our work? By examining the data, what are our learning needs?*

No other key to success has had such an impact as school personnel truly understanding the context of the students' community. Understanding context is to the school community much like market research is to the business community. Who is out there? What do they want? How can we meet their needs? This includes a deep understanding of ethnic, racial, religious, and other related issues within the community. In addition, socioeconomic and parent education levels must be considered. What community resources are already in place, and which agencies provide services? How can the school connect with the community networks and build on those resources to develop good communication and quality educational opportunities for all the constituents? Barth says in *Improving School From Within* (1990) that educators should create the kind of school that they would want their children to attend. That school needs to reflect the students and the community.

In addition to understanding the school community context, the organizational culture of the school must be addressed. Step on most school campuses, and staff members can be heard to complain about "wasted time" in staff meetings and inservices. Worse yet are the horror stories of committee work and subsequent recommendations being tossed aside as the school leader makes an authoritarian decision that everyone thought would be in the decision-making realm of the committee. Improving process in the school can be described as the professional development for the system. As people grow and change, so do the systems of their organizations. On the flip side of the coin, it has long been recognized that sometimes changing attitudes and beliefs begins with changes in behaviors. Instituting processes that reflect a learning community can begin to change the people and the culture in the organization.

Designer: Planning Professional Development

It is important for the principal to learn about effective professional development and make decisions using the context and the needs of the school.

> Designer—Planning: Focused Questions
> How do we design effective professional development?
> What professional development plans will help us reach our target?
> What is the balance and infusion of inside and outside expertise?

In this era of high-stakes testing, No Child Left Behind (2001) mandates, and public scrutiny, no one needs to remind today's principals that they are highly accountable for the instructional program. If the bottom line is improved student learning, then educators should focus on students and not just learning new teaching strategies for professional development. So, instead of starting with the teacher and classroom techniques, effective principals understand the power of knowing the students well as learners and unique individuals. In *The Results Fieldbook: Practical Strategies From Dramatically Improved Schools,* Schmoker (2001) provides powerful examples of schools and districts that have made gains "[w]hen teachers regularly and collaboratively review assessment data for the purpose of improving practice to reach measurable achievement goals" (p. 1).

According to Calhoun (2002), using data can be initially frightening "because it requires that we juxtapose our practice and our students' performance against exemplary research-based practices and high levels of student performance attained in similar settings" (p. 20). This can be worrisome for some staffs. However, she argues that Action Research, which collaboratively engages teachers, can be "used as a school improvement tool or individual professional development option" (p. 23). Creating a variety of group opportunities within the learning community can be effective. It is more supportive for individuals to be a part of a collaborative effort. The collective focus of the staff will lead to the greatest gains for the students. *How do we design effective professional development? What professional development plans will help us reach our target?*

In a results-driven school culture, the focus is on learning. Student data is analyzed continuously, and a review of the data produces a basis for narrowing the focus and addressing the achievement gaps the data shows. Benchmarks are developed to measure student progress and make the necessary adjustments in the classroom to ensure growth. Professional development plans are created based on these real needs to reach targets for improvement. This is a huge change from the traditional course of professional development focused on new materials, curriculum, and teaching strategies.

Resources and plans are created with this focus in mind. A principal must be ready to plan for, understand, and support the ongoing needs as the learning community grapples with new learning and change. A conscious effort to balance inside knowledge with outside knowledge helps connect the school to the larger community while building the capacity of the teachers to value the knowledge gained through experience (Fullan, 1993: Lieberman, 1996). *What is the balance and infusion of inside and outside expertise?*

Implementer: Taking Action

Taking action is about making changes. Principals need to know "how" and "when" to help initiate the most appropriate changes.

Implementer—Taking Action: Focused Questions
How do we take action?
What are the supportive conditions for professional development?
What tools will help sustain the action?

Researchers agree on many of the facets of change in education. There are phases to the process, change definitely takes time, different types of changes can be implemented, and some schools are especially resilient to change (Fullan, 1993; Fullan & Stiegelbauer, 1991; Goodlad, 1983; Lieberman, 1995b; McLaughlin & Talbert, 1993; Tyack & Cuban, 1997). There are multiple processes for action to create change and the appropriate professional growth. *How do we take action?*

As the professional learning community begins and continues the ongoing process of professional development, there will be various needs for resources such as time, materials, research, and expertise as well as various tools. *What are the supportive conditions for professional development? What tools will help sustain the action?*

Reflective Leader: Evaluating Results

No one would consider taking a journey in unfamiliar territory without occasionally referring to the map, checking for guideposts, and determining progress to the destination. For professional development, each trip is different due to the human nature of the individuals involved.

Reflective Leader—Evaluating: Focused Questions
What progress have we made?
How does our progress inform our practice?
How do we check for understanding?

Reflective leaders constantly consider their actions and gather feedback from others when necessary. Reflection becomes a habit for effective leaders and learning communities. Wanting to know what progress is being made and how that progress is informing practice is critical to the study and reflection on actions. A principal as reflective leader must model a continuous process of inquiry and reflections on actions. A reflective leader asks the following questions of professional development actions: *What progress have we made? How does our progress inform our practice? How do we check for understanding?*

Human brains are wired to observe, consider the information, and then make meaning out of it. Using the process of reflection allows for constructing greater connections and meaning. Periodically checking for understanding not only builds insight but also allows us to share with others and clear up any potential misunderstandings. This evaluation of efforts is critical to finding out what has been accomplished and what needs continued attention. Too often, there is not an established reflection and evaluation process in place to focus the efforts on what has been the clear effect on student achievement.

At the end of each chapter, we have included key points as a summary. Take a moment now and review the key points for Chapter 1. This chapter has served to introduce the model for principal leadership and professional development used throughout this book. We invite you to think deeply about your own school as you begin this journey.

KEY POINTS OF CHAPTER 1

- Professional development is the critical leverage point for change in schools and increased student learning.
- The professional development leader needs to share leadership and build the school culture collaboratively to effect change.
- Professional development is defined as a collaborative learning process that nourishes adult-learner-centered growth in the context of job-embedded work that results in improved student learning.
- High-quality professional development has critical components that must be addressed if professional educators are to grow and schools are to improve.
- Focused Questions will serve to anchor the principal and the professional learning community with continued focus and improvement of student learning.
- There are four critical roles for the principal as a professional development leader: Builder, Designer, Implementer, and Reflective Leader.

Note: At the end of the book, see Resources A and B and Recommended Readings and Web sites. These are meant to be helpful to leaders as they pursue the professional development process.

CHAPTER TWO

The Principal as Builder

Building the Capacity of the Professional
Learning Community

Education is not preparation for life; education is life itself.

—John Dewey

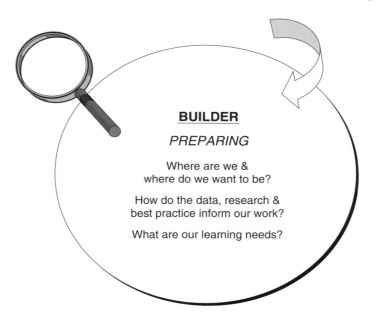

BUILDER

PREPARING

Where are we &
where do we want to be?

How do the data, research &
best practice inform our work?

What are our learning needs?

Principal's Scenario

The Chavez School leadership team meeting was about to begin. Juanita had contacted each member by phone and asked him or her to attend. One teacher was still on vacation with her family and would not be back in time for the meeting. All the other members agreed to attend. Most were planning on working at the school that day anyway to prepare for the fall semester. Juanita briefly told each member about the conversation with Mike and about the idea of a long-term professional development process to improve student learning.

The leadership team was composed of one teacher from each grade level, two specialists, an instructional assistant, and Juanita. Most of the team members were veteran teachers; however, one of the specialists was only in her third year. The team members had developed norms for their meetings that encouraged full participation of each member and open, honest discussions. The team met monthly and reported back to other staff members and parents in formal and informal ways.

In preparing for the meeting, Juanita asked herself, "What is it we need to know to be able to create the best possible long-term plan that will really make a difference?" She pulled out the stacks of student assessment information, circled key scores, and asked Joan, the school secretary, to put the information into computer program spreadsheets. From the Internet, Juanita downloaded an article about high-quality professional development programs and the National Staff Development Council standards and mailed them to the team members with the request that they read them before the meeting. She asked each teacher to bring a copy of the district student grade level standards appropriate to his or her grade level. And finally, she made copies of the vision statement adopted by the school community the previous year.

Juanita:	Thanks for coming to the meeting. I want to make it perfectly clear that I do not have the answers, but I do have a lot of questions.
Yen (laughing):	This reminds me of last year when we worked on the shared vision statement. We finally agreed that it was perfectly okay to learn together.
Juanita:	Yes, and you were all wonderful as we began to lay the foundation for our professional learning community. Now, we need to move to the next step of making

	"learning together through a cycle of inquiry" an important part of our school culture and the basis for our long-term professional development plan.
Anna:	I went to five district staff development sessions last year, and they were all a waste of time. I could have better spent the time working in my classroom. At least my students would have benefited more.
Yen:	That is a good argument for creating a school professional development plan based on our students' needs. We can target in our plan what will benefit our students most.
Jorge:	No matter what we plan and do, it will not make a bit of difference if we don't begin to close the achievement gap between groups of students. I spent some time looking at the assessment data, and I think there are some kids getting shortchanged.
Juanita:	Jorge, why don't you lead us in a discussion about the assessment data and point out the patterns you see? We have some of the scores on spreadsheets, so we can sort the data in a number of ways and create tables or graphs to help us visually understand the data. We can also begin to brainstorm a list of other information we need to fully understand what is happening in our school.

As in most endeavors, valuable time and effort spent in preparation creates the groundwork for the action that follows. In this chapter, the focus is on building and preparing the learning community to take action. Initial assessment and capacity building are keys to an effective long-range professional development plan.

> Where are we, and where
> do we want to be?

There is almost universal agreement that adults rarely learn more than superficial information in traditional types of inservice programs or from motivational speakers (Fullan & Stiegelbaur, 1991; Lieberman & Miller, 1999; Little, 1989; Sparks & Hirsh, 1997; Speck & Knipe, 2001). New skills, attitudes, and beliefs are developed from participating in meaningful experiences with immediate application. Constructing knowledge is a key component of deep learning.

Throughout schools across the nation, teachers complain about inservices and professional development days as a waste of time that could be better spent working in their classrooms. The message is the concern for immediate relevancy to the work they do. Teachers often feel overwhelmed with the complexity of their work and pressure of meeting mandates. Anything they perceive as distracting from that focus is often dismissed as unimportant. This is a particular dilemma for educators. New learning takes time, especially in the beginning stages, and many educators are unwilling to devote that time unless the results are assured. Often, success comes through a process of trying, testing, and revising rather than through immediate assurances. An essential goal for the principal, therefore, is improving the school's abilities to use high-quality professional development to drive change in practices and school improvement, thus clearly striving to reach the vision of improved student achievement.

The isolation of teachers behind individual classroom doors is not only lonely, but unproductive as well. Teachers believe that they must solve problems on their own rather than use the expertise of the group. As Speck and Knipe (2001) state, "When the culture of an organization is collaborative, each teacher has a built-in network of support" (p. 58). A culture of collaboration is not just about starting conversations to bring about change. It permeates how the organization functions and what decisions are made on a day-to-day basis. The two main nemeses of collaboration are desire and time. These are addressed, discussed, and solved in collaborative cultures. Another issue to be addressed is that no one school will ever look exactly like another school. There are no lockstep formulas to follow. As Starratt (1996) puts it, "Every school that restructures itself as a learning community will be unique" (p. 77). However, assessing the degree to which the school embraces a collaborative collegial culture is a starting point that can begin to provide a pathway toward becoming a true learning community.

The principal and other site leaders can use the key components of high-quality professional development (see Chapter 1) to assess the school culture and set goals for professional development planning. A good starting place for assessing the school culture is to use the High-Quality Professional Development Rubric (see Table 2.1) to holistically score the school and determine the current level of professional development.

Table 2.1   High-Quality Professional Development Rubric

Key Component	Beginning	Basic	High-Quality
Focuses on learning and sustaining improved student learning	The school does not have a professional development plan, or it is centered on teacher experiences unrelated to targeted improved student learning. The focus for professional development activities is determined outside the school community. New school improvement plans or changes are tried but may be abandoned within a short time when they apparently do not work.	Professional development is part of a larger school plan that targets federal and state requirements for student achievement. Broad areas for improvement are selected annually and supported with categorical funds that also include new materials. The cycle repeats each year as required by law. Some resources are allocated for long-term changes.	Professional development at the school is focused on success targets through analysis of student learning needs and teacher practices. A plan is in place to improve student achievement, and this is the goal of all professional development efforts. Changes are fully implemented and supported with a plan for resources and appropriate evaluation.
Emerges from student data and the need to improve student results	Areas of concern are identified only through statewide testing results or large-scale initiatives such as reading improvement. There is little involvement of school staff in the planning of professional development activities.	A representative school council or leadership team selects areas of concern for the school plan by analyzing various forms of schoolwide and individual classroom data. Efforts are made by the planning team to make the professional development relevant and contextual.	Specific areas of concern are identified through analysis of various forms of schoolwide and individual classroom data and inquiry into student work and results. A collegial commitment to professional development that is relevant and contextual results from the analysis.
Nurtures collegiality and collaboration among teachers, other staff, and the principal	The school culture is one in which teachers work individually or with a specialist to solve classroom problems. Methods of solving	The culture of the school is one of support and concern. New teachers are teamed with veteran teachers or mentors to talk about	A sense of collegiality and collaboration among teachers, the principal, and the school community is the essence of the

Key Component	Beginning	Basic	High-Quality
	problems are set and experimentation is rare or prescribed by outside sources.	their practice, observe each other, and share what they know about teaching and learning. The school staff works together on curriculum issues usually as grade level or subject teams. Opportunities for conversations about practice exist in the school and are sometimes part of the professional development activities, but sustained, routine engagement is rare.	school culture. Sharing professional knowledge and grappling with tough student achievement and learning issues are the norm. The issue of teacher isolation has been addressed. Colleagues are routinely engaged around real learning issues that exist within their classrooms and school. The professional development agenda emerges from colleagues recognizing the needs and issues. The culture of collegiality and collaboration gives each teacher and principal the ongoing support needed as changes in teaching practices and content take place.
Develops shared leadership, resources, and inside/outside support	Frequent criticism of professional development activities is voiced and reflects concerns regarding relevance to classroom practice. Professional growth plans are provided only to teachers who are not meeting district expectations	Some staff members prepare professional growth plans. Both inside and outside expertise are used in the activities. School experts share knowledge through formal district activities such as mentor programs and district	A broad-based feeling of ownership exists at the school, which allows for deeper understanding of the critical issues that need to be addressed. Professional growth plans are continuous and focused.

(Continued)

Table 2.1 (Continued)

Key Component	Beginning	Basic	High-Quality
	per the evaluation process. Resources for professional development are extremely limited or determined by others outside of the school. Professional development strategies are consistently provided by mentors within the district or are provided by outside consultants.	inservices. Outside sources are usually obtained from attending conferences or workshops and sharing with other staff members at faculty meetings.	Appropriate use of resources is viewed as a powerful means to help carry out professional development plans. The staff taps sources of inside as well as outside expertise for support, including research and best practices to nourish and infuse the professional growth opportunities.
Utilizes research with a foundation in standards and accountability	Professional development is generally geared around textbook adoption cycles. Standards for student achievement are in place but rarely used as a means to examine student work. The accountability system for the school is whatever is used by the federal and state guidelines.	Student achievement standards are used to assess student progress and prepare professional development activities. Most staff members feel accountable for improved student learning. The focus is on meeting federal and state mandates.	Professional development is substantiated by research. A research-based plan of action grounded in student achievement standards provides a foundation for the work. The school community holds itself accountable to outcomes based on improved student learning.
Deepens teachers' content knowledge and teaching practices	Professional development sessions generally provide workshops for teachers to learn non-content-specific activities that can be used to enhance the classroom curriculum. Classroom instruction	Subject content and teaching practices form the basis of most professional development activities. Some grade level or subject area teams share specific content knowledge. Some	Deepening teachers' understanding of specific content knowledge as well as teaching practices is a goal of the professional development plan. Teachers routinely share

Key Component	Beginning	Basic	High-Quality
	is teacher centered. Content knowledge is rarely shared among teachers, and teacher isolation regarding subject area content exists.	subject area teachers use student-centered, project-based lessons.	knowledge about content. Content-specific knowledge gives teachers rich experiences in what they are teaching as well as integrating the strategies of how they deliver the content. Learning experiences in the classrooms meet high expectations for student-centered learning.
Centers on the adult learner through job-embedded work, options, and learning styles	Almost all teachers receive the same professional development that has been predetermined by a publisher, consultant, etc. The content of the professional development activity may focus on classroom issues, but not use real student work. Most professional development work-shops are regularly scheduled and presented in a traditional format of information, practice within the session, and evaluation.	Teachers self-select professional development activities. Some activities include using student work to assess needs. Discussions are about relevant issues, but most teachers engage in the same few types of professional development. Some individuals implement in the classrooms the strategies learned during professional development.	Professional development is centered on what each teacher needs to know and be able to do. Teachers are engaged in grappling with their daily practices. Well-focused options offer teachers experiences based on their own learning needs and styles of learning. Ongoing job-embedded daily professional growth honors the developmental levels and experiences of teachers as they tackle specific classroom and subject matter learning issues. Differentiated professional

(Continued)

Table 2.1 (Continued)

Key Component	Beginning	Basic	High-Quality
			development plans are in place to meet individual needs and address the scope of the necessary learning (content), how adult learners acquire knowledge (process), and the career stages and style of learning for each staff member (context).
Requires ongoing inquiry, practice, and reflection to inform practice	Professional development is episodic and may include various motivational speakers. Efforts to engage in reflection occur only at the end of a professional development session. Teachers are not engaged in the cycle of inquiry.	Some teams at the school are engaged in the cycle of inquiry and report their findings to the entire staff. Teachers are asked to use journals to reflect about teaching and learning. There is a pattern and consistency to professional development throughout the school year and may include study groups, peer coaching or other long-term strategies.	Ongoing inquiry, practice, and reflection are used to inform practice in order to sustain and integrate strategies that make a difference for student achievement. A cycle of inquiry into practice by examining student work and results data creates a school culture that continuously reflects on practice. The ability to study, act, and inform critical teaching and learning issues, continuous improvement, and the means to reach those goals. Professional development is seen as

Key Component	Beginning	Basic	High-Quality
Evaluates progress and accounts for student learning by examining results	Professional development evaluation occurs only at the end of sessions and is basically concerned with affective feedback from the participants or thoughts on how they might use the new concept or strategy. Annual statewide district test results are used to provide the general focus for professional development activities the following year.	In addition to evaluation and feedback at the end of a session, periodic evaluations of professional development include self-reports of whether the new strategy or practice is being implemented in the classrooms. The results are used to determine the next steps in more fully implementing the new strategy or practice.	a daily facet of teachers' real work rather than presented as an episodic one-time event. Evaluation of professional development as a means of making progress toward improved student achievement results is consistently used. Evaluating whether professional development makes a difference for teacher practices and affects student learning points to what needs to be done or changed. The school community, as a way to determine whether the professional growth that is taking place is worthy of the efforts, embraces accountability for actions and results.

PAUSE

Pause: Assess your school using the rubric.

Now that you have gathered some baseline assessment according to the rubric about your school's professional development practice, you are ready to complete the picture. This chapter outlines the various categories that can be used to add information regarding the culture indicators, such as standards, mandates, research, best practices, staff learning styles, and expertise, to build a more complete snapshot of the school and to set goals.

NATIONAL LEGISLATION AND DISTRICT AND STATE STANDARDS

According to legislators, educators, critics, and supporters, this is the age of accountability for schools. Recent federal legislation, No Child Left Behind (2002), has provided to states and local districts a complex and comprehensive agenda for shoring up what many believe is a sagging educational system. Considered an educational reform plan, it includes the requirement that all states must develop standards for students in reading and math immediately, and ultimately in science as well. States must then assess the annual progress of students toward meeting the standards.

Standards are everywhere. In educational terms, we have standards for student achievement as well as expectation standards for adult and organizational learning. Students are expected to meet or exceed content and performance standards. In other words, these standards are what students need to know about and what they need to be able to do regarding the subject area. Aspiring teachers and administrators meet or exceed certain adult standards to obtain credentials. Universities use program standards to improve educator preparation programs. In addition, associations, such as the National Staff Development Council, provide standards for their areas of expertise.

Proponents of standards claim that their use in schools helps "level the playing field" by ensuring access by all students to core curriculum. Standards are visible reminders of key concepts. Not only are the standards the base of the educational program but they are also well-known by all stakeholders as well. Teaching for standards attainment creates a determined focus for teaching and learning. Professional development can be wrapped around particular standards, improving knowledge, and strategies to make the standards more accessible to all students. Standards can create a coherent view of the educational experience without standardizing the learner (Darling-Hammond, 1997).

On the other hand, critics of the use of standards in schools believe the curriculum is limiting and that the apparent loss of local control removes the instructional context from the school community. Creativity is stifled, and the art of teaching can be reduced to checking off boxes. Externally imposed standards may not be part of a larger systemic reform package.

Although the debate rages on, student achievement standards are a way of life for most students in most schools in most states. Most states have adopted standards for student achievement and the aligning curriculum. In addition, many local districts have added standards to the state efforts. More recently, assessments, report cards, and grades have been aligned with standards in the attempt to maintain a cohesive educational program for students. Some educators may resist standards, but it appears acceptance is growing (Glatthorn, 2000).

In fact, standards can inform the work of educators on an almost daily basis. Student achievement standards are the large chunks in the core curriculum around which other learnings can be built based on the local context of the school and the interest of the community. Adult standards can serve as opportunities for gaining new knowledge. For example, most state teacher and administrator professional standards now require technology skills. Standards for programs, subject areas, or school improvement efforts provide comparison bars for expectations. Local and state standards must inform the work of professional development.

DEALING WITH MANDATES AND EXPECTATIONS

There is little doubt in any educator's mind that standardized testing has become one of the most widely used mandates for today's schools. In the past decade, many states have developed assessment systems designed around nationally normed tests and/or specific content standards tests. Some statewide assessment systems include school rankings and rewards and/or sanctions for improvement goals. School comparison results are reported in local media. Popham (2001) refers to this as "scoreboard-induced motivation." The stakes are high for schools. The public tends to be impatient when it comes to school improvement results.

Although "high-stakes" testing may not provide the most reliable data for instructional decision making (Popham, 2001), it can be used to look for patterns of results for the instructional program. Then, using performance data and local measures, educators can refine the search for student outcome results and focus improvement objectives.

Most colleges and universities require minimum expectations of grade point averages and standardized entrance exam scores for students to matriculate. There is a tradition of university requirements driving high school expectations. In 1892, the National Education Association's Committee of Ten established uniform college entrance requirements. The committee's report set the course for expectations of the high school curriculum (Kliebard, 1995). In many states, such as California, these requirements also include passing marks in particular high school classes. In addition, most states now require a high school exit exam for graduation and the accompanying diploma. Various mandates and expectations must be considered when planning professional development.

CURRENT GOALS AND CONTEXT FOR CHANGE

Standards and external expectations by themselves are not the "silver bullets" for improving schools. Even with clear goals about what students should learn, reform efforts must center on improving teaching to make an impact on student learning (Darling-Hammond, 1997; Stigler & Hiebert, 1999; Willis, 2002). Goals for professional development must directly relate to developing high-quality teaching in every classroom and use local measures to study the results. There is a tendency for American educators to become defensive regarding the notion that teaching needs to be improved. It is a simple mistake to assume that it means that teachers are incompetent. Stigler & Hiebert (1999) argue, in their study of mathematics teaching in Germany, Japan, and the United States, that the commonly used teaching methods make a huge difference for the student experience. In addition, those methods differ in each country, making them appear cultural. American mathematics teachers spend a great deal of time teaching isolated skills rather than teaching for conceptual understanding.

If teaching is going to improve, then the school culture must embrace the idea of trying new methods and measuring results.

Developing this context for change is challenging and requires leaders who firmly believe that taking responsible risks is productive (Costa & Kallick, 2000). According to Stigler & Hiebert (1999), the cultural change that is needed is educators engaged in "generating and sharing knowledge about teaching" (p. 12). Changing the culture of the school to one that continually seeks to improve the quality of teaching should be the bottom-line goal for any professional development plan. School leaders can build group support that shares knowledge and encourages taking risks as a part of the normal process.

TOOLS FOR UNDERSTANDING STANDARDS AND GOALS

How well do all the educators understand the requirements, standards, mandates, and expectations? The professional learning community must be centered on the necessary elements for the school system as well as the local context of the community and the specific needs of the students. A balance must be achieved. This allows for the professional learning community to focus on improved student learning and meet external expectations.

To assist the principal and other school leaders in making reasonable decisions about "Where we are and where we want to be," mandates, standards, and requirements need to be clearly charted and understood by everyone. Using the Examining Expectations tool (see Table 2.2) can help provide a visual chart of the necessary expectations for improving student learning. Use the chart to answer these questions: What are the federal requirements? What are the state standards? What are the local mandates? What are the graduation/promotion expectations?

How do the data, research, and best practice inform our work?

COLLECTING AND USING DATA

Knowing the students well can lead to the appropriate decisions for classroom instruction. Careful analysis of student data is essential to make informed decisions regarding pedagogy, content, and strategies. One of the most important steps in establishing a meaningful professional development program is learning how to consider data

Table 2.2   Examining Expectations

Federal Requirements	State Standards	Local Mandates	Graduation/Promotion Requirements

together as a school community. As teachers, staff, parents, and the principal work to understand the data, they also come to have a deeper understanding regarding their own learning needs. Data is a powerful tool!

Serious tension often appears among stakeholders regarding the subject of data. Oversimplified reports and newspaper accounts about test results can be fertile ground for growth of suspicion and mistrust. Parents and community members are concerned about how "their" school compares with others. Teachers fear being held to only one measure of accountability. Principals are thrust into uncommon spotlights, defending or basking in results. Often, the community still has no clue how to fix a problem or what might have worked this time. The truth of the matter is that student achievement and growth are more complex than one measure can offer. The school must marshal an arsenal of information to use for effective decision making. Then it must be counted, sorted, categorized, analyzed, and meaning constructed from it.

A professional learning community tests theories and assumptions, measures results, and tries again. This cycle of inquiry generates new knowledge that informs the practice. Collecting data is no longer a one-shot event that occurs either at the beginning or the end of the school year, but becomes an ongoing process that has more to do with the work than with outside mandates. Teachers collect and analyze classroom performance measures, collaborative teams pore over various results, and the school continually solicits feedback from the students and community. Data moves away from being a form of punishment to a vehicle for improvement. In *The Results Fieldbook* (2001), Schmoker provides examples of schools and districts that have embraced collaboratively reviewing assessment data to improve teaching and, ultimately, student achievement. The "formula" is almost simplistic, yet that first step of real collaboration is sometimes too huge of a leap of faith for many staff members. School leaders can stay focused on the school goals by developing team plans for collaboration and use the assessment data to inform the work.

What are our learning needs?

LINKING TEACHER KNOWLEDGE, PROFESSIONAL DEVELOPMENT, AND STUDENT GROWTH

Teachers are expected to provide differentiated instruction in the classroom to help each student grow. The principal needs to consider the school staff in much the same way. Individuals are in different career stages and have different developmental needs (Speck & Knipe, 2001). The professional development needs of a new teacher can be completely different from the needs of the veteran teacher. One-size-fits-all type of inservice rarely is the key to sustained growth. Personalized plans can help keep the focus on the individual. Many principals sort the staff members into categories of assistance through self-assessments and general observations. Career Stages and Developmental Needs (see Table 2.3) is a model for understanding the phases of an individual teacher's career as well as the developmental needs of that stage. Knowing where each teacher stands relative to this model is helpful in differentiating the professional development strategies.

A recent report from the National Commission on Teaching and America's Future (2003), titled *No Dream Denied: A Pledge to America's Children,* argues that the teacher shortage problem for today's schools

Table 2.3   Career Stages and Developmental Needs

Career Stage	Developmental Needs
Formative years (1–2 years)	Learning day-to-day operations of classroom and school
Building years (3–5 years)	Developing confidence in work and multifaceted role of teaching
Striving years (5–8+ years)	Developing professionally and achieving high job satisfaction
Other issues: Crisis periods Complacency Career wind-down Career end	 Teacher burnout and need for renewal Complacency sets in and innovation is low High status as a teacher without exerting much effort Retirement

SOURCE: Based on the work of Burke, Christensen, & Fessler (1984); Christensen, Burke, Fessler, & Hagstrom (1983); Feiman & Floden (1980); Newman, Dornburg, Dubois, & Kranz (1980); Ponticell & Zepeda (1996); Speck & Knipe (2001).

is not the unsuccessful recruitment of teachers but rather the high beginning-teacher attrition rates. In the book *New Teacher Induction: How to Train, Support, and Retain New Teachers* (2003), Breaux and Wong provide seven steps for structuring an induction program with checklists, suggestions, and examples. Teacher induction, which includes "systematic training and ongoing support for all new teachers, commencing BEFORE the first day of school and continuing for several years" (p. 123) is different from the typical orientation-type programs offered to most teachers when they begin in a school district. According to the authors, "Effective induction programs not only retain highly qualified new teachers; they also ensure that these teachers are teaching effectively from the very first day of school" (p. vi). Understanding the career stages of teachers is necessary to design effective professional development that truly supports each teacher's needs.

In addition to adult learners being in various stages of career development, there are also common concerns held by individuals in an organization regarding implementation of any innovation. In *Taking Charge of Change* (Hord, Rutherford, Huling-Austin, & Hall, 1987), the authors describe seven stages of concern that users may have about an innovation and point out that the stages are not

Figure 2.1   Stages of Concern

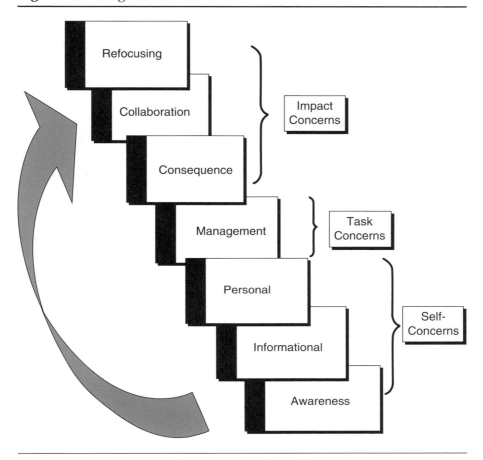

Adapted from Hord, Rutherford, Huling-Austin, & Hall (1987).

mutually exclusive. The stages in order are awareness, informational, personal, management, consequences, collaboration, and refocusing. Even more telling is the normal progression of the "developmental nature" of the stages. Initially, individuals will often have self-concerns as they move from the awareness level to requesting more information about the change (informational) and wondering how the change will affect them (personal). As commitment grows, the concern is more likely to be about the task and how it might be implemented (management). Ultimately, individuals will move into wanting to know the impact of the innovation on the students (consequences), the group (collaboration), and generating new ideas for improvement (refocusing). Knowledgeable school leaders use their understanding of these stages (see Figure 2.1) to ask questions of staff members, measure the responses, and facilitate movement to a higher stage. For example, an individual who is worried about whether she will actually be able to do what is expected is demonstrating personal concern and may need encouragement or to learn sequential skills to implement the innovation. If these are intense concerns and are unresolved, the individual will likely resist the change. Support for implementation can be varied for staff members at each level of concern.

CURRENT RESEARCH

Consistently applying the findings of the most recent research on teaching and learning to the context and needs of the school is essential. There has been a wealth of knowledge created in the last decade about how individuals learn, the function of the brain during the learning process, and strategies for improving content knowledge and instruction. It is important to belong to organizations that offer information about current research.

In challenging times, such as during budget woes, there is a tendency to pull inward and drop outside contacts (Thomas, 2003). Often, when the dust settles on budget cuts, the principal may be the only instructional leader on the staff other than the classroom teachers due to the reduction of specialists. It is all the more important to build outside networks to assist in understanding research and staying current. For example, university-school partnerships and networks can also play a role to ensure that current research is shared as well as to provide the opportunity to participate in generating new research-based information.

ENGAGING IN INQUIRY

In a recent report from the Bay Area School Reform Collaborative, or BASRC (Center for Research on the Context of Teaching, 2002), it was concluded that using a cycle of inquiry actually changes the culture of the school. The collaborative serves as an intermediary for school reform efforts by providing support, coaching, and expertise. Although some student achievement results were mixed during the first phase of the initiative, "where inquiry became an accepted dimension of teachers' professional community, new forms of leadership, accountability for all students, problem-solving skills and expectations about teachers' learning came about" (p. 18). The long-term success for school change based on continuous inquiry is promising. See Chapter 5 for more information regarding BASRC efforts using the cycle of inquiry.

LEARNER-CENTERED AS COLLABORATIVE PRACTICE

According to Eaker, DuFour, and Burnette in *Getting Started: Reculturing Schools to Become Professional Learning Communities* (2002), "Schools that function as professional learning communities are *always* characterized by a collaborative culture. Teacher isolation is replaced with collaborative processes that are deeply embedded into the daily life of the school" (p. 5). Focusing the organization on continuous improvement allows for a type of collaboration that Starratt (1996) refers to as "a communal sense of self-efficacy" (p. 174). A strongly held belief that improvement comes through working together is an idea that feeds on itself. Roles can become more fluid as various leaders step forward. Goodlad (1983) called this a "self-renewing system." More recently, Lambert and colleagues (1995) referred to a "continually renewing place." The adults are also learners in schools.

LEARNING STYLE

Understanding learning preferences can help a school leader prepare for effective professional development. It has long been recognized that students learn through different perceptions and often rely on certain physiological or environmental features to help build meaning for new learning. Proponents of Howard Gardner's Multiple Intelligence theory understand that aptitudes come in many forms (Gardner, 1985) and that no two people sitting through a lecture perceive it exactly the same way. Prior knowledge about the subject can certainly create a particular lens, but so can natural, individual differences.

The traditional way of looking at learning styles divides along the lines of senses. For example, a visual learner prefers the input to be in graphic or pictorial form. Often, graphic organizers, charts, and written language assist in the learning. An auditory learner can often learn best by hearing the new information. By listening and making connections aurally and then talking through the new learning, this kind of learner can better categorize the input. The kinesthetic learner is more physically active than the others appear to be in the learning process and uses touch and movement to assist.

Another way to consider learning style is to reflect on the thinking process. Does the learner imagine the whole or use a step-by-step process? Do the examples need to be concrete or abstract?

Actually, learning is much more complex than this, but for decades, classroom teachers have varied their teaching to meet the needs of students with different types of intelligences and learning styles. Unfortunately, adult learning is often relegated to simple "sit and listen" sessions with some graphics or activities thrown in.

Interestingly, most adult learners can identify their own styles by measuring against a standard. Simple self-assessments are available at no cost at a number of Internet sites. There are also inventories available on the market based on self-assessments. Whatever the school is currently using to better understand student learning can be used to focus the adult learners in the organization. The question to ask is *How do you learn best?*

TEACHER EXPERTISE

Another self-assessment for teachers that is helpful in understanding the preparations for professional development planning is the level of expertise with any particular concept. Has a teacher taken any training or had experience in a specific content area or with a particular instructional strategy? Matrix for Professional Development Planning (see Table 2.4) is a form that can be used to combine various bits of self-generated information about teachers for individual, team, and school professional development planning. A principal and leadership team using this wealth of information can utilize an individual teacher's expertise and influence a differentiated design that meets the learning needs of each teacher. Site-based expertise is more valuable than outside resources because it is routinely available and geared toward the specific focus of the school.

Table 2.4 Preparing for Individual Professional Development Plans

School Team _____

Teacher's Name	Career Stage	Learning Style	Previous Training	Current Needs Generated From Looking at Student Data	Expertise or Talents to Share

49

KEY POINTS OF CHAPTER 2

- Initial assessment and capacity building are keys to preparing the learning community to take action.
- The High-Quality Professional Development Rubric can be used to assess the school culture and target goals.
- Understanding legislation, standards, and mandates clarifies the direction of a professional development plan.
- Collecting and using data informs decision making about student learning and professional development.
- Understanding individual differences and learning needs can help build the capacity of the learning community.
- Knowing the staff well (career stage, learning style, expertise, etc.) will assist in the preparations for creating an effective professional development plan.

The Principal as Designer

Developing Focus, Plans, and Resources

When teachers have convincing evidence that their work has made a real difference in their students' lives, the countless hours and endless efforts of teaching seem worthwhile.

—Richard Sagor

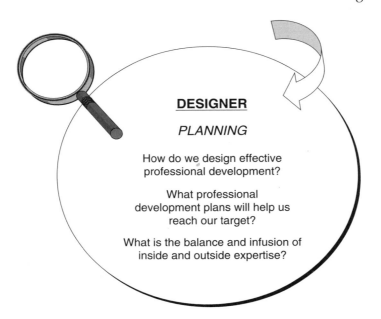

DESIGNER

PLANNING

How do we design effective professional development?

What professional development plans will help us reach our target?

What is the balance and infusion of inside and outside expertise?

Principal's Scenario

Juanita took inventory of the accomplishments of the Chavez school leadership team and school staff during the past few months. They analyzed standardized test data, district performance data, report card grades, and student class work and had conducted surveys of parents, teachers, and students. The team members expressed mutual satisfaction that they had learned a great deal about the students by discussing and considering the achievement data.

The teachers selected key student achievement standards to compare to student performance. It was clear that literacy was the main issue for most students. By disaggregating the data, teachers were able to observe a pattern of low performance in reading comprehension and vocabulary, especially for lower socioeconomic students.

In addition, several staff meetings were used to keep all staff informed of the team's activities and for teachers to self-assess their professional development needs. Each teacher provided information about his or her areas of expertise, years of experience, and learning style.

An evening parent meeting provided the opportunity for the leadership team to share the findings and solicit input into the planning.

None of these accomplishments was easy. Several of the veteran staff members questioned the need for any professional development and requested instead that the time and money that would have been used for professional development be made available for teachers to work in their classrooms and buy supplies. However, several other members of the leadership team and other teachers had become vocal supporters of creating a school professional development plan, and during the last meeting, Juanita was pleased they had shared their thoughts and concerns.

Jorge: Look, we have examined the standards, several different data points, and it is clear that most of our students need something different to happen to reach grade level proficiency in literacy. This is even more evident when we disaggregated and looked at certain groups of students.

Mike: We reviewed our vision, and we all agreed that the education of every student is important to all of us. We can provide the change necessary in our classrooms that Jorge is talking about. A long-term plan with real consistency that really improves student learning should be our goal.

Anna: Well, I'm excited about the prospect of finally having some professional development that would be meaningful for us here at Chavez School.

Yen: Yes, and we have also discovered we have plenty of expertise on the staff.

Janet: Well, I'm going to state this again, according to the union contract, teachers need to be paid for working outside their normal day.

Juanita: I have been working with the district to earmark certain funds for our professional development plan. We certainly can also use the valuable district resources. Let's look at a variety of site-based, job-embedded professional development options and see what might work for our focus on improving literacy.

> **How do we design effective professional development?**

It is important for a professional development plan to be well designed. In 2001, the National Staff Development Council revised its standards for professional development to cover the categories of context, process, and content. These standards can guide the design stage of a professional development plan. The National Staff Development Council Standards for Staff Development (see Table 3.1) offers greater detail. This chapter will include some strategies for meeting the context, process, and content of professional development.

Table 3.1   Standards for Staff Development (revised, 2001)

Context Standards
Staff development that improves the learning of all students:

- LEARNING COMMUNITIES: Organizes adults into learning communities whose goals are aligned with those of the school and district.

- LEADERSHIP: Requires skillful school and district leaders who guide continuous instructional improvement.

- RESOURCES: Staff development that improves the learning of all students requires resources to support adult learning and collaboration.

Process Standards
Staff development that improves the learning of all students:

- DATA-DRIVEN: Uses disaggregated student data to determine adult learning priorities, monitor progress, and help sustain continuous improvement.

- EVALUATION: Uses multiple sources of information to guide improvement and demonstrate its impact.

- RESEARCH-BASED: Prepares educators to apply research to decision making.

- DESIGN: Uses learning strategies appropriate to the intended goal.

- LEARNING: Applies knowledge about human learning and change.

- COLLABORATION: Provides educators with the knowledge and skills to collaborate.

Content Standards
Staff development that improves the learning of all students:

- EQUITY: Prepares educators to understand and appreciate all students, create safe, orderly and supportive learning environments, and hold high expectations for their academic achievement.

- QUALITY TEACHING: Deepens educators' content knowledge, provides them with research-based instructional strategies to assist students in meeting rigorous academic standards, and prepares them to use various types of classroom assessments appropriately.

- FAMILY INVOLVEMENT: Provides educators with knowledge and skills to involve families and other stakeholders appropriately.

SOURCE: The National Staff Development Council (2001)

VISION AND BELIEFS OF THE LEARNING COMMUNITY

Although strong site leadership is essential for making improvements at a site, a principal cannot do it alone. Sharing the leadership for the school's efforts begins with a shared vision of "how things should be." Each person brings his or her own vision to any situation, and to assume that everyone at the school has the same set of beliefs would be faulty. Discussions of what individuals believe, what the community needs, and what are the goals of the organization are crucial to bring about a collective vision for the school. This essential first step in planning is often overlooked because the school has a slogan or written mission statement. However, whether creating a new vision or revisiting the current vision, the school community needs to be in at least conceptual agreement regarding the vision of the school. Armed with a shared vision, the plan can begin to take shape.

SHARED LEADERSHIP

Who is involved in providing shared leadership for the various elements of the plan? The principal has the opportunity to build broad support for the change and professional learning that is needed to improve practices by ensuring a larger group takes ownership. Various teachers and school community members can add leadership direction to improve the process and outcomes.

In an effort to clarify the focus for improvement and ultimately the professional development that will make that improvement happen, the school community must examine all the available data and even generate additional information if necessary. Many times, the steps taken to clarify the focus are more of a problem-finding rather than problem-solving quest. Questions can help the search: What does this mean? Why do we suppose this is the result? How can we find out more about this? It is important to remain nonjudgmental and include as many of the staff and community as possible in the "search." Generally, student improvement targets become obvious, especially in light of the emphasis on student achievement standards of the past decade. Chapters 2 and 4 also provide discussion of issues of shared leadership and examples of strategies for narrowing the focus for improved student learning.

| What professional development plans will help us reach our target? |

PROFESSIONAL DEVELOPMENT IMPACT AND USE

We know that professional development must be adult-learner focused and relevant. But in a greater sense, the process of professional development can make the difference in long-term implementation. Table 3.2 illustrates types of professional development activities and the level of use and impact.

In designing professional development plans, the level and impact must be considered. The types of professional development that include feedback, coaching, reflection, and inquiry are more effective. The principal needs to be knowledgeable about the strategies that will lead to greater success in improving student learning. In addition, according to Fullan (1993), "The best organizations learn externally as well as internally" (p. 22). The combination of inside knowledge and outside knowledge is powerful when applied to school improvement.

The learning cycle shows that for new strategies, teachers need opportunities to move from awarenes to exploring new techniques, to implementing them in the classroom, getting ongoing support and coaching, and then sharing and reflecting. Principals must understand that if teachers are given only awareness sessions on a new strategy, less than 5% will be remembered or implemented in the classroom (see Figure 3.1). Understanding the impact and level of usage (awareness to implementation and refinement) of new teaching strategies and knowledge is important. It is this ongoing support from inside and outside that helps sustain the learning. By practicing and applying the new strategy in the classroom, the implementation rate goes up 5% to 15%, but with ongoing support, modeling, and coaching, implementation goes up to 85% to 90%. Continued application and refinement with reflection increase the adoption rate of a new strategy to 95%.

Sustainability is a huge issue for schools. According to Fullan (1991), systemic change can take 5 to 10 years. Change that is dependent upon one leader at a school is doomed if that leader leaves. Building broad-based support through a learning community that is engaged in professional development processes that support a cycle of inquiry will increase the possibility that successful change will be sustained.

Table 3.2   Professional Development Processes: Impact and Use

Type	Length	Level of Use	Level of Impact
One-time workshop	Episodic	Awareness of new idea or strategy	Little or none Less than 5%
Series of workshops	2–3 days	Awareness, practice	Beginning use Less than 5%
Series of workshops	3 months– 1 year	Awareness, practice Beginning implementation	Implementation Developmental level Less than 10%–15%
Conferences	Periodic	Awareness and sharing	Little or none Less than 5%
Summer institutes	Periodic	Awareness, development, practice, reflection	Little or none Less than 10%
Practice, feedback, coaching	Ongoing	Ongoing coaching	Continued use 85%–90% use
Job embedded	Daily	Research into practice	Inquiry into practice 85%–90% use
Cycle of inquiry action Research	Ongoing	Research into practice	Study of issue Understanding

SOURCE: Adapted from the research of Joyce & Showers (2002) and Speck & Knipe (2001).

> What is the balance and infusion of inside and outside expertise?

INSIDE KNOWLEDGE (JOB-EMBEDDED) MODELS AND TOOLS

Using Data, Research, and Needs to Target Goals

In the book *Reflective Practice to Improve Schools,* the authors discuss the difference between "externally generated knowledge" and

Figure 3.1   Learning Cycle and Implementation Levels

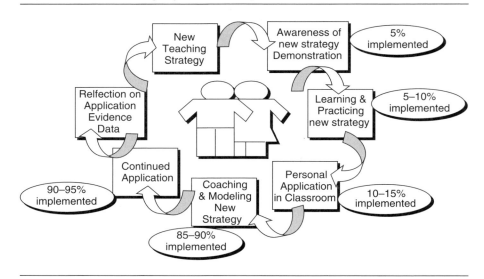

Based on Joyce & Showers (2002).

"internally created knowledge." Referring to knowledge that is generated by the research community and shared with practitioners, the authors state that it is "technical-rational or content knowledge." On the other hand, "contextual knowledge," they opine, is based on reflective practice and adapting the research community's findings and suggestions to fit the school's unique context (York-Barr, Sommers, Ghere, & Montie, 2001, p. 10). The authors further argue that "Lived experience is perhaps the most powerful influence on the formation of beliefs and values, which are the driving force behind actions" (York-Barr et al., 2001, p. 12).

Contextual knowledge is gathered through the process of comparing the school's actual work with the goals set by the school. Outside research can guide the internal inquiry; however, it is the actions of the staff that will make the difference. A school community engaged in using data, research, and needs to inform the practice will be constantly creating new knowledge in a cycle of inquiry.

Peer Coaching, Mentoring

According to the author of *Peer Coaching for Educators*, "Peer coaching is a simple, nonthreatening structure for peers to help each other improve instruction or learning situations" (Gottesman, 2000, p. 5). Gottesman advocates for a supervisory model that incorporates peer coaching to change the culture of the school, create a more professional experience for teachers, and engage teachers in continuous problem solving. Using the motto "No Praise, No Blame," the feedback given from one peer to another is specific and nonjudgmental. With some initial training and practice, peer teams can refine their skills in everyday situations following this five-step model:

1. The Teacher Requests a Visit,

2. The Visit,

3. The Coach Reviews the Notes and Lists Some Possibilities,

4. The Talk After the Visit,

5. The Review of the Process. (Gottesman, 2000, p. 33)

Ultimately, after the initial investment in training and as trust builds among the peer teams, the process is quite cost-effective. Peer observations can be conducted during the coach's prep period, with class coverage by specialists or by combining classes for an instructional period. The largest benefit, however, is the fact that teachers are conducting collegial work as they problem solve together.

Peer coaching is a structure that pairs teachers in similar situations. Another model of assistance is mentoring, which matches a less experienced teacher with one of greater experience. Expert guidance of one adult to another is the basis of this model. Many districts have formalized this type of assistance through programs that release veteran teachers from their classroom duties for at least part of the day to meet with other teachers, provide model lessons, or coteach in an advisee's classroom. Key to this strategy is the recognition that adults react differently to advice from "experts."

Some principals can be genuine coaches for teachers. Trust and expertise are important components of this scenario. It is especially important to separate the role of coaching for improvement from the role of evaluator. Districts that are actively involved in using both formative and summative teacher assessments based on standards, goals, or portfolios may have already taken steps to ensure that teachers can be perfectly honest with the coach without fear of that honesty appearing in the year-end, formal written evaluation.

Study Groups

Bambino (2002) describes her experience as a Critical Friends Group (CFG) coach in a recent article. The National School Reform Faculty (NSRF) through training and support presents the CFG concept. Each school site CFG meets monthly with up to 12 educators to discuss student work and the teaching that produced it. The coach for each group is trained to facilitate colleague sharing and use the NSRF protocols. The key is "building the trust needed to engage in direct, honest, and productive conversations with colleagues about the complex art of teaching" (Bambino, 2002, p. 25).

Study groups generally schedule regular meetings and choose the focus for the study by considering the school goals. Leadership responsibilities are often rotated, or the logistics for the group are taken care of by a facilitator. In Evergreen School District in San Jose, California, many of the study groups are districtwide groups made of individuals with common interests. Other groups have a single school focus. The groups meet during an early student release time that is set aside for professional development. The district provides resource support in the forms of expertise and literature for each group's study.

The Annenberg Institute for School Reform conducted principal study groups to provide the opportunity for principals to discuss student, teacher, and principal work. The insights to the power of reflection, shared accountability, giving and receiving feedback, in addition to modeling ongoing learning were reported in an article by Nancy Mohr, who served as a facilitator to several groups (Mohr, 1998).

Action Research Cycle

Action research is described as a process of inquiry that is guided by real work and involves the individuals who are taking the action (see Figure 3.2). Generally, a problem or concern is identified and questions formulated. The researchers collect data, try new actions, and collect more data to attempt to answer the questions. Analysis and reflection lead to better understanding of the work and the progress. According to Fullan (2000), successful schools had teachers and administrators who "recultured" their schools by forming an "assessment literate" professional learning community, which means "1) the ability of teachers, individually and together, to interpret achievement data on student performance; and 2) teachers' equally important ability to develop action plans to alter instruction and other factors in order to improve student learning" (p. 582).

Figure 3.2   Action Research Cycle

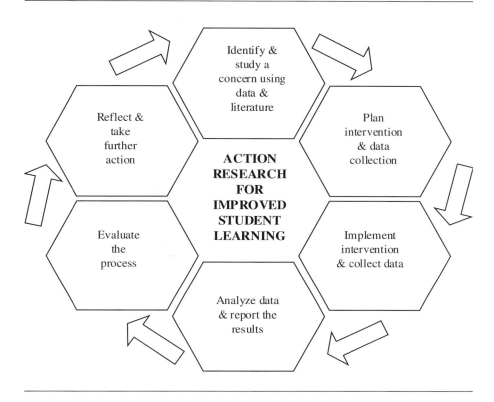

Noguera (2001) suggests that action research provides the opportunity to challenge assumptions and engage in conversations about complicated issues. Data can assist the school community in overcoming denial and rationalization.

The reality is that using action research within a school community can be a messy process, especially in the beginning. A school team may falter the first time through the action research cycle as it defines the area of study or analyzes the data, but participation in the process is a powerful learning experience, and team members generally emerge excited about the next cycle.

In the Urban High School Leadership program at San Jose State University, participants attend as school teams. The academic goals of the program for the participants are earning a master's degree in education from San Jose State University and qualifying for a California Administrative Services credential. However, the focus for the program is developing leaders who will change schools by engaging in collaborative inquiry. Each school team develops an action research project by analyzing data, selecting a school problem to study, establishing the questions to answer, and, through literature review and implementing some kind of action, answer the questions.

Collaboration Around Student Work

Fullan says the most powerful professional development is teachers talking with other teachers about student work and comparing it to standards (2003). The simple process of sitting together as a grade level team or subject area department and discussing actual student work can offer powerful results, especially when led by a facilitator or documents that measure quality such as a scoring rubric. Questions can be raised about how to get particular results with students or what part of the curriculum needs to be strengthened or enhanced. These conversations should end with a suggestion to try in the classrooms before the next collaborative meeting and the commitment to gather additional student work. The focus is to discuss the results of teaching efforts and develop the flexibility to try new ideas and then measure results.

Teachers at Evergreen Valley High School in San Jose, California, analyze student work and develop strategies for moving students forward by using a technique developed by the Santa Cruz New Teachers Project. Teachers sort student work into four piles representing ranges of more than one year below standard to exceeding standard. Then, one sample is chosen from each pile, and the actual performance of the representative student is described using the work and the content standard. Finally, strategies for each of the four students are developed. Even though this technique uses one representative student for each level, teachers are able to use the strategies they develop with groups of students in the classroom.

Reflective Practice

For centuries, individuals have reflected on the day's events in journals or diaries. These important documents offer the subsequent reader great insight into historical events, unspoken thoughts, and deeper understanding of the individual's context. At the time, however, journal writers create greater meaning for themselves by analyzing all parts of the situation: facts, feelings, reactions, goals, and dreams. What if individuals began to reflect together to construct information about a situation? York-Barr and her colleagues (2001) present a four-level model they call "The Reflective Practice Spiral" in the book *Reflective Practice to Improve Schools.* The levels the authors describe as "resulting in a cumulative effect on school wide practice" (p. 12) begin with the individual and move to partner, team, and schoolwide. Each level offers specific benefits and strategies for implementing.

Self-examination can include a journal that can be reread for insights or an assessment tool to measure progress toward skills, attitudes, or beliefs. The act of committing to writing reflective thoughts can open avenues of discussions and considerations that do not emerge in normal conversations.

Personal Learning Plan

Breaking Ranks: Changing an American Institution, a 1996 Commission on the Restructuring of the American High School report of the National Association of Secondary School Principals in partnership with the Carnegie Foundation for the Advancement of Teaching, outlined 13 priorities for renewal and areas of support for high schools. The item "Professional Development: Helping School Staff Members Fulfill Their Potential" called for personal learning plans for the adults in the schools.

Tremont Community Unit District 702 in Illinois began using "professional growth plans" in 1997. Teachers are allowed to direct their own professional growth (Peine, 2003). After conducting a self-assessment based on standards and best practices, each teacher chooses a focus area. Using a defined format and with the school leader's support, a plan for improvement is designed. Documentation of implementation and monitoring of the plan includes workday plans, summary reflections, and work artifacts. In Tremont Community Unit District 702, the formative and summative evaluations of each professional growth plan substitutes for a more traditional type of teacher evaluation. Two-minute growth plan updates at staff meetings are required by each individual or groups to encourage the concept of the learning community.

In California, the Beginning Teacher Support and Assessment (BTSA) program was designed in 1992 to meet the varied needs of new teachers during their first 2 years in the classrooms. In this program, a "support provider" is assigned to guide a beginning teacher and work with assessment data. An important component of the BTSA program is the California Formative Assessment and Support System for Teachers (CFASST), which outlines a 2-year cycle of inquiry, observation, experience, assessment, and the Individual Induction Plan (IIP). The IIP is a one-page chart that serves as a professional development plan for each teacher. The six areas of the IIP are teaching strengths, teaching growth needs (strength and needs are based on the California Standards for the Teaching Profession), growth goals, student outcomes, implementation plan, and resources that support the goals (see http://www.btsa.ca.gov). It is a simple yet powerful tool to focus the teacher and all the other supporters on the basic goals of improvement:

- Creation of assessments, curriculum, rubrics, and instructional strategies (e.g., Understanding by Design, Dimensions of Learning)
- Staff expertise (trainer of trainer)
- Observation, implementation, practice, and feedback

The principal and leadership team can use a similar graphic organizer for a personal professional development plan (see Table 3.3). By committing to writing the various phases of planning, the document can be a map for individual growth. The graphic organizer includes these points: self-assessment, targeted student learning, current conditions, expectations, goals, resources, and reflection.

OUTSIDE KNOWLEDGE MODELS AND TOOLS

Using outside expertise to bring awareness and understanding regarding new instructional strategies, curriculum, and assessment ideas provides an infusion of new knowledge to a school. A principal and the shared leadership team need to balance "inside" job-embedded professional development work with "outside" infusion of expertise and information. Attending outside expert workshops and conferences provides a team of faculty members along with the principal the opportunity to explore new ideas and strategies that might help improve their schools' achievement. Attending and participating together is a powerful way to become aware of the possibilities that can be brought back to the school for further in-depth study and application. The research of Joyce and Showers (2002) tells us that unless we apply our new learnings, we will only retain less than 5% of what we learned. University partnerships, subject matter networks, and educational associations are a rich resource for outside learning, sharing, reinforcing, and reflecting on professional growth efforts to improve student success. This outside continuous support

Table 3.3 Personal Professional Development Plan

	Targeted Student Learning:
Name _____	
Team _____	Data:
Date _____	
Self-Assessment:	
• Career Stage _____	Goal:
• Learning Style _____	
• Other _____	
Current Conditions & Expertise:	Relationship to Expectations:
Myself:	Federal:
	District:
	School:
Team:	Standards:
	Assessments:
Professional Development Goal:	Resources to Support Professional Development Goal:
Action | Evidence	
Short-Term:	Reflection on Progress:
Long-Term:	Review Date _____ Revision Date _____

SOURCE: Adapted from the California Beginning Teacher Support and Assessment (BTSA) program.

and reflection on progress causes a school to focus its work and understand the depth of what needs to change.

Subject Matter Projects, Networks, and Regional Collaboratives

It has been argued that the key to creating change is developing supportive networks for collaborative problem solving and inquiry (Lieberman & McLaughlin, 1992). Networks that operate outside of the school are usually focused on a particular reform or subject area. For example, the Coalition of Essential Schools (CES) Network facilitates discussions, list serves, and meetings to share knowledge about the reform. Some networks are linked to state agencies, such as the California Subject Matter Projects.

Regional collaboratives can be formed to address a particular issue or to pool expertise and resources. Many times, these collaboratives are generated by either county or regional education agencies. In addition, districts can form collaborative communities within a district or among groups of districts. By adopting modern technologies to stay connected through e-mail, Web sites, and videoconferencing, the networks can meet the need of participants even though the sites might be rural or remote.

Inservice, Conferences, Training

Attending an inservice or conference is often the best approach to understand theory or gain awareness about an issue, especially if the individual attending has some site responsibilities for dissemination of information upon return to the school. Although widely accepted as a professional development strategy, the main benefit is to the individual who attends the inservice or conference and only to the degree that the information is put into practice.

The "Train the Trainers" approach is to send one or more staff members to a training for the express purpose of creating a cadre of site level trainers. Not only is this strategy more cost-effective than continually bringing in outside consultants, but a staff member can lend tremendous credibility to any new opportunity.

University Partnerships and Professional Development Schools

University partnerships open the opportunity for shared expertise. Many research institutions are eager to work with practitioners in learning more about effective practices. University professors can often be a tremendous resource for action research. With this type of partnership, the practitioners can gain insight into the most current literature, procedures for action research, and outside views of the work. These partnerships can result in increased content knowledge and classroom strategies.

Professional Development Schools develop a balance between theory and practice by becoming the site for both the university learning and the hands-on opportunity for the staff (Abdal-Haqq, 1998). The seamless fabric of this partnership is powerful for both the university and school communities.

The merits of some kinds of professional development can be weighed depending on the context of the school, particular issues raised by analysis of student data, and budget. The Merits of Selected Types of Professional Development (see Table 3.4) is a partial listing of types of professional development and their cost-effectiveness. Selecting a professional development strategy would depend on the career stage of the individual teacher and the expertise of the individuals involved.

PAUSE

Pause: Consider the professional development that would best fit your school context.

PEDAGOGY AND CONTENT KNOWLEDGE

Deep understanding of content will change how the teacher approaches the subject in the classroom. Elementary teachers are often criticized for having only superficial knowledge of some content areas, and secondary teachers are accused of focusing on the content rather than the student. The most effective teachers balance their understanding of child development and the subject. In addition, teachers make subject matter more meaningful for students by using appropriate pedagogy. Helping teachers understand how to teach their content area using certain tools, exercises, and links to prior knowledge can be the basis for effective lessons.

To help students meet high standards, teachers must know their students well, build lessons that scaffold the learning, and create assessments that provide necessary feedback. Teachers who possess deep content and pedagogy knowledge are able to keep lessons flexible and responsive. Professional development plans must include opportunities for teachers to develop content knowledge, instructional strategies, and appropriate use of assessments.

Table 3.4   Merits of Selected Types of Professional Development

	Type of Professional Development	Brief Description	Cost Effectiveness	Career Stage	Level of Expertise
Inside knowledge	Peer coaching	Pairs or small teams of colleagues who plan together, observe each other, and provide specific feedback to one another	Initial investment for materials and training and perhaps recurring costs for substitutes		
	Mentoring	Matching a less experienced teacher with one of greater experience who provides assistance	Recurring costs for training and salaries		
	Study groups	Groups meet regularly to study a concern, innovation, book, or to discuss student work and the teaching that produced it	Initial investment for materials and training		
	Action research	A process by which practioners engage in collecting and analyzing data to generate new knowledge and information	Few costs involved Possible release time for participants		

	Type of Professional Development	Brief Description	Cost Effectiveness	Career Stage	Level of Expertise
	Collaboration around student work	Grade level teams or departments use student work to guide discussion about trying new strategies in the classrooms	Few costs involved Possible release time for participants		
	Reflective practice	Self-examination by an individual or a group to create greater meaning and construct information about a situation	Few costs involved		
	Personal learning plans	Written plan for personalized professional development	Few costs involved		
Outside knowledge	Subject matter projects, networks, collaboratives	Resources and networking opportunities outside the school site	Perhaps some recurring costs for memberships and meetings		
	Inservice, conferences, trainings	Individuals attend event and bring back information to the site or develop a cadre of trainers	Recurring costs		
	University partnerships	University and school staff share expertise though joint projects or research	Initial investment for materials and training		
	Professional development school	School site becomes the locus of university learning and hands-on practice	Initial investment for materials and training		

KEY POINTS OF CHAPTER 3

- The National Staff Development Council has standards to guide professional development planning.
- To design high-quality professional development, it is important to understand the types of professional development and the impact on the adult learner.
- All professional development plans should be focused on the target of improved student learning.
- Various models and strategies can be used as alternates to traditional inservice.
- A balance of "inside knowledge" and "outside knowledge" is a powerful combination for making change.
- By understanding content, pedagogy, and developmental levels of the students, teachers can help make subject matter more meaningful for students.

The Principal as Implementer

Taking Action

Leaders are the architects of improved individual and organizational performance.

—Douglas Reeves

IMPLEMENTER

TAKING ACTION

How do we take action?

What are the supportive conditions for professional development?

What tools will help sustain the action?

Principal's Scenario

The Chavez School professional development leadership team is about to convene, and Jorge, as chair, has the agenda ready after reviewing it with Juanita, the principal, and other team members. The agenda for the meeting focuses on the critical question around how the professional development planning will be carried out.

Jorge: We have developed a wonderful professional development plan, but I'm concerned that we, as a team and school, can't implement it. Where are we going to get the time, resources, and support for our professional learning? Maybe we've spent too much time planning and not enough doing? Let's work through the agenda and see what you think?

Janet: As the union rep, I want to be sure that teachers get the support they need and we don't spend teachers' time ineffectively. What incentives are you going to have for teachers?

Tanya: Look, we've invested a lot of time analyzing student achievement data, researching best practices and ideas, and formulating a professional development plan, so let's get doing it. You know the stuff about job-embedded professional development, why don't we start practicing it? I think the team, teachers, and Juanita as principal supports the plan, so let's take action!

Yen: Yes, we've developed the shared leadership and collaboration, now we need the time to get it done. You all know what I shared last week at our meeting about using time differently. Let's take the plan and look at the next 3 years of implementation, using time differently, to get at the achievement we want for students. I'm tired of planning too—let's get moving!

Juanita: Listen, I know all of you have a lot invested in making the plan work. I do too! My concern is do we have the processes, strategies, and tools available to use to take action? I will assure you that I will deal with the district office, support your efforts, and shield you from outside demands and get resources that can help.

Jorge: The rest of you are being a little silent. What's the matter? I know your silence according to our norms says that you agree. So, what are the next steps of getting the plan into action?

The leadership team members turned to the copy of the plan and began to review it. After an hour of discussion, an outline of action steps had unfolded, but not without some intense debate. Juanita couldn't help but think about how she was really going to ensure the conditions, resources, and support of the professional learning that this ambitious leadership team had put together to assure increased student achievement. The principal's role was crucial, and she wondered if there were tools available that the team could use rather than be reinvented.

How do we take action?

If any thing is to happen as a result of all the professional development planning, the principal's role as an implementer of action brings this component of focused efforts to the improvement process. As an implementer of action, the principal must collaboratively help focus the action to get results if the school ever expects to close the achievement gap and raise the bar of expectations. The link between establishing a culture of collaboration and accountability within the school is based on relationships developed over time and founded on trust (being honest) and integrity (keeping one's word). Implementing an ongoing professional development plan requires systematic steps and scaffolding to support change efforts. The "Focused Question" that is answered in this chapter is: *"How do we take action?"* Certain conditions, models, strategies, and tools must be present if high-quality professional development is to be carried out. This chapter will emphasize the conditions, supports, and various models, strategies, and tools that can be used by a principal to take the action necessary that will lead to improved professional practices and student achievement. Implementation represents all the professional development planning put to action.

What are the supportive conditions
for professional development?

CONDITIONS FOR TAKING PROFESSIONAL DEVELOPMENT ACTION

The conditions under which professional development takes place are critical factors in successful implementation. As a principal works toward implementing plans, the following conditions need to be in place (see Figure 4.1):

- Collaborative environment
- Shared leadership
- Time
- Incentives
- Resources for support

Each of these conditions offers a firm foundation for supporting the professional action work. Each will be described briefly to provide the principal with key points to review as implementation takes place. Conditions for Professional Development Action (see Table 4.1) provide a simple tool for a principal to use as a review chart of what conditions are or might be in place as action is taken.

COLLABORATIVE ENVIRONMENT

Collaboration and trust are hallmarks of conditions that must be present for learning communities to develop and teachers to grow, but these are not easy conditions to establish. Most schools are organized in ways that isolate teachers so that collaboration is not easily established or sustained. Working within their classrooms on a daily basis with students, teachers do not have a lot of time for interacting with colleagues or developing trust with other teachers and administrators. Teachers' experiences and their collective understanding of trust and collaboration vary. The skills associated with continuous collegial interactions must be nurtured within the school. Professional development, like school reform efforts in general, works best as a collaborative effort when teachers, administrators, classified staff, students, and parents trust one another and can work together over a sustained period of time.

Figure 4.1   Conditions for Professional Development

**RESOURCES
&
TOOLS FOR
SUPPORT**

INCENTIVES

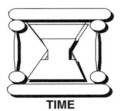

TIME

SHARED LEADERSHIP

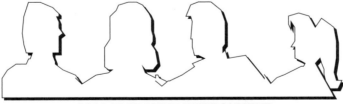

COLLABORATIVE ENVIRONMENT

Table 4.1   Conditions for Professional Development Action

Collaborative Environment	What Currently Exists?	What Needs Improving?
	Grade level teams Dept./discipline teams Action research teams Assessment teams Schoolwide councils Parent/community groups Exhibitions of student work Schoolwide portfolio/report Other:	
Shared Leadership	Representative Leaders	Responsibilities
	Grade level Department level Interdisciplinary teams Action research teams School community Other:	
Time	Use of Available Time	Possible Use—Plan
	Balanced calendar Summer, before school starts Periodic schedule days Faculty meeting Grade level meetings Department meetings Common planning time Before school, late starts Release time within the day After school, evening Saturday/weekends End of school, summer institutes Staff retreats Banked time Alternative grouping Alternative scheduling School-university partnership Other:	

Incentives	*What Drives Individuals to be Involved*	*What is Available to Involve Individuals, Teams, & School?*
	Use real-life events of teaching as a source Instructional materials Supplementary materials related to training Time Space (facilities) Equipment or technology (computer and software) Capacity to videotape lessons Acknowledgment of work efforts by school/district and board Stipends and credit hours Refreshments (lunch, dinner, or treats) Planning time Release time for inter/intra school visits Substitute time for teachers to plan Opportunities to attend conferences as teams Grade level planning time Release time for coaching (peer or expert) Release time for conferences with principal and others Other:	
Resources/Support	*What Resources/Supports?*	*School/District & Community*
	New instructional materials Supplies Facilities (conditions to work) Time (see incentives above) Technology sources (equipment, software, list servers, etc.)	

(Continued)

Table 4.1 (Continued)

Resources/Support	What Resources/Supports?	School/District & Community
	Access to expert advice/training Subject-matter networks Other networks Critical friends Access to peers expertise (modeling, coaching, & sharing) Structured tools & protocols University & business partnerships University classes Grants Journals & research Responsive & supportive Administration Regulatory flexibility	

As schools become learning communities, trust and collaboration are developed and modeled. Teachers need structured opportunities to collaborate on decisions, problems, and new ideas within an atmosphere of mutual trust and respect. Even motivated teachers are unlikely to sustain innovations in their own classrooms without the support, trust, and involvement of colleagues. The school as a whole is even less likely to improve without productive interactions and trusting relationships among the teachers. The pull of individuals within the learning community is the sense of vision, purpose, and shared values rather than the fear of negative consequence, which seems to be a driving force in many of the current educational reform mandates.

Trust must permeate the organization for teachers to collaborate and take charge of their own professional development. Principals must model daily the attributes of trust by consistently keeping their word, telling the truth, and acting in alignment with their own and the schools' expressed values. This represents one of the largest challenges of transformational leadership for a principal. Fullan (2003) describes this extensively in his new book, *Moral Leadership*. A principal helps to promote trust by providing support for teachers' efforts, helping them stay focused on student achievement and sharing leadership and power to carry out change efforts. Teachers need to trust each other as they work together for school improvement. Coaching requires the ultimate trust of receiving feedback and reflecting. Trust can take fear out of the context for learning. Teachers must believe that they can learn new ways to teach and assess. Beliefs are built on trusting people, including their integrity and commitment. Like collaboration, trust must be nurtured step-by-step and reinforced constantly by leaders and teachers at the school and district level.

Personal conversations, well-planned meetings, school newsletters, newspaper articles, site councils, up-to-date Web sites, and a continuous information flow build trust with parents and the community. Parents need to know what changes are taking place within the school that will affect their children, and schools need to solicit parents' feedback to consider before implementing major changes. Parents need to trust that teachers and administrators will retool constantly as do other professionals (doctors, lawyers, and engineers) to keep up with changing times and expanding knowledge. Parents understand that as professionals, teachers cannot operate with knowledge they gained when they graduated from college two or more decades ago to meet the needs of today's students. Just as doctors do not operate on the knowledge they had when they left medical school years ago, teachers cannot effectively function without updating their skills. Parents must trust that when teachers are involved in professional development, they are developing skills and abilities to meet the learning needs of their students. They should be informed about the relevance of new knowledge in the following areas:

- Instructional strategies and how students learn
- Content knowledge
- Uses of technology
- Changes in student population and greater diversity, and how teachers will meet these changing needs
- New demands on schools to create informed citizens and productive workers

When teachers leave their classrooms for continued learning, parents must trust that teachers' professional growth will ultimately benefit their children.

Collaboration is never easy, and breaking down isolation is difficult. Fullan (1993) discusses the issues of isolation, autonomy, and collaboration. Teachers guard their solitude because it gives them a territory to call their own, provides them with an opportunity to get work done, and shields them from unwanted scrutiny. Although leaders understand a teacher's desire to work alone, one teacher cannot meet the increased academic performance needs of students without reaping the benefits of intellectual support from colleagues who share research, analyze student work together, use technology, develop new curricula, and update their teaching strategies.

Hargreaves and Dawe (1990) caution against "contrived collegiality" when administrators impose superficial forms of collaboration upon a school culture that is still isolationist at heart. Schools need to foster genuine collaboration that stems from committing to shared goals and recognizing the necessity to work together to achieve them. Again, common time to work together is a means for fostering collaboration among teachers when they work as grade level teams sharing lessons, creating team units, or reading a book together and reflecting on its implications for their school. Collaboration is also evident when committee members use consensus building to make decisions on curriculum or school budgets. As mentioned before, two of the most powerful forms of teacher collaboration are involvement in designing and implementing professional development and peer coaching. In the context of their working together, learning skills such as group facilitation, conflict management, and other group process skills helps develop and sustain teachers. Their collaborative efforts break the norm of isolation found in schools. Different schools approach collaboration development in various ways, but it is important for teachers and the principal to acknowledge the significance of collaborative work as they nurture the relationships that strengthen collaboration.

Collaboration within the school is important; however, collaboration should extend beyond the school to inform teacher practice. Teachers can collaborate at the district level with other teachers who share their concerns and restraints. Through state or national collegial networks such as the National Writing Project (or other subject matter projects) or the Coalition of Essential Schools (educational philosophies and instructional methods), teachers and principals share problems and successes that transcend the boundaries of districts or regions. Their involvement provides them with opportunities to develop, implement, and discuss new approaches in a safe and supportive environment. Networks provide members with opportunities to attend conferences, publish articles, and exchange information through discussions, correspondences, electronic list serves, newsgroups, and other formats. Teachers can interact with experts and peers at different times by exchanging e-mail, asking questions, sharing experiences and discussing issues. The community of learners in networks reduces teacher isolation and increases collaboration without regard to location and time.

SHARED LEADERSHIP

Shared leadership provides the basis for the development and ongoing, broad, inclusive leadership of a school professional development plan. The principal, by sharing leadership and involving teacher leaders, grade level, or department team leaders as well as including district and outside expertise in the professional development process, helps build ownership in goals, plans, and actions. The issues of shared leadership have been covered in Chapter 2 in developing the school culture and as a key condition for professional development action.

TIME

If student achievement is to improve, then teachers need time to engage in the Learning Cycle: learn, practice, implement, observe, and reflect (see Chapter 3, Figure 3.1). "Time is our number one most valuable non-renewable resource" (Sommers, personal communication, March 28, 2003). Currently, educational reform movements fail because there is not the long-term commitment to professional development for teachers who need to be sustained on a year-round basis. New instructional practices intended to improve student success often fail to be implemented because the professional development plans of schools are sporadic, time constrained, and lack focus (Speck & Knipe, 2001). These professional development activities do not give teachers enough time to understand the new strategy, practice, implement, receive coaching, and collaboratively reflect on their practice with other teachers. No wonder little changes in schools! We need to look at professional development time and learning for teachers in a different way that is balanced throughout the year. Ongoing job-embedded (within the daily school work) professional development offers the necessary time for teachers to learn and collaborate that will sustain change over time and improve student achievement (Daniels, Bizar, & Zemelman, 2001; Sparks & Hirsh, 1997). How do we get time for professional learning in our schools?

The traditional 9-month school calendar is an artifact of our agrarian 19th- and early-20th-century past, when students worked in the fields to harvest the crops (Stenvall, 2001). This archaic school calendar limits the potential learning of not only the students but also the teachers. Cooper, Nye, Charlton, Lindsay, & Greathouse (1996) have documented the loss of 3 months of learning during the summer vacation months for students. Teachers generally have very sporadic summer learning for themselves unless they initiate it individually through a summer institute, network, or university work. These are separate, discrete activities based on the individual teacher's motivation and use of personal time. When school ends in late May or early June, teachers might have a short inservice day about a new curriculum or textbook adoption but then are left alone for the long summer. Just before school starts in late August or after Labor Day, teachers are generally infused with a rapid-fire string of professional development activities completed in 1 or 2 days in preparation for the start of the new school year. The intent of these professional development activities is to ensure a great start to a new school year and to help meet the goals of the school and district. Research tells us that this type of temporary infusion of learning for teacher development does not work (Darling-Hammond, 1997). What follow-up to the initial learning is done? Reform conducted on the fringes of the school year and day will never become an integral part of the school. Time, the school calendar, and school day issues for professional development must be addressed if true school reform is to take place.

Examining the school calendar and the use of time during the school day for long-term, job-embedded professional development can drive meaningful change. In *The Teaching Gap*, Stigler and Heibert (1999) ask us to "imagine what would happen if we were to take the millions of dollars spent every year to 'reform' American education, much of which has little effect on classroom practice, and use it to provide the time and resources teachers need to improve teaching" (p. 3). What are the professional development opportunities for teachers to have quality professional development on a year-round basis or balanced calendar?

Research and proven practice provides several models for reallocating time within the year for learning and quality professional development. Each of the possible options will be briefly discussed in the following sections: balanced calendar and year-round education, expanded professional development hours and days, accumulated or banked time, alternative grouping, alternative scheduling, expanded staffing, and school-university partnerships.

Balanced School Calendar and Year-Round Education

The option of a balanced school calendar with year-round education should be explored more extensively than it is currently, to provide quality time for professional development without having the teachers leave the classrooms and their students. More districts and schools should explore the use of a balanced or single-track, year-round calendar, which shortens the summer vacations and expands periodic breaks during the school year (see Figure 4.2). Professional development plans and activities can be spaced throughout the year, providing ongoing opportunities for teachers rather than the sporadic one shot during the beginning-of–the-year teacher inservice days (Speck & Knipe, 2001). Using a balanced calendar, teachers can be introduced to a new professional development, such as an instructional strategy or literacy program, then practice it, observe, and be coached during the first 9 weeks of school. Then, at the first break (vacation and/or intersession 2–3 weeks), which allows for immediate remediation or enrichment for students, teachers can continue with professional development by continuing training, observing other teachers, or doing clinical teaching with students and debriefing with fellow teachers during the intersession. The periodic breaks in the school calendar allow for teacher and student rejuvenation as well as engaging in ongoing learning and reflection on teaching practice. Business certainly understands the need for professional development and the time to carry it out. No organization can survive without continual learning to improve the process and outcomes.

This balanced calendar uses time for professional development in a critical leverage point way that is completed during the day periodically rather than after school, in the evening, or on the weekends, when teachers are already tired from a full day of teaching. The long-term effect of systematic professional development carried throughout the year yields a sustained effect on changing and improving teaching practices (Joyce & Showers, 2002). Professional development

Figure 4.2   Traditional vs. Balanced Year-Round Calendar

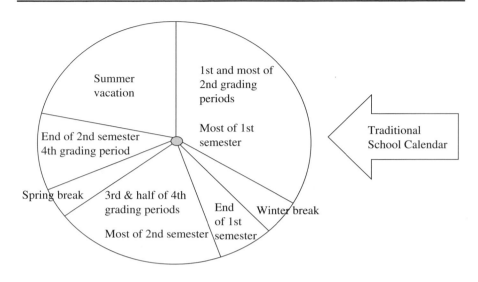

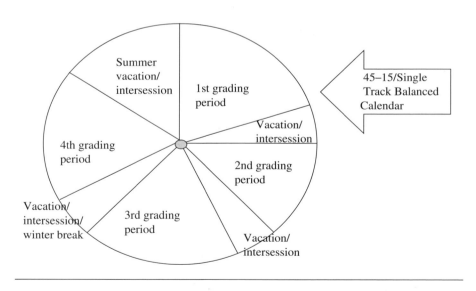

can no longer be a one-time event, but is intertwined into a balanced work year for teachers and their practice.

The other benefit of the single track, year-round calendar besides teachers' professional development is increased learning for students. It is an important recognition of the amount of learning loss students experience over the summer. Learning loss is diminished for students with shorter summer breaks (Cooper et al., 1996). In addition, teachers use less time reteaching material or establishing classroom management when students have not had an extended 3-month summer break from learning and school. Teachers and students are better served by a single-track, balanced, year-round calendar with continuous learning than by the traditional school calendar. Educators should take a serious look at the school calendar year and how it is used. Finding the time for continuous professional development over the entire year is possible in a revised school calendar year.

Expanded Professional Development Hours and Days

Districts can extend the teachers' contract to include additional hours or days for professional development. The extended contract buys time during the summer for workshops, seminars, curriculum development, and planning, and during the school year, it adds hours for follow-up (Hackmann & Berry, 2000). It also buys time for coaching and collaboration, which provides the time needed for learning and concept implementation for teachers. Collaboration time for purposes of writing curriculum and refining assessment strategies is also an excellent investment for schools.

Accumulated or Banked Time

Increasing instructional minutes during the week to accumulate or bank release minutes can be used as a block of time each week for professional development (Zepeda, 1999). Some states require waivers to implement this strategy. Schools using banked time have developed an effective block of time each week or month to do substantial intense professional development work with their teachers.

Alternative Grouping

Working with colleagues, teachers bring students together in large groups other than single classes to provide release time for designated teachers. Team teaching, regularly scheduled assemblies, or community service learning offers a means to release teachers and expand the time available for professional development (Zepeda, 1999).

Alternative Scheduling

Altering the master schedule to give teams of teachers common planning time for professional development and collaboration is another action a principal can take to provide quality time. This alternative scheduling can be done under different configurations, such as common planning time at the start or end of the day; use of block scheduling with teacher-scheduled prep periods; and adding an extra period to the schedule so that blocks of time can be available at different times of the day for different teams of teachers (Hackmann & Berry, 2000).

Expanded Staffing

A school can use regular substitute teachers to release teachers to work on their professional development during the school day. This may include the use of a floating substitute who can move from class to class within in a school and release teachers for observations, coaching, mentoring, or other types of job-embedded professional development activities. This floating substitute should be a consistently scheduled individual who knows the curriculum and students well enough to carry on regular learning activities in the classroom while the teacher is involved in professional development. A further way to expand staff is for administrators to occasionally volunteer to release teachers as a demonstration of clear support for their professional development work. Administrative leaders who help expand staff time for important work by subbing in classrooms also benefit themselves by teaching and participating with the students in the classroom (Speck & Knipe, 2001).

School-University Partnership

This approach is very comprehensive and allows for university students or faculty to cover teacher's classrooms. Professional development activities tied to the school-university partnerships inform teachers and university practice in a reciprocal way as those involved share university research and classroom practices (Darling-Hammond, 1997). Teachers, student teachers, and university faculty work together on teaching and learning issues to expand their knowledge and abilities. These types of partnerships play an enriching role for both the school and the university in a systematic way. San José State University has exemplary school district and university partnerships in the Teacher Leadership, Triple L Teaching Collaborative, and Urban High School Leadership Programs, where cohorts of teacher teams participate in educational leadership. Working collaboratively on school team action research projects, the team members truly make a difference in teaching and learning in their schools. The Southern Maine Partnership, coordinated by Miller, is another fine example that has been in existence for some time influencing schools and the university (Lieberman & Miller, 2001, chap. 7).

Given all considerations for the use of time for professional development, educators are reminded that there are constraints to be negotiated in the change process. The legislature, the state department of education, the teachers union (including bargaining agreements), the school board and community, and district policies are all fluid parts of a changing system. The use of time must be addressed if teachers are to transform schools and learning for students. The National Education Commission on Time and Learning in its 1994 report, *Prisoners of Time,* states, "We cannot get there [improved student achievement] from here with the amount of time now available and the way we now use it. Limited time will frustrate our aspirations. Misuse of time will undermine our best efforts" (p. 9). The commission designated the 6-hour school day and 180-day school year as the "unacknowledged design flaw in American education" and a "foundation of sand" for our educational system. Further, the report asserts that "both learners and teachers need more time, not to do more of the same, but to use all time in new, different, and better ways. The key to liberating learning lies in unlocking time" (p. 10).

Time is an essential factor in turning schools into continuous learning communities. If educators and boards refuse to tackle alternative schedules, they are stuck with what they have had in the past: periodic, shallow, or episodic professional development activities that have little or no sustaining effect on a teacher's practice in the classroom. Time is an important element for continuous learning. Adequate time for professional learning must be allotted. Teachers may be required by their state to take professional development hours to renew their teaching licenses, or they may earn salary increases for taking college units or advanced degrees. This is a catch-as-catch-can system. This patchwork nature of professional development will have to change. Continuous learning opportunities must become part of teachers' everyday working lives and part of every school's institutional priorities. Closing the achievement gap as well as raising the expectation bar for students will not happen without the critical element of time for professional learning.

Incentives

Most teachers are intrinsically motivated to keep learning, but how is this motivation sustained for teachers throughout their careers? What incentives or recognition will be meaningful for teachers? Recognition in its various forms is an acknowledgment from within the school and district of the valuable work of teachers. Teachers often respond that time and appreciation as well as a need to be treated as professionals are ways to recognize their efforts for continuous professional development. Treating teachers professionally and recognizing their efforts may range from providing materials, a dinner or refreshments at an activity they are sponsoring, release time to work with others on a unit of curriculum, or formal recognition at a school board meeting. Stipends, supplementary materials related to a training they attended, and/or equipment such as computers or software for participating in development activities are incentives for teachers that provide real and visible rewards for their work in professional growth. These incentives recognize that the teacher has participated in and is open to new learning. Publicly recognizing teachers' professional development efforts without creating animosity is important by tying the teacher's success to the overall school improvement efforts. Below is a brief summary of possible incentives, but a principal or staff should not be limited by these suggestions: Create more of your own.

Here are possible incentives for teachers engaged in professional development:

- Instructional materials
- Supplementary materials related to training
- Equipment or technology (computer and software)
- Capacity to videotape lessons
- Acknowledgement of work efforts by school or district and board
- Stipends and credit hours
- Refreshments (lunch, dinner, or treats)
- Planning time
- Release time for inter- or intraschool visits

- Substitute time for teachers to plan
- Opportunities to attend conferences as teams
- Grade level planning time
- Release time for coaching (peer or expert)
- Release time for conferences with principal and others
- Other incentives you have found successful

Time, however, remains the greatest incentive that teachers need. Building time for quality professional development within a teacher's workday or year is crucial. Superintendents, board members, and principals who commit to recognizing and honoring teachers for their continued learning for school improvement legitimize professional learning in the eyes of teachers, administrators, parents, and communities.

Pause: What conditions for taking professional development action are in place at your school?

PAUSE

RESOURCES FOR SUPPORT: OUTSIDE & INSIDE

Teachers need access to adequate as well as enriching resources, such as research, effective practices from inside and outside their schools, assistance by accomplished practitioners as coaches, and creative ideas of experts on subject matter, instructional methods, and school organization. Resources are fundamental to supporting reform efforts and influence teacher and administrator abilities to implement change (Guskey, 2000). Lack of resources or spreading resources so thin that they have little impact may hinder the implementation of a well-designed professional development plan. Targeting resources where they can make the greatest impact is a strategic way of using limited resources in schools and districts. Without the proper resources, teachers can become disillusioned with the innovations because materials, books, supplies, equipment, software, technology, or facilities are not available to help them implement what they have learned and are ready to apply.

Professional development cannot take place without proper resources made available to teachers in the implementation stage. Use of the computer and the links it can make for teachers electronically are fairly unexplored resources for information and assistance. The use of list servers and e-mail allows teachers with common interests to

Table 4.2   Matrix of Teaching Expertise

Teacher Name	Grade/Level	Improvement Focus	Expertise to Share
Example Elementary Isabel I. Jose L. Ann W. Continue to list other staff:	Primary 4–6 2–4	Literacy Math Science	Literacy circles Math manipulatives Hands-on science unit
Example High School Mike Jamina Shana Steve Continue to list other staff:	11th English 11th History 11th English 11th History	Interdisciplinary curriculum	Writing Cooperative learning Literature Problem-based learning

share information and ideas, but to be most useful, teachers need consistently functioning, up-to-date technology and easy access. Again, nothing is more frustrating for a motivated and passionate teacher trying to implement new strategies than lack of the proper resources. Leaders must assure teachers that their professional development work is important by providing the necessary resources and support.

Review of inside resources is an important step. A principal needs to know who on the teaching staff has expertise in various curricular, instruction, or assessment areas. By using a matrix that lists the staff members' names and then listing the areas of focused improvement, including curricular areas, instructional strategies, and assessment techniques, the principal can create a tool to help analyze who has strengths on the staff. These individuals can then share their expertise with other staff members by sharing, modeling, and coaching others (see Table 4.2). This allows the staff the opportunity to take the initiative and leadership around an area of improvement in which they have some expertise and can help other teachers become more proficient. The use of teachers within the school serves to validate important work and provide readily available support for implementing new ideas. It supports the collaborative culture that is being developed within a school. By using the information the matrix provides, teachers are engaging their own expertise, ideas, values, and energies in the learning process; thus professional development shifts to building capacity rather than demanding compliance.

What tools will help sustain the action?

STRATEGIES AND TOOLS: BUILDING CAPACITY AND SUPPORTING THE WORK

There are multiple ways to build capacity within a school learning community. The tools and strategies, when used in a purposeful way to carry out a school professional development plan for improvement, provide specific means and opportunities to reinforce the importance of professional learning.

Whole Staff Conferences With Focused Questions

Whole staff conferences are a means for the entire staff to meet to discuss specific goals and progress. Usually 2 to 3 hours allows for planned interaction or instruction around specific goals. Teachers can learn a new concept, read a professional journal article and discuss its implications for classroom practices, view a video, participate in "Teacher Walks" (see below) or spend time in grade level discussions. Teachers are expected to dialogue about what they are learning, and Focused Questions (see Table 4.3) help with the discussions. A summary of the discussions should be compiled, shared, and disseminated to all teachers.

Focused Grade Level Sessions

Grade level or subject area sessions can become the heart of carrying on new learnings in professional practice. Teachers come together on a weekly, biweekly, or monthly basis to review and discuss strategies they have learned at staff conferences or workshops or one identified by the team they are studying. During the grade level sessions, teachers can analyze student work and the progress of their

Table 4.3   Whole-Staff Conference Focused Questions

What are the critical questions teachers need to be discussing with regard to our school improvement plan?

Use guiding questions during staff conference and meeting to focus the work of school improvement efforts.

Focus for September: Goals for year? Student achievement based on data? Plans for year?

Getting Started:

- What do I need to know about my students?
- What information and student work will I collect to make sure my students are learning?
- What will I learn from my students' work?
- From my learning, what assessment do I need more practice with?
- How do I create lessons to meet my students' needs?
- How will I use the results of my assessments to change my instruction and to help modify my students' learning?
- Who on the teaching staff has some experiences that they can share, model, or coach me on?

Focus for October:
Focus for November:
Focus for December: (Midyear check in)
Focus for January:
Focus for February:
Focus for March:
Focus for April:
Focus for May: What progress have we made, and what is the evidence?

learnings from their previous meeting. The discussion should be clearly focused on what did and did not work and what changes need to be put into place for continued progress. Teachers share their student work and strategies that are focused on the professional development goal, not random areas of interest (see Table 4.4).

Teacher Walks

"Teacher Walks" is a hands-on vehicle for viewing and learning purposeful instruction around the improvement goals. Teachers with the principal, as teams or individuals, visit other grade level

Table 4.4   Focused Grade-Level Meeting Summary

Team Chair: _____ Members present: _____

Date: _____

Meeting room: _____

Recorder: _____

Focus of grade-level meeting: _____

Teaching strategy discussed: _____

Summary of grade-level meeting: (sharing, learning, etc.)

Grade-level needs: _____

Next steps or tasks before next grade-level meeting: _____

teachers' classrooms and explore ideas by viewing teaching sessions or demonstrations of what is working in their classroom to improve student success. Much like the experience of medical interns in teaching hospitals, "Teacher Walks" are coordinated by the principal and based on the principle of learning together as the "Teacher Walk" takes place.

"Teacher Walks" are similar to the *Walkthrough*, which is "a protocol developed originally by [Anthony] Alvarado and his colleagues in New York City's Community District 2 (Elmore & Burney, 1997) and modified and promoted by the Institute for Learning at the University of Pittsburgh (Institute for Learning, 1997)" (Lieberman & Miller, 2001, p. 226). The protocol begins with a discussion of learning standards. In the case of the University of Pittsburgh model, these especially emphasize the students' capacity to learn rigorous intellectual habits and content, learning as apprenticeship, and habits of "accountable talk." Following the discussion, the participants tour the school, entering its classrooms and other work spaces, looking for and examining student work, talking with students and teachers, and in all of these activities searching for evidence of the "principles of learning" (University of Pittsburgh model) in practice. Following the *Walkthrough*, participants discuss their findings with each other, offering evidence from their notes to support the judgments they make. "Then one of their number, typically the principal, writes a post-*Walkthrough* letter to the teachers summarizing the findings" (Lieberman & Miller, 2001, p. 226).

Teacher Visitation and Observation

Teacher visitations to another teacher's classroom can be facilitated by the principal using a simple form such as the Classroom Visitation Request Form (see Table 4.5) to coordinate the classroom visit.

Teachers can observe demonstrations of specific strategies (literacy circles, math manipulatives, etc.) by experienced or lead/mentor teachers. The Teacher Observation Form (see Table 4.6) helps structure the classroom visit with prompts: What I observed, What I learned, What I intend to study for possible implementation, and Questions. Teachers can then test out and practice strategies within their own classrooms. Teachers should keep videotapes of the demonstrations for future study so that they can review the specific strategy. Demonstration, practice, and reflection on practice help the process of changing instructional strategies. There are other observation protocols available for looking at classroom

Table 4.5   Classroom Visitation Request Form

Name of teacher: _____

Visitation date requested: _____

On-site: _____ Off-site: _____

Location: _____

Time: _____ to _____

Information:

Teacher to be visited: _____

What I plan to observe: _____

How does this observation fit with grade-level or school goals? _____

Classroom coverage needed: Yes _____ No _____

– –

Visitation Confirmation

Name of teacher: _____

Confirmation of visitation to teacher: _____
Date: _____ Time: _____ to _____

_____Coverage cannot be arranged for you at the requested date and time.
Please select a different date and/or time.

_____
Principal's Signature

Table 4.6   Teacher Observation Form

Name of teacher: _____ Name of teacher observed: _____
Date: _____ Lesson focus: _____

What I observed	What I learned	What I intend to study for possible implementation	Questions ???????????
			e.g., What do I want to know more about?

teaching and providing feedback (see Resource B, "Recommended Web Sites").

Professional Growth Seminars and Specialized Study Groups

Professional Growth Seminars can be used 2 to 3 times a year as a means of going into depth in an identified area of instructional need. Teachers can become part of a "specialized study group." In the professional seminars, new knowledge, including research, is shared, and teachers then reflect, self-evaluate, collaborate, and problem solve to improve specific teaching practices/strategies. Teachers can select sessions based on their needs. Teachers who have expertise in identified areas will lead the sessions. Protocols can be designed to help the facilitators.

Information Sharing and Journal Articles

Journal articles or text excerpts focusing on current teaching practices can be shared periodically with teachers. The weekly bulletin could include important shared thoughts by teachers to reinforce the ongoing work. Keeping current through regular professional reading and sharing allows for constant integration of new information and trends. Larger articles can be "jigsawed" during group meetings.

Personal Professional Learning Journals

Each teacher on the staff keeps a professional learning journal following staff conferences, grade level sessions, and other learning experiences. These personal reflections can serve to clarify, raise questions, and reflect on new learnings and how they are practiced within the classroom. Using "Focused Questions" after each session can help guide the reflective writing and help support the focus of the new learning. Personal journal insights can be voluntarily shared with peers, teams, and schoolwide when appropriate.

Inter/Intra School District Visitations

Interdistrict or intradistrict visitation provides teachers with an opportunity to visit and see the classrooms of other teachers practicing successful strategies. A roving substitute teacher can be hired once or twice a week to help with classroom visitation, thus freeing the teacher for the visit. Off-site visitations can provide new insights about teaching strategies that have not been used at the site. The observation of the new teaching techniques in action is a powerful learning experience and provides an incentive to return and to try the practice within the teacher's own classroom. The teacher observation form, as previously mentioned (Table 4.6), and the school visitation form (see Table 4.7) are easy means of organizing and capturing information from visitations.

New Teacher Support Team

New teachers need additional support, and a new teacher support team can help. The beginning teacher support programs offer additional assistance and should be coordinated with the ongoing school efforts so that there is not a duplication of efforts. New teachers need immediate support in classroom management and lesson designs. Teachers teaming to support new teachers are a critical help. The California Beginning Teacher Support and Assessment (BTSA) program and the New Teacher Center (NTC) provide excellent examples of new teacher support teams. Veteran teachers often discover that the role of mentoring a new teacher is invigorating and rewarding, so the benefit is mutual (Moir & Bloom, 2003).

Expert or Coaching Partners

Initial expert coaching can be used to model and facilitate the development of coaching partners to help implement and practice new learning in a safe and supportive collegial environment. All teachers within a school can be assigned coaching partners. The purpose of the coaching partnership is to build a working relationship that will allow for planning together, observing each other, and reflecting on each other's practice. Partners should be matched to allow for sharing of successful instructional practices. Initial coaching training by an expert needs to take place for the coaching partners to understand their roles and develop their skills. Remember that the element of reinforcement of learning through coaching is one of the most powerful forms of seeing teaching practices change and adopting new instructional strategies. Without an element of coaching, new learning is not practiced, reinforced, or adjusted and does not become a part of the teaching repertoire.

Table 4.7   School Visitation for Principal and Teacher

Name of school: _____ Principal: _____

Date: _____ Location: _____

Purpose of School Visit—Topic: _____

– How did the principal and teachers gain support for this change?

– How did the principal and teachers deal with specific problems during implementation?

– What would the principal and teachers consider the strengths of the change?

– What areas would the principal and teachers caution you to be aware of and provide support for implementation?

– How are the principal and teachers working together to maintain the momentum of their efforts?

Reflective Questions:

– What have you learned about the process of school improvement?

– How will you use this information in your school/classroom?

– What outcome do you hope to achieve in your school/classroom?

Action Research Teams: Inquiry Cycles

In communities where inquiry is a regular way of working, not a project or strategy, groups of teachers and student teachers engage in joint inquiry and construction of knowledge through conversation and other forms of collaborative analysis and interpretation. Through inquiring, talking, and writing, they make their tacit knowledge more visible, call into question assumptions about common practices, and generate data that make possible the consideration of alternatives (Lieberman & Miller, 2001, chap. 4). Part of the culture of inquiry communities is that analysis work includes collegial talk, grappling with data and results, and clarifying learning that is made visible and accessible day-to-day. It is different from teachers being "trained" in workshops. Using inquiry means that teachers challenge the purposes and underlying assumptions of educational change efforts rather than simply helping to specify or carry out the most effective methods for predetermined ends. Teacher leadership is fostered by "questioning" and "challenging the system"; thus there is a leadership consequence of inquiry-based professional development. Inquiry both stems from and generates questions. "[Teachers] learned to look to their own practice as a powerful source of learning" (Lieberman & Miller, 2001, p. 66). This exemplifies the type of teacher learning taking place at International High School and the Urban Academy in New York. Ancess, in Lieberman & Miller (2001), explains how, specifically, organizational learning at these schools meant a continuous cycle of broad-based faculty understanding of their own and their colleagues' learnings. Applying the lessons learned to their own practice and adapting the structures of the school's organization and pedagogy provided supports for the changes demanded by the new knowledge:

> Teacher learning can be characterized as problem solving or inquiry that starts with teachers' particular goals for their students. (p. 75)

> Because teachers had the opportunity to create new knowledge and to apply it to their school's daily life, they had the opportunity to create and recreate their school culture and community each day, helping it to achieve a closer correspondence to its values and vision and increasing their investment in it. (p. 76)

Student performance mapped against their teacher's goals for them was the most powerful catalyst for teacher learning. It defined the content and determined the direction of teacher learning. . . . [Faculties] who were dissatisfied with the performance of their students brought their knowledge of their students to the problem of improving student performance and acquired new knowledge and developed strategies to apply it to their situation. (pp. 76–77)

Teachers did this by using a cycle of inquiry through action research. Action research is also addressed in Chapter 3 (see Figure 3.2).

Mentor Teachers

Utilizing mentor teacher expertise with the professional development plans of the school provides another source of support. Focusing the work of the mentor on the key improvement goals of the school and how the mentor can help by mentoring teachers in specific areas targets the work.

Uses of Technology

The uses of technology can be a tremendous resource in professional development processes. Integrating the following types of technology can help enhance the school's and teachers' collaborative work:

- Communication via e-mail, instant messaging, chat rooms, message boards, list servers, etc.
- Research information via Internet and Web sites
- Minimize paperwork and documentation through electronic portfolios and files
- Manage data and analysis software for easy access and disaggregation of the data

School Portfolio Development

The development of a comprehensive school portfolio provides a process that requires the documentation of the whole change effort. It should be viewed as part of the professional development process as it is job-embedded in the ongoing work of the school. It should not be viewed as a separate process, but as an integral part of the teachers' and principal's ongoing efforts. It is a tool to highlight the successes and focuses the work on areas of need. As a tool that demonstrates progress, the school portfolio has become a professional development process tool. An example is the Bay Area School Reform Collaborative (BASRC), which has seen significant results using school portfolios (Center for Research on the Context of Teaching, 2002).

Responsive and Supportive Principal/Administration

A principal and an administration that is responsive and supportive of teacher professional development at all levels through meeting teachers' learning needs is critical. The trust and collaborative environment will not be sustained if the actions and words of the administration are not supportive and timely. Help with regulatory flexibility and bureaucracy are important leadership interventions. These interventions can keep enthusiasm, momentum, and innovative action that improve teaching and student learning (Lieberman & Miller, 2001).

PLANNING TO KEEP PROFESSIONAL DEVELOPMENT FOCUS: USING A MATRIX OF ACTION

Professional development planning must be ongoing and consistent throughout the school year. Looking at a Matrix of Action (see Table 4.8), a principal can help keep the focus on professional development and the key areas of improvement. The use of this matrix helps reinforce the efforts for change on the long-term continued support of growth in each teacher. The consistency and support builds capacity in each staff member. There is a recurring emphasis on improving practice to improve student achievement.

Table 4.8   Professional Development Plans Matrix of Action

Focus of professional development:_____
Directions: Use the chart as a map of the school actions over time to see the focus of the professional development plan and action. Do not be limited by these columns; add your own.

Monthly Plan	*Faculty Meetings*	*Grade-Level Meetings*	*Visitations Classroom/ School*	*Coaching*	*Mentors*	*Other Areas*
Summer						
September						
October						
November						
December						
January						
February						
March						
April						
May						
June						
Summer						

KEY POINTS OF CHAPTER 4

- A principal needs to understand the supportive conditions (collaborative environment, shared leadership, time, incentives, and resources) necessary to create ongoing job-embedded professional development at a school site.
- Time for learning is critical, and there are various ways to find the time for teachers to engage in the Learning Cycle (learn, practice, apply, model, coach each other, and reflect on progress).
- Teachers need a variety of incentives and resources to support their efforts in professional growth.
- Tools and strategies help focus the professional development work so that it is planned and systematic.
- School leaders who are responsive and supportive of teacher professional development are critically needed.

CHAPTER FIVE

The Principal as Reflective Leader

Evaluating Results

Reflecting on one's own work enhances meaning. Insights and complex learning result from reflecting on one's experiences.

—Art Costa

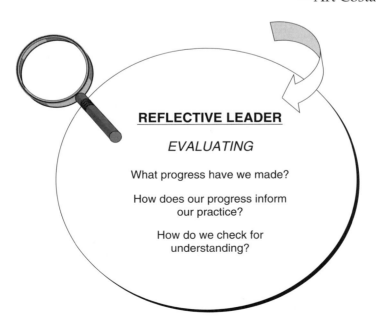

REFLECTIVE LEADER

EVALUATING

What progress have we made?

How does our progress inform
our practice?

How do we check for
understanding?

Principal's Scenario

The faculty meeting at Chavez School looked different in January. The meeting was being held in several classrooms to review student work and give input on the progress that the school was making on the professional learning and its effect on student achievement. The school leadership team had designed the faculty meeting with a specific goal of continuing to reinforce job-embedded learning, which affected student achievement. All were wondering and asking themselves, "Is what we are doing helping, or not helping? Are we doing it because it's easy for us, or because it's good for the students? What are we doing that changes our practices and affects students, especially the lowest achieving? Are our practices really reflecting what our goals are?"

Juanita: This is our midpoint check in on the progress we are making on our professional learning and its effect on student achievement. The leadership team has designed a protocol as part of the cycle of inquiry for you to look at several pieces of student work and assess them in relation to how your new learning has affected student achievement. Anna will elaborate and take it from here.

Anna: You know, I used to think professional development was about sitting, getting an idea or making something, and taking it back to my classroom to use the next day. Our leadership team has caused a paradigm shift in my thinking about how and why I learn as a professional. Today, we are going to reflect on our progress by looking at student work, and then we are going to ask ourselves individually and collectively how this assessment informs our teaching practices. Last, we want to check that we all understand the professional learning work and its effect on student achievement. With this end in mind, let's get started.

The leadership team, with the protocol divided up with various grade level teams, departed to different classrooms to review the student work. Juanita, as principal, was a little nervous about the outcomes because she had invested so much time in seeing that the leadership team looked at research and best practices and implemented their ideas. There was the nagging question in her mind: "What would the district office, parents, and the few dissenting teachers say if there was no progress shown after all of this hard professional development planning and work?" Time would tell, but she was committed to the long-term and no wavering or jumping on the next bandwagon. She was convinced that the quality of teaching and teacher learning have tremendous influence on student success.

> What progress have we made?

REFLECTION IN AND ON ACTION: EVALUATION

A principal as reflective leader is an expansion of Schon's (1983, 1991) notion of teacher as "reflective practitioner." As a reflective leader, a principal must model a continuous process of inquiry and reflections on actions. Principals as reflective leaders constantly consider their actions by gathering data and feedback from multiple sources to assess the progress of the school. Reflection in action and about action must become a habit for effective leaders and learning communities. A professional development plan must have this reflective evaluation piece. Evaluation is a means to assess the progress of the school's and the faculty's joint efforts together and whether it is affecting student achievement. Wanting to know what progress is being made and how that progress is informing practice are critical to the study and reflection on actions. This is collegial accountability and reflection that develops in a school learning community culture. As the school year progresses, the principal and teachers must ask the following questions: *What progress have we made? How does our progress inform our practice? How do we check for understanding?* It is this constant mantra of *How do we know we are progressing, and what is the evidence* that should drive professional development plans and assessments to improve student achievement.

While it is critically important that principals reflect on professional development through evaluation, it is equally important for principals to reflect on their own learning and the results that are being produced in the schools. Significant change happens only when the principal has a mental model about reflection on practice. The school change efforts benefit from regular periods of reflection by the

Figure 5.1 School Cycle of Inquiry

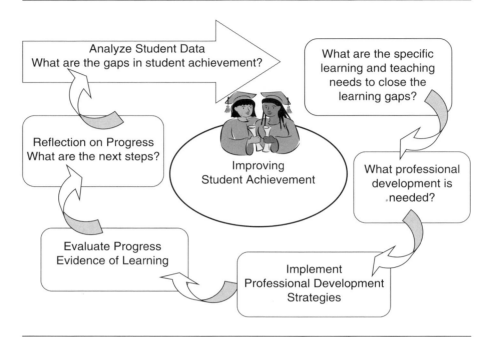

principal and its leaders. Understanding the needs of a principal's own professional development and reflection is an essential piece for fostering continuous learning and improvement.

Evaluation of efforts and reflection on practice are critical to finding out what has been accomplished and what needs continued attention. The School Cycle of Inquiry (Figure 5.1) provides a lens by which to reflect on progress.

Each cycle of inquiry ends with a reflective component that asks for not only self-study but also evidence. This practice of acknowledging what has been learned and what needs to be studied triggers the next cycle of inquiry for continuous improvement. The school community, including the principal, uses reflection as a continuous inquiry improvement process. Data generated by actions need to be examined and analyzed for results.

> It is important to reinforce the idea that professional development and accountability are reciprocal processes demanding high engagement in both policy and practice, and that the long-term objective of investing in educator's skills and knowledge is to increase the capacity of schools to solve

Figure 5.2   Bay Area School Reform Collaborative (BASRC) Cycle
of Inquiry

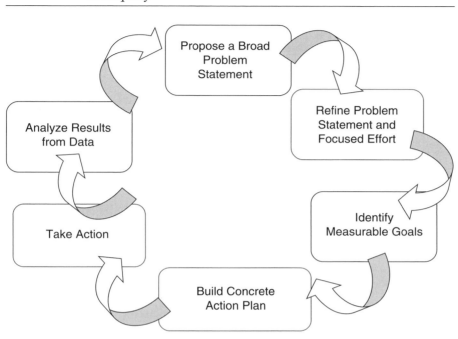

pressing problems through the application of best practice,
not just to implement someone else's solutions. (Elmore,
2002a, p. 12)

The Bay Area School Reform Collaborative (BASRC) is an example of an evidenced-based school reform effort that has used evolving
patterns of inquiry to build capacity for change at both school and
classroom levels. The BASRC cycle of inquiry seeks to "reculture"
schools in ways that support whole-school change. Using a school-
based cycle of inquiry to inform school reform efforts and marshal
diverse forms of knowledge to support teachers' learning and change
is the overall BASRC strategy (McLaughlin, with Zarrow, cited in
Lieberman & Miller, 2001):

The cycle of inquiry required of BASRC schools is intended to
help schools pose, investigate, and respond to questions about
policies and practices and has six steps [see Figure 5.2]. The
first two steps have to do with selecting and narrowing a

question for investigation. The next step is to identify measurable goals. This step recognizes that setting specified targets as a measure for success is critical in determining the success or failure of an action. The fourth and fifth steps include creating and implementing a particular action— connecting knowing and doing. The sixth step is to collect and analyze results from data generated by the action taken. Finally, the cycle connects back to the first step as the problem statement is refined in light of new evidence. Simply put, BASRC's cycle-of-inquiry aims to inform schools about what they are accomplishing in terms of their focused reform effort and consequences for students. (p. 80)

The BASRC cycle of inquiry used by schools has begun to mature into an accepted, iterative process of data collection, analysis, reflection, and change. Learning communities are developing in which teachers are generating knowledge and creating the source of learning. The whole school is both the site of inquiry and the focus of change, the community that incorporates most of the faculty rather than a smaller group of reformers. "Discourse about students' standards-based achievement and expectations about evidence are commonplace rather than exceptional" (McLaughlin, with Zarrow, in Lieberman & Miller, 2001, p. 81). Knowledge of teacher practice has made teachers more powerful as consumers of knowledge and school reform efforts. Finally, BASRC findings have shown that school level inquiry adds meaning to classroom-based inquiry but that classroom-based research needed to be situated in school level inquiry if it were to add up to coherent knowledge for school decision making and progress. Thus, inquiry and action in BASRC schools saw the development of confident learning at the school sites by teachers and principals about practice versus the norms of privacy and individualism characteristic of schoolteachers (Lortie, 1975). These communities of teacher learners are engaging in a social process of active participation in inquiry that reflects about current practice and habits of inquiry based on data and evidence that prompts change at school and classroom levels (Rogoff, 1994; Wenger, 1998).

RESULTS-ORIENTED EVALUATION

There is a dire need to move away from measuring professional development success by numbers of participants. Simply put by

Sparks and Hirsh (1997), "Results-driven education for students requires results-driven staff development for educators" (p. 5). Rarely do evaluations of professional development move beyond an accounting of the event and the accompanying tally of numbers, whether or not the participants enjoyed themselves, or a brief feedback opportunity with no examination of long-term effects (Guskey, 2000).

Historically, many professional developers have considered evaluation a costly, time-consuming process that diverts attention from important planning, implementation, and follow-up activities. Others believe they simply lack the skill and expertise to become involved in rigorous evaluations. As a consequence, they either neglect evaluation issues or leave them to "evaluation experts" who are called in at the end and asked to determine whether what was done made any difference. The results of such a process are seldom very useful (Guskey, 1998, p. 36).

Principals who are committed to professional development need to demonstrate whether the professional development activities and processes have made any difference for the school and make that information available to other principals, district office administration, parents, and teacher leader groups. Encouraging principals to network and share their information about what works in the classroom is essential to their own professional growth.

Generally, educators plan and implement but fail to evaluate whether what they are doing makes a difference for the individuals and the system involved in professional development. It is important for a school community to stop and analyze the progress they have made by evaluating the outcomes of their efforts. A constant question should be: "Has the professional development process produced the expected outcomes?" Bull and Buechler (1996) summarize some key evaluation questions educators should be asking about professional development:

> All the rhetoric about professional development and school improvement, all the theories about program design and peer coaching, all the action research and collaboration in the world ultimately give way to a single question: Is professional development working? To be more specific: Is professional development reinvigorating teachers? Is it expanding their repertoire and improving their ability to teach? Is it leading to new roles and responsibilities for teachers within the school organization? Is it contributing

to a richer, more positive school culture? Most importantly, is professional development leading to improved student performance? (p. 27)

In other words, is the outcome of the professional development initiative worth the human and fiscal resources that have been invested? Systematic evaluation of professional development, which is purposeful and results driven, is needed if it is to be supported by the school board, administrators, teachers, parents, and the community.

EVALUATION FOCUS: IMPROVING STUDENT LEARNING

Most schools do not have a formalized, consistent process for evaluation of professional development designs, programs, activities, or events (Sparks, 1998; Guskey, 2000). The common practice is to plan a professional development program and begin implementation without an agreed-upon set of expectations of what "full" implementation and success looks like. The rigor of evaluating it is almost nonexistent. The traditional questionnaire survey of participants after an inservice as to whether or not they found the speaker interesting, visual aids helpful, and other parts of the activities interesting does not get to the heart of whether the professional development brought about change in teacher behavior and increased success for students (Loucks-Horsely, Hewson, Love, & Stiles, 1998).

Sparks and Hirsh (1997) emphasize the importance of the shift in evaluating professional development from teachers' perceptions regarding their needs to a focus on student learning:

> Ultimately, systemic change efforts must be judged by their contribution to student learning. It is no longer sufficient to determine the value of staff development efforts by assessing participants' perceived satisfaction with those efforts. While participants' satisfaction is a desirable goal, assessment efforts must also provide information about changes in on-the-job behavior, organizational changes, and the improved learning of all students. (p. 41)

Multifaceted, long-term evaluation that examines professional development in some depth and tries to determine its effect on teachers and students is needed (Bull & Buechler, 1996). Evaluation designs need to be started in the early part of the professional development planning process and continue after the particular professional development activity is completed (Guskey, 1998, 2000; Killion, 2002). Evaluation should provide information about the implementation process and document effects, especially on student achievement. Evaluation reports not only provide information to teachers and the principal, but are an important tool to inform parents and the community on the progress that is being made at the school. When parents and school board members see the hard evidence and results of professional development, then there is less skepticism about future release time or noninstructional time being devoted to professional development activities.

The need for concrete evidence that professional development is making a difference is important for maintaining credibility with teachers, leaders, and the community. A formal evaluation process demonstrates that the school is interested not only in teacher growth but also the growth for students. Professional development needs an ongoing evaluation process to ensure that goals are being achieved, needs are being met, and resources are being used wisely (Zepeda, 1999). Without systematic evaluation of efforts based on hard data, it is almost impossible to determine whether the changes are sustainable. And more important, did the professional development activities improve teachers' abilities to increase student achievement?

How does our progress inform our practice?

ELEMENTS OF EVALUATION PLAN

An evaluation plan for professional development should include the following elements, as described in Figure 5.3.

Needs Assessment

What Does the Current Student Achievement
Data Show as Learning Gaps?

Student achievement data, properly analyzed and disaggregated, will show clear learning gaps among the students. The data analysis is the focus of the needs assessment for what changes, and learning needs to take place to improve student achievement in the targeted areas. Planning for professional development before clarifying the

Figure 5.3   Elements of Evaluation Plan for Professional Development.

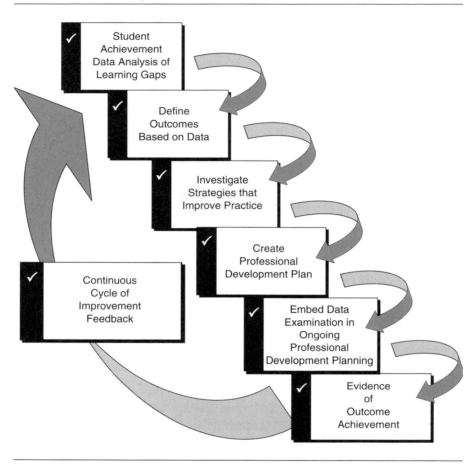

learning gaps will not provide the necessary development that is needed to improve the student learning results. Data analysis and commitment to understanding the importance of data are keys to the needs assessment. It can no longer be what teachers would like to learn, but what is needed based on the data.

Outcomes

What Are the Student Achievement Outcomes?

An evaluation plan should begin with the end in mind by focusing on what the expected outcomes are for student achievement. If a principal and teachers want to see results, there must be specific targeted outcomes. This focus must be on expectations for student achievement based on the current analysis of data and learning gaps. Designing an evaluation plan is similar to backward planning: Start with the end in mind (Wiggins & McTighe, 1998).

The Professional Development Evaluation Plan (see Table 5.1 later in chapter) is a tool that a principal and school can use to set specific plans for reaching outcomes and having specific evidence of results. This tool provides for a systematic way of planning the evaluation process. The components and questions regarding professional development and its evaluation can be organized and clarified by using the guide. It is intended to help a principal and teachers focus on the desired outcomes first and then develop the activities that will meet those outcomes, rather than planning the activity and hoping for the outcome, which is usually the case. Evaluation planning helps focus on the outcomes rather than the activities (Guskey, 2000).

Professional development plans typically have a wide range of goals, but they are often not articulated as outcomes. How would you describe your successes with professional development activities and plans? What changes have occurred? By whom? Generally, professional development results are reported as activities completed (conducted series of workshops or summer institute) rather than accomplishments (higher student achievement rate in problem solving). Outcomes for professional development can be described as new abilities (knowledge, skills, strategies, attitudes), by a variety of individuals (teachers, students, administrators), organizations (departments, teams, schools, districts), and areas (teaching, leadership, change management).

> Being clear about desired outcomes, articulating what they would look like if they were present, not only lays important groundwork for evaluation but also causes the program to be more focused and purposeful. (Loucks-Horsely et al., 1998, p. 221)

Learning Needs of Teachers

What Learning and Teaching Strategy Needs
Do Teachers Have? How Does That Influence
the Creation of the Professional Development Plans?

Teacher learning and teaching strategy needs must be identifiable based on the student achievement data. The gaps in learning show areas that should be targeted for professional development. Then the professional development plans will be set up to provide for the learning needs of the teachers. Examples of teacher learning needs and strategies might be in the area of literacy, where teachers need research-based strategies in fluency and reading comprehension skills to improve student results. The need for learning the new literacy strategies should be based on the recent student data that show poor performance in these specific areas. A well-grounded professional development plan can be created by reviewing and using the High-Quality Professional Development Key Components and Rubric (see Chapters 1 and 2) as guides in the planning process.

Evidence of Progress

What Evidence Will Be Used to Assess Progress?

The evaluation process needs to be accomplished in a variety of ways to provide information on the progress of the participants and define whether the outcomes have been met. To help understand the impact of the professional development plan and activities, a wide range of evidence is needed. Evidence from participants in the form of surveys, interviews, observations, lesson analysis, performance tasks, student work, and focus groups can provide data that contribute to the evaluation process. The type of data collected will depend on the outcomes to be measured as a result of the professional development plan. Clearly stated outcomes for professional development help frame the short- and long-term data collection process. If, for example, the outcome is to improve students' reading scores, it would be important to gather data substantiating teacher strategies that develop students' abilities to read (i.e., Has the use of a teaching strategy increased student capacity in reading? How would we know? What evidence do we have?).

Evaluation baseline data on students (i.e., achievement scores, grades, attendance rates, and discipline rates), teachers (i.e., assessment of current knowledge, teaching skills, learning styles, and attitudes), and the school (i.e., related procedures, policies, roles, and the extent of teacher collaboration) are needed in the initial stages of planning to provide beginning data to compare with the results of the professional development work. Also, these initial data give a clearer picture of the status, abilities, and needs of the students, teachers, and school and should be reviewed as the plan is developed.

Developing a plan without understanding student achievement and teacher and school levels of need does not address the specific professional growth requirements for expected outcomes. Understanding the abilities and needs of participants in professional development is critical and can easily be identified through the collection of baseline data. Failure to assess the current status and level of professional development of participants condemns the process to "one-size-fits-all" professional development. Further, it builds resentment among participants because their individual abilities and knowledge are not recognized and valued.

Pause: Think about the elements of an evaluation plan you may already have in place. What do you still need?

PAUSE

THE PROFESSIONAL DEVELOPMENT EVALUATION PLAN

The Professional Development Evaluation Plan is a tool to be used in creating an effective evaluation plan (see Table 5.1). First, the baseline data of current student achievement is stated (Needs Assessment), in combination with the expected student achievement outcomes identified (Expected Outcomes), the learning needs of teachers are correlated to the outcomes (Teacher Learning Needs), and finally, the evidence of progress is specified in relation to student outcomes (Evidence of Progress). This Professional Development Evaluation Plan provides a framework for finding out whether professional development is working. Sets of questions are provided as guides under each element. These are not meant to be restrictive and can be expanded upon by a school's context and need.

ASSESSING PROGRESS USING THE PROFESSIONAL DEVELOPMENT RUBRIC

The High-Quality Professional Development Rubric (Figure 2.1) introduced in Chapter 2 should be used to assess progress. Individual teachers, teams, and whole-school assessment by using the rubric and charting progress can inform the professional development evaluation. A quick survey of teacher perspective adapted from the rubric can give the principal and professional development planning team feedback on progress (see Table 5.2). A caution should be noted here that the survey gets at teacher perspectives for feedback and should inform the professional development plan, but student achievement data is the ultimate outcome. The survey provides immediate feedback on teacher perceptions as a means of informing practice and

Table 5.1   Professional Development Evaluation Plan

Data *Analysis of Learning Gap* *Needs Assessment*	*Define Expected* *Outcomes*	*Teacher Learning Needs* *Investigate Strategies* *Improving Practice*	*Embedded-Data* *Examination*	*Evidence of Progress* *Outcome Achievement*
What does the current student achievement data analysis show as learning gaps?	What are the student achievement expected outcomes?	What learning and teaching strategy needs do teachers have? How does that influence the creation of the professional development plans? 1. Is it expanding the teaching repertoire and improving teachers' ability to teach? 2. Is it leading to new roles and responsibilities for teachers within the school organization? 3. Is it contributing to a richer, more positive school culture? 4. Most important, is professional development leading to improved student performance? How do you know?	How is data examination embedded in ongoing professional development planning and action?	What student achievement evidence will be used to assess progress? Benchmarks? How is the High-Quality Professional Development Rubric used in evaluation?

Table 5.2   Survey of Teacher Perspective of High-Quality Professional
Development

Survey

Teacher Perspective of High-Quality Professional
Development Informing Practice

Directions: Given your experience with the professional development
provided, what is your perspective about how it is progressing? Your input
will help inform our professional development practices. Please rate each
question and make any comments.

For each question, circle the number that best represents the answer as it
relates to the current professional development program based on the scale below.

1	2	3	4
Never	Seldom	Usually	Always

1. Do you see it providing a clear focus on learning and sustaining
   improved student learning?

   1   2   3   4

2. Has the plan and action emerged from student data and the need to
   improve student results?

   1   2   3   4

3. Is the professional development work founded on a sense of collegiality
   and collaboration among teachers, other staff, and the principal?

   1   2   3   4

4. Does the plan use shared leadership, resources, and inside/outside support?

   1   2   3   4

5. Is it research based, with a foundation in standards and accountability?

   1   2   3   4

6. Has it deepened teachers' content knowledge and teaching practices?

   1   2   3   4

   Which areas? (Be specific):_____

7. Is it centered on the adult learner through job-embedded work, options,
   and learning styles?

   1   2   3   4

8. Is it requiring ongoing inquiry, practice, and reflection to inform practice?

   1   2   3   4

9. Is it evaluating progress and accounting for student learning by
   examining results?

   1   2   3   4

10. Comments that will inform practice: _____

adjusting the professional development work. Clear benchmarks for student progress and achievement need to be specified by the teachers and principal in the professional development evaluation plan based on the focused work.

> How do we check for understanding?

EMBEDDED-DATA EXAMINATION IN ONGOING PROFESSIONAL DEVELOPMENT PLANNING

During the implementation process, participants should document their involvement, including types of training, follow-up coaching, and feedback and impact on learning. Principals as leaders already have many sources to help with this in-depth evaluation, such as questionnaires, peer observations, school records and reports, student portfolios, student performance, and achievement tests. Clearly delineating the data to be used to assess progress provides the evidence and results, which can be used to determine the next steps for action. Looking at results becomes part of the professional development plan as it reinforces ownership in the success of the process and anticipated outcomes. When individuals are engaged in analyzing the data, they inform their own practice and understanding (Lieberman & Miller, 1999; Sagor, 1992; Schmoker, 1996). Examining evidence of progress helps validate the efforts and resources expended to close the achievement gap.

The evaluation process provides informed results of the professional development initiative. It does not allow the typical responses of "We think it is working" or "We feel good about it." Evaluating the progress made by teachers and students and reporting it helps inform the school's continuous improvement cycle. It clearly focuses the school and teachers on the needed next steps. Evaluation provides for informed decision making about the learning needs of teachers to improve student achievement that should be incorporated into the professional development plan.

The evaluation process must include feedback for teachers, the use of data to show evidence, and data about student progress or lack of it. Evaluation serves as a means to observe, reflect, and analyze the work. Principals and teachers need to focus on the evaluation processes and results as soon as they begin to plan for professional development. Unfortunately, too often, educators buy into reform initiatives because of the hype around the program. The first question should be: "Is the objective to improve student achievement, and how will that be demonstrated?"

Evaluation data collected will help inform decision making using both formative (ongoing feedback) and summative (final summary) data. Common formative assessment tools include informal and formal classroom observations by colleagues and principal, construction of teaching portfolios, student portfolios, and student achievement on standardized tests. An example of a summative assessment is the traditional year-end evaluation or summary report. The evaluation will inform future work as each assessment event, in itself, provokes new learning, leading to enhanced teaching practice as a natural outcome of engaging in the assessment (Guskey, 1998; Killion, 2002; Sparks, 1998).

Effective evaluation programs should have both long-term and short-term objectives (Rutherford, 1989). Short-term objectives usually target changes in teacher behaviors, in the school, or in the curriculum, while long-term objectives focus on improvements in student achievement or behavior. Professional development can be justified only if its ultimate goal is to improve education for students. Monitoring results has proven to be a major factor for achieving success in schools and districts. Results-oriented professional development planning requires that the theory and research presented, modeled, and practiced in workshop or inservice settings be supported with on-the-job coaching to promote transfer to the workplace and to facilitate change in teacher behavior that will effect student achievement.

The professional development evaluation process has implications for principals as they provide leadership for their school's continuous improvement. Principals must help create a sense of ownership and risk taking by teachers as professional development initiatives are designed and implemented. For example, teacher-driven action research involves teachers who identify teaching/learning issues of importance, try out new methods, and determine their effect on student learning, without fear of a negative evaluation by the principal regarding their efforts (Sagor, 1992). The results of their research often lead to a further cycle of inquiry, which deepens the teacher's knowledge and understanding. It is a self-renewing process that models taking action on new learnings and examining results. Monitoring continuous improvement of teachers' learning through effective evaluation procedures also reinforces results and accountability. We can no longer afford professional development activities that do not have measurable results. Although each person may be willing to be personally involved, the administrative and teacher leadership are responsible for school and districtwide accountability and results.

Continuous improvement in schools must be an ongoing cycle of inquiry that looks at data and the professional development program to determine whether progress is being made. Inquiry into what is working or not working in the professional development program encourages a process of ongoing feedback. Adjustments can be made to meet the needs of the teachers as they learn new skills and practice them in the classroom. Through the evaluation process, teachers learn to examine their teaching, reflect on practice, try new practices, and evaluate their results based on student achievement. This ongoing reflection must be seen and nurtured as a part of the professional development process.

WORD OF CAUTION ON EVALUATION AND DOCUMENTATION

Teachers and principals can be overwhelmed by evaluation and documentation processes. There must be a caution raised about not having documentation become too burdensome. The easy forms and frameworks provided in this book are intended to help structure and assist a busy principal in providing high-quality professional development. The tools and forms should be of great benefit if used with this caution in mind of not overemphasizing documentation of activities and increased paperwork. Ways should be found to correlate required reports, teacher evaluation, and program and school evaluation so that one focused report can be made. Teachers and principals need to use their time wisely, and paperwork that does not lead to student achievement must be kept to a minimum.

REFLECTION INFORMS PRACTICE AND RAISES FOCUS ON STUDENT ACHIEVEMENT

The process of ongoing reflection and evaluation provides the principal with a means to process the variety of actions and efforts taking place within a school. Wanting to know whether plans, resources, and new learnings are affecting practice is important. By reflecting on practice, a principal and school wants to know whether professional learning is getting the results. The ultimate question must be: "What evidence is there of increased student achievement?" A reflective journal, writing prompt before a faculty meeting starts, or other ideas generated by teachers can help make their reflective process a habit and share some reflective thoughts publicly, if appropriate. The Reflective Thought! (see Table 5.3) is a sample that can be used to spark reflection and sharing.

THE PRINCIPAL'S OWN PROFESSIONAL DEVELOPMENT

As stated earlier in the beginning of this chapter, while it is critically important that the principal reflect on professional development through evaluation, it is equally important for principals to reflect on their own learning and the results they are producing in schools. The principal must be the lead learner in the school, fostering professional learning but taking time to nurture his or her own learning. What are the ways for principals to model professional learning and their own professional development? Here is a sample of ideas:

- Modeling learning together with teachers focused on specific school goals and learning needs
- Attending and participating in teacher professional development
- Seeking coaching and a reflective coaching partner
- Meeting with other principals as colleagues and discussing and grappling with issues and data (e.g., Minneapolis district formed professional learning communities for principals and gave up one principal meeting a month to accommodate principal learning)
- Developing job-embedded professional development opportunities in a principal's workday
- Joining professional associations, such as Association for Supervision and Curriculum Development (ASCD); principal associations (NASSP or NAESP); and networks, such as Harvard's Principal's Network, Association of California School Administrators (ACSA), Principal's Academy, and alumni networks
- Attending conferences, workshops, meetings, and summer institutes or academies where new information and updates are provided
- Reading journals and other research materials

Table 5.3   Reflective Thoughts!

Writing Prompts for Reflection:
    What's new about what you are learning since last we met?
    How is the new strategy affecting student learning and achievement?
    What evidence is there of increased student achievement?
    What insights would you like to share with colleagues?

- Taking and reflecting on self-assessment tools
- Continuing university work or school university partnership work
- Using the principal's evaluation process to set professional learning goals and seek support to achieve the goals.
- Others (This list is not exhaustive of what's available for principals learning. Please add to it. We would like to know your additions.)

Principals must make their own professional learning a priority; otherwise, they fail to model the importance of learning as a professional. Too often, we have seen principals who fail to be continuous learners and condemn their schools to the past as well as their leadership. Alvarado (1998), from his work in New York, clearly states it: "Professional development is the job." The principals' abilities to lead depends to a large part on keeping current, developing their leadership abilities, and working with teachers to increase professional learning. A focus on how to support one's own learning as principal is critical to efforts aimed at improving student learning. By asking principals to examine their own practices in context with their school and expected professional standards, principals will increase their knowledge about their school, teachers, and students, become informed about their capacities, and receive guidance about what they need to do next to support themselves and the school. Changing practice is a complex, long-term effort involving both technical and moral clarity and change (Stokes, in Lieberman & Miller, 2001). Principals need to model this!

KEY POINTS OF CHAPTER 5

- Reflection on practice is a continuous process that informs the individual's as well as the school's practice and focuses next steps for the cycle of improvement.
- Data analysis and results of student achievement must inform planning and actions.
- The School Cycle of Inquiry is a process tool for continuous improvement.
- Professional development plans should be targeted based on student achievement data and learning gap needs.
- Learning and teaching strategy needs of teachers must be identified based on student achievement data and be the basis for professional development planning.
- Evaluation of progress must be clearly focused with specific multiple pieces of evidence.
- While it is critically important that principals reflect on professional development through evaluation, it is equally important for principals to reflect on their own learning and the results they are producing in their schools.

CHAPTER SIX

The Principal as Change Agent

The Challenge for the Future

I wonder how many children's lives might be saved if we educators disclosed what we know to each other.

—Roland Barth

Leadership & Learning

What lessons have been learned about high-quality professional development and building capacity for increased student achievement?

How does this new knowledge influence your practice as a principal and professional development leader?

What challenges do you see for the future?

Principal's Scenario

It was August again, and Juanita was standing in the hallway of Chavez School, thinking what was so different about what she saw now compared with what she'd imaged 12 months ago. Even though these were the last days of summer and teachers and students had not returned, she could see the difference. The leadership team members had invited a board member to visit the school, and as she waited, she said aloud, "What really made the difference? What would the leadership team, teachers, district office, parents, and the community say now?"

Mike: Hey! There's Juanita thinking aloud again! Remember what happened last year at this time when I caught you talking to yourself and imagining? Does it look different?

Tanya: Come on Mike, don't give her a bad time. She's kept us focused, as a leadership team and school, and allowed us to see the importance and impact of professional learning and our leadership role. You have to admit things are different around Chavez, but we have some big challenges left.

Anna: Yes! We haven't arrived yet, but what a great learning journey. We've brought Roberto, the board member, to see the progress of our work during the last school year and at our summer institute. He's interested in how seriously we are taking our own professional learning and what impact it has had on student achievement.

Roberto: Yes, several parents and the superintendent have mentioned your progress, but I wanted to see it myself and talk with the leadership team. As a board member as well as a businessman, I'm interested in knowing whether what you are doing really sustains increases in student achievement and how changes in your practices will help you continually improve.

Juanita: I think you will be surprised how the leadership team has assembled an action plan and multiple forms of evidence.

Mike: Wow! Who would believe we are not just focused on standardized test scores and workshops to fit them. We've learned a few things about high-quality professional development and learning, but there's still more to learn. Let's get going so we have time to share with Roberto! Juanita, are you coming, or are you still dreaming?

Juanita: You've got me! (laughter) But I think we've got something here, and I believe we can keep it rolling. Right? Leadership and learning are very intertwined, and as principal, I've learned a lot by working with all of you! We've deepened our teaching practices, enhanced our professional learning, and provided persuasive evidence to support our work.

What lessons have been learned about
high-quality professional development and
building capacity for increased student achievement?

LESSONS LEARNED FOR LEADERSHIP

Professional development is a powerful means to improving schools and student achievement. Elmore (2002a), in *Bridging the Gap Between Standards and Achievement: The Imperative for Professional Development in Education,* states that "the use of professional development is at the center of the practice of improvement. It is the process by which we organize the development and use of new knowledge in the service of improvement" (p. 32). As you assess your new learnings and their application to your school, think about the following questions:

- What lessons have been learned about high-quality professional development and building capacity for increased student achievement?
- How does this new knowledge influence your practice as a principal and professional development leader?
- What challenges do you see for the future?

Reflecting on lessons learned and applying them to your unique school and teachers will help build the learning community capacity you need to reach your goals of increased student achievement. Pause

Figure 6.1   Focused Questions: Principal as Professional
Development Leader

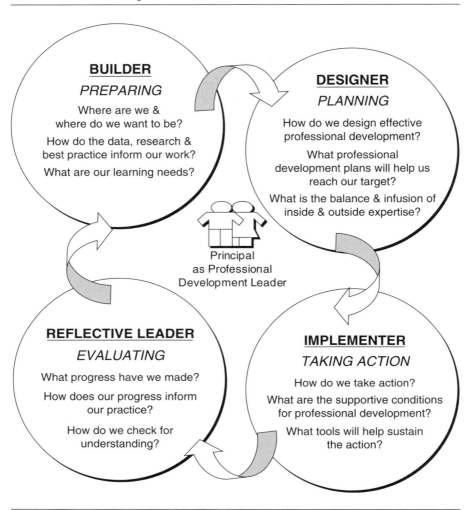

a moment and look at Figure 6.1, "Focused Questions: Principal as
Professional Development Leader." Use this visual as an overview
guide to understanding the big picture of the role of the principal as
a leader in professional development. It provides a large summary
map for meeting the challenges of continual professional learning
that a principal and learning community can use to help guide
their learning journey. Closing the knowledge gap of what quality
professional development content and processes are must be rooted

within the learning community, thus increasing the capacity of the school to solve pressing achievement gaps.

> How does this new knowledge influence your practice as a principal and professional development leader?

INFLUENCE THE QUALITY OF TEACHING AND LEARNING: LEADERSHIP MATTERS

As a professional development leader within a school, the principal knows that it is critical that teachers have the knowledge and skills they need to help students learn. A substantial body of research suggests that one of the most important school determinants of student achievement is the quality of teachers (Darling-Hammond, 1999; Shields, 1999). If the most effective way to improve student achievement is to improve the quality of teachers, then improving the quality of teaching and learning will lead to increased student achievement by all students, and particularly for the most disadvantaged (Darling-Hammond, 1999). The current reauthorization of the 2001 Elementary and Secondary Education Act, No Child Left Behind, is further evidence that teacher quality has emerged as a top federal education priority (U.S. Department of Education, 2002). Teachers, as a critical element in student achievement, must have the opportunity, resources, and support to develop professionally. The leadership role of the principal with other teacher leaders in designing, implementing, and evaluating high-quality professional development *matters*. Leaders influence the quality of professional learning within a school by the continuous dialogue, structures, and assessments that are used to focus on results: increased student achievement. Sparks (2002) summarizes the leader's influence when he states,

> Leaders matter because they can affect the fundamental choices, mental models, and sense of efficacy of those with whom they interact. They are particularly powerful in leading communities of learning when they stand with others as equals and partners to assist them in creating that, which initially may have been viewed, as impossible—schools in which all students and staff members learn and perform at high levels. (p. 14)

MAKE PROFESSIONAL DEVELOPMENT AN INTEGRATED PART OF THE OVERALL SCHOOL PLAN

Professional development will have its greatest impact if and when it is an integral part up front of the overall school improvement planning process. According to a recent study conducted for The Pew Charitable Trusts by SRI International (David & Shields, 2001), research on seven urban school districts implementing standards-based systemic reform, known as the "Pew Network," found that schools that communicate ambitious expectations for instruction supported by a strong professional development system are able to make significant changes in classroom practices. This report shares the original theory of standards-based reform (see Figure 6.2) and takes the creation of ambitious standards, aligned assessments, and accountability as the starting place for increasing student achievement. But the researchers modified the standards-based reform theory after results showed that districts that had ambitious standards for students as a starting place for improving instruction with high expectations for instructional practice and professional development up front got better results. The researchers go on to say, "Across the Pew Network districts, the greatest strides occur where the adults also have opportunities to learn" (David & Shields, 2001, p. 45). By aligning a high-quality professional development system with the school improvement plan, there is a cohesiveness of focus and support to make the necessary change in practice to significantly increase student achievement. Principals as professional development leaders must keep this in mind and provide the leadership initiative to make it happen.

What challenges do you see for the future?

THE CHALLENGE: IMPLEMENT HIGH-QUALITY PROFESSIONAL DEVELOPMENT COMPONENTS INTO SCHOOL PRACTICE

The challenging task for the principal as a professional development leader along with teacher leaders is not to tell teachers what best practices are, but to create opportunities for teachers to discover through a vital learning community important new knowledge and practice. This journey of discovery by teachers and the principal

Figure 6.2   The Original and Modified Theories of Standards-Based Reform

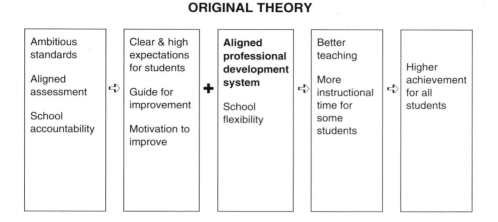

ORIGINAL THEORY

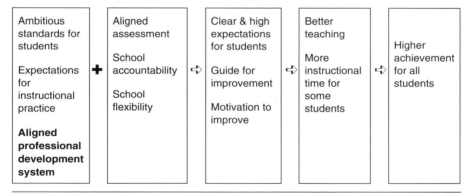

MODIFIED THEORY

SOURCE: David & Shields (2001).

through high-quality professional development should display the characteristics shown in Figure 6.3.

PRINCIPAL'S JOURNEY MAP OF DISCOVERY OF HIGH-QUALITY PROFESSIONAL DEVELOPMENT

This journey of learning through using the components of high-quality professional development will help you, as principal, meet

Figure 6.3   High-Quality Professional Development Key
              Components

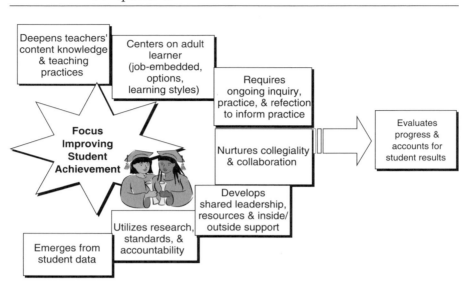

the challenges principals and teachers face. All students deserve
high-quality teachers and learning experiences so that they can reach
their full potential as learners. The Principal's Journey Map for
Professional Development (see Figure 6.4) provides a visual summary of the ideas that have been presented in this book. Although
the journey map may look linear, the process of the journey is
interwoven. As a visual, it highlights key points that a principal
and teachers can use as guideposts in reviewing their actions and
keeping a focus.

CONCLUSION: MEETING THE CHALLENGE FOR THE FUTURE: IMPERATIVE TO CREATE IT!

Given what we know about high-quality professional development
practices, the school and the principal as a collaborative professional
development leader currently have the capacity to create the professional learning community that will produce the results. Barth (2001)
says it this way: "If you want to predict the future, create it! This

Figure 6.4   Principal's Journey Map for Professional Development: Discovery of High-Quality Professional Development

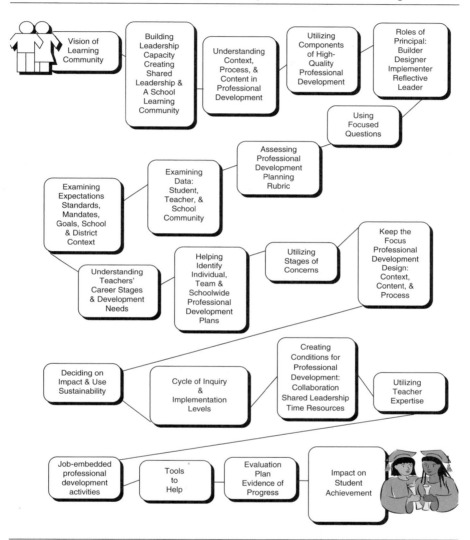

is precisely what school people now have the opportunity—and imperative—to do" (p. 213). As a principal, you can wait no longer to act on this knowledge. We know you will make a difference for teacher learning and student achievement. We hope this book has inspired you as well as given you helpful research, ideas, strategies, and tools. Happy journey!

KEY POINTS OF CHAPTER 6

- Professional development is a powerful means to improving schools and student achievement, and the principal is a key leader influencing the quality of teaching and learning.
- Focused questions about professional development helps keep the principal on target and guides the school's learning journey.
- The leadership role of the principal with other teacher leaders matters in providing high-quality professional development.
- Professional development will have its greatest impact if and when it is an integral aligned part up front of the overall school improvement planning process.
- The Principal's Journey Map for Professional Development provides a visual summary integrating the high-quality professional development components into the daily work and professional learning of the principal as professional development leader.

Resource A: Recommended Readings

Bredeson, P. (2003). *Design for learning: A new architecture for professional development in schools.* Thousand Oaks, CA: Corwin.

Darling-Hammond, L. (1997). *The right to learn: A blueprint for creating schools that work.* San Francisco: Jossey-Bass.

Elmore, R. (2000). *Building a new structure for school leadership.* Washington, DC: Albert Shanker Institute. Available: www.shankerinstitute.org/Downloads/building.pdf.

Elmore, R. (2002). *Bridging the gap between standards and achievement: The imperative for professional development in education.* Washington, DC: Albert Shanker Institute. Available: www.shankerinstitute.org.

Guskey, T. R. (2000). *Evaluating professional development.* Thousand Oaks, CA: Corwin.

Killion, J. (2002). *Assessing impact: Evaluating staff development.* Oxford, OH: National Staff Development Council.

Lieberman, A., & Miller, L. (Eds.). (2001). *Teachers caught in the action: Professional development that matters.* New York: Teachers College Press.

National Staff Development Council. (2001). *Standards for staff development* (Rev. ed.). Oxford, OH: National Staff Development Council.

National Staff Development Council. (2002). *By your own design: A teacher's professional learning guide.* Available: www.enc.org/pdguide or www.nsdc.org.

Sparks, D. (2002). *Designing powerful professional development for teachers and principals.* Oxford, OH: National Staff Development Council. Available: http://www.nsdc.org/educatorindex.htm.

Speck, M., & Knipe, C. (2001). *Why can't we get it right? Professional development in our schools.* Thousand Oaks, CA: Corwin.

York-Barr, J., Sommers, W. A., Ghere, G. S., & Montie, J. (2001). *Reflective practice to improve schools.* Thousand Oaks, CA: Corwin.

Resource B: Recommended Web Sites

ON THE WEB

The professional educational associations, government centers, and regional educational lab networks listed below provide online resources and links to a variety of professional development current research and practices. Suggested Internet resources are intended to provide ongoing updated information for professional development ideas and planning.

Professional Educational Associations

American Educational Research Association
http://www.aera.net

Association for Supervision and Curriculum Development
http://www.ascd.org

National Staff Development Council
http://www.nsdc.org

American Association of School Administrators
http://www.aasa.org

The National Association of Elementary School Principals
http://www.naesp.org

National Association of Secondary School Principals
http://www.nassp.org

National Middle School Association
http://www.nmsa.org

National School Board Association
http://www.nsba.org

Government

United States Department of Education
http://www.ed.gov/
http://www.ed.gov/inits/teachers/development.html

National Center for Educational Statistics (NCES)
http://nces.ed.gov/

Educational Resource Information Center (ERIC)
http://ericir.syr.edu/ (also known as AskERIC)

Regional Educational Lab Network

Links to 10 U.S. Regional Educational Labs
http://www.relnetwork.org

Appalachian Educational Laboratory (AEL)
Specialty: Rural Education
http://www.ael.org

North Central Regional Educational Laboratory (NCREL):
Specialty: Technology
http://www.ncrel.org

Northwest Regional Educational Laboratory (NWREL):
Specialty: School Change Process
http://www.nwrel.org

Western Regional Educational Laboratory (WestEd):
Specialty: Assessment and Accountability
http://www.wested.org

Mid-Continent Regional Educational Laboratory (McRel):
Specialty: Curriculum, Learning, and Instruction
http://www.mcrel.org

Pacific Region Educational Laboratory (PREL):
Specialty: Language and Cultural Diversity
http://www.prel.org

Northeast and Islands Laboratory at Brown University (LAB):
Specialty: Language and Cultural Diversity
http://www.lab.brown.edu

Mid-Atlantic Laboratory for Student Success (LSS):
Specialty: Urban Education
http://www.temple.edu/departments/LSS

SouthEastern Regional Vision for Education (SERVE):
Specialty: Early Childhood Education
http://www.serve.org

Southwest Education Development Laboratory (SEDL):
Specialty: Language and Cultural Diversity
http://www.sedl.org

NATIONAL REPORTS

National reports provide current perspectives on professional development. Frequently, professional developers search for documents to show others who question the new approach to professional learning, and these Web sites are helpful resources. The documents listed below are important current resources with a national perspective.

Professional Development: Learning From the Best: A Toolkit for Schools and Districts Based on the National Awards Program for Model Professional Development
http://www.ncrel.org/pd/

A National Plan for Improving Professional Development: National Staff Development Council
http://www.nsdc.org

National Commission on Teaching and America's Future (2003). *No dream denied: A pledge to America's children.* **Washington, D.C.**
http://www.nctaf.org/

Educational Information

Annenberg Institute for School Reform
http://www.annenberginstitute.org

California Beginning Teachers Support and Assessment (BTSA) Program
http://www.btsa.ca.gov

Coalition of Essential School
http://www.essentialschools.org

EdSource
http://www.edsource.org

Education Trust
http://www.edtrust.org

Education Week
http://www.edweek.com

Harvard Education Letter
http://www.edletter.org

New Teacher Center
http://www.newteachercenter.org

RAND Education
http://www.rand.org

School Services
http://www.ssc.com

References

Abdal-Haqq, I. (1998). *Professional development schools: Weighing the evidence.* Thousand Oaks, CA: Corwin.

Alvarado, A. (1998, Winter). Professional development is the job. *American Educator, 22*(4), 18–23.

Bambino, D. (2002, March). Critical friends. *Educational Leadership, 59*(6), 25–27.

Barth, R. S. (1990). *Improving schools from within.* San Francisco: Jossey-Bass.

Barth, R. S. (2001). *Learning by heart.* San Francisco: Jossey-Bass.

Bennis, W., & Nanus, B. (1985). *Leaders: The strategies for taking charge.* New York: Harper & Row.

Breaux, A. L., & Wong, H. K. (2003). *New teacher induction: How to train, support, and retain new teachers.* Mountain View, CA: Harry K. Wong.

Bull, B., & Buechler, B. (1996). *Learning together: Professional development for better schools.* Bloomington, IN: Indiana Education Policy Center.

Burke, P. J., Christensen, J. C., & Fessler, R. (1984). *Teacher career stages: Implications for staff development* (Whole No. 214). Bloomington, IN: Phi Delta Kappan Educational Foundation.

Calhoun, E. F. (2002). Action research for school improvement. *Educational Leadership, 59*(6), 18–24.

Center for Research on the Context of Teaching. (2002, October). *Bay Area School Reform Collaborative Summary Report.* Stanford, CA: Author.

Christensen, J., Burke, P., Fessler, R., & Hagstrom, D. (1983). *Stages of teachers' careers: Implications for professional development.* Washington, DC: National Institute of Education. (ERIC Document Reproduction Services No. ED 227 054)

Coleman, J., Hoffer, T., & Kilgore, S. (1982). Cognitive outcomes in public and private schools. *Sociology of Education, 55,* 65–76.

Commission on the Restructuring of the American High School. (1996). *Breaking ranks: Changing an American institution.* Reston, VA: National Association of Secondary School Principals.

Cooper, H., Nye, B., Charlton, K., Lindsay, J., & Greathouse, S. (1996). The effects of summer vacation on achievement test scores: A narrative and meta-analyic review. *Review of Educational Research, 66*(3), 227–268.

Corcoran, T. B., & Wilson, B. L. (1986). *The search for successful secondary schools: The first three years of the secondary school recognition program.* Philadelphia: Research for Better Schools.

Costa, A. L., & Kallick, B. (Eds.). (2000). *Discovering & exploring habits of mind*. Alexandria, VA: Association for Supervision and Curriculum Development.

Daniels, H., Bizar, M., & Zemelman, S. (2001). *Rethinking high school: Best practice in teaching, learning, and leadership*. Portsmouth, NH: Heinemann.

Darling-Hammond, L. (1997). *The right to learn: A blueprint for creating schools that work*. San Francisco: Jossey-Bass.

Darling-Hammond, L. (1999). Target time toward teachers. *Journal of Staff Development, 20*(2), 31–36.

David, J. L., & Shields, P. M. (2001, August). *When theory hits reality: Standards-based reform in urban districts* (SRI Project P07270 developed for Pew Charitable Trust). Menlo Park, CA: SRI International.

DuFour, R. (2003, Winter). Leading edge. *Journal of Staff Development, 24*(1), 77–78.

Eaker, R., DuFour, R., & Burnette, R. (2002). *Getting started: Reculturing schools to become professional learning communities*. Bloomington, IN: National Educational Service.

Edmonds, R. (1979). Effective schools for the urban poor. *Educational Leadership, 37*, 15–24.

Elmore, R. (2000). *Building a new structure for school leadership*. Washington, DC: Albert Shanker Institute. Available: www.shankerinstitute.org/Downloads/building.pdf.

Elmore, R. (2002a). *Bridging the gap between standards and achievement: The imperative for professional development in education*. Washington, DC: Albert Shanker Institute.

Elmore, R. (2002b). Hard questions about practice. *Educational Leadership, 59*(8), 22–25.

Elmore, R. (2002c, February). *Leadership as the practice of improvement*. Presentation at The Association of American School Administrators (AASA) Conference, San Diego, CA.

Elmore, R., & Burney, D. (1997). *Investing in teacher learning: Staff development and instructional impact in Community School District #2, New York City*. Cambridge, MA: Consortium for Policy Research in Education, Harvard Graduate School of Education; New York: National Commission on Teaching and America's Future, Teachers College, Columbia University.

Feiman, S., & Floden, R. (1980). *What's all this tale about teacher development*. East Lansing, MI: The Institute for Research on Teaching. (ERIC Document Reproduction Service No. ED 189 088).

Fullan, M. (1993). *Change forces: Probing the depths of educational reform*. Bristol, PA: Falmer Press, Taylor & Francis.

Fullan, M. (1999). *Change forces: The sequel*. Bristol, PA: Falmer Press, Taylor & Francis.

Fullan, M. (2000, April). The three stories of education reform. *Phi Delta Kappan, 81*(8), 581–584.

Fullan, M. (2003, February). *Leading in a culture of change*. Presentation at the National Association of Secondary School Principals Annual Conference, San Diego, CA.

Fullan, M. G. (with Stiegelbauer, S.). (1991). *The new meaning of educational change* (2nd ed.). New York: Teachers College Press.

Gardner, H. (1985). *Frames of mind: The theory of multiple intelligences.* New York: Basic Books. (Rev. ed. 1993)

Glatthorn, A. A. (2000). *The principal as curriculum leader: Shaping what is taught & tested.* Thousand Oaks, CA: Corwin.

Goodlad, J. I. (1983). *A place called school: Prospects for the future.* New York: McGraw-Hill.

Gottesman, B. (2000). *Peer coaching for educators* (2nd ed.). Lanham, MD: Scarecrow.

Guskey, T. (1998). The age of our accountability. *Journal of Staff Development, 19*(4), 36–43.

Guskey, T. R. (2000). *Evaluating professional development.* Thousand Oaks, CA: Corwin.

Hackmann, D. G., & Berry, J. E. (2000). Cracking the calendar. *Journal of Staff Development, 21*(3), 45–47.

Hargreaves, A., & Dawe, R. (1990). Paths of professional development: Contrived collegiality, collaborative culture, and the case of peer coaching. *Teaching and Teacher Education, 6,* 227–241.

Hord, S. M., Rutherford, W. L., Huling-Austin, L., & Hall, G. E. (1987). *Taking charge of change.* Alexandria, VA: Association for Supervision and Curriculum Development.

Institute for Learning. (1997). *Walkthroughs: Developing a learning community* (Version 7). Pittsburgh: University of Pittsburgh, Learning Research and Development Center.

Joyce, B., & Showers, B. (2002). *Student achievement through staff development* (3rd ed.). Alexandria, VA: Association for Supervision and Curriculum Development.

Killion, J. (2002). *Assessing impact: Evaluating staff development.* Oxford, OH: National Staff Development Council.

Kliebard, H. M. (1995). *The struggle for the American curriculum* (2nd ed.). New York: Routledge.

Lambert, L. (May, 2002). A framework for shared leadership. *Educational Leadership, 59*(8), 37–40.

Lambert, L., Walker, D., Zimmerman, D., Cooper, J., Lambert, M. D., Gardner, M. E., & Ford-Slack, P. J. (1995). *The constructivist leader.* New York: Teachers College Press.

Lieberman, A. (1995a). Practices that support teacher development: Transforming conceptions of professional learning. *Phi Delta Kappan, 76*(8), 591–596.

Lieberman, A. (Ed.). (1995b). *The work of restructuring schools: Building from the ground up.* New York: Teachers College Press.

Lieberman, A. (1996, November). Creating intentional learning communities. *Educational Leadership, 54*(3), 51–55.

Lieberman, A., & McLaughlin, M. (1992). Networks for educational change: Powerful and problematic. *Phi Delta Kappan, 73*(9), 673–77.

Lieberman, A., & Miller, L. (1992). *Teachers—their world and their work: Implications for school improvement.* New York: Teachers College Press.

Lieberman, A., & Miller, L. (1999). *Teachers transforming their world and their work.* New York: Teachers College Press.

Lieberman, A., & Miller, L. (Eds.). (2001). *Teachers caught in the action: Professional development that matters.* New York: Teachers College Press.

Lightfoot, S. L. (1983). *The good high school: Portraits of character and culture.* New York: Basic Books.

Little, J. W. (1989). District policy changes and teachers' professional development opportunities. *Educational Evaluation and Policy Analysis, 11*(2), 165–179.

Little, J. W. (1993). Teacher professional development in a climate of educational reform. *Educational Evaluation and Policy Analysis, 15*(2), 129–151.

Lortie, D. (1975). *School teacher.* Chicago: University of Chicago Press.

Loucks-Horsely, S., Hewson, P., Love, N., & Stiles, K. (1998). *Designing professional development for teachers of science and mathematics.* Thousand Oaks, CA: Corwin.

McLaughlin, M., & Talbert, J. (1993). *Contexts that matter for teaching and learning: Strategic opportunities for meeting the nation's education goals.* Stanford, CA: Center for Research on the Context of Secondary School Teaching.

Meier, D. (1995). *The power of their ideas: Lessons for America from a small school in Harlem.* Boston: Beacon.

Mohr, N. (1998, April). Creating effective study groups for principals. *Educational Leadership, 55*(7), 41–44.

Moir, E., & Bloom, G. (2003, May). Fostering leadership through mentoring. *Educational Leadership, 60*(8), 58–60.

National Commission on Teaching and America's Future. (2003). *No dream denied: A pledge to America's children.* Washington, DC. Available: http://www.nctaf.org/.

National Education Commission on Time and Learning. (1994). *Prisoners of time: Report of the National Education Commission on Time and Learning.* Washington, DC: Author. Also available: http://www.ed.gov/pubs/PrisonersOfTime/.

National Staff Development Council. (2001). *Standards for staff development* (Rev ed.). Oxford, OH: Author.

Newman, K., Dornburg, B., Dubois, D., & Kranz, E. (1980). *Stress to teachers' midcareer transitions: A role for teacher education.* (ERIC Document Reproduction Services No. ED 204 321)

Noguera, P. (2001, September/October). *Solving problems with "action research."* Harvard Graduate School of Education, Harvard Education Letter.

Peine, J. M. (2003, Winter). Planning, measuring their own growth. *Journal of Staff Development, 24*(1), 38–42.

Ponticell, J. A., & Zepeda, S. (1996). Making sense of teaching and learning: A case study of mentor and beginning teacher problem solving. In D. McIntyre & D. Byrd (Eds.), *Preparing tomorrow's teachers: The field experience* (pp. 115–130). Thousand Oaks, CA: Corwin.

Popham, J. W. (2001). *The truth about testing: An educator's call to action.* Alexandria, VA: Association for Supervision and Curriculum Development.

Rogoff, B. (1994). Developing understanding of the idea of communities of learners. *Mind, Culture and Activity, 1*(4), 209–229.

Rutherford, W. (1989). *How to establish effective staff development programs: Tips for principals.* Reston, VA: National Association of Secondary School Principals.

Rutter, M. (1983). School effects on pupil progress: Research finding and policy implications. In L. S. Shulman & G. Sykes (Eds.), *Handbook of teaching and policy.* New York: Longman.

Sagor, R. (1992). *How to conduct collaborative action research.* Alexandria, VA: Association for Supervision and Curriculum Development.

Sagor, R. (2000). *Guiding school improvement with action research.* Alexandria, VA: Association for Supervision and Curriculum Development.

Schmoker, M. (1996). *Results: The key to continuous improvement.* Alexandria, VA: Association for Supervision and Curriculum Development.

Schmoker, M. (2001). *The results fieldbook: Practical strategies from dramatically improved schools.* Alexandria, VA: Association for Supervision and Curriculum Development.

Schon, D. (1983). *The reflective practitioner.* New York: Basic Books.

Schon, D. (Ed.). (1991). *The reflective turn: Case studies in and on educational practice.* New York: Teachers College Press.

Senge, P. M. (1990). *The fifth discipline: The art & practice of the learning organization.* New York: Doubleday.

Shields, P. M. (1999). *Teaching and California's future: The status of the teaching profession 1999.* Menlo Park, CA: The Center for the Future of Teaching and learning and SRI International.

Sparks, D. (1998). Making assessment part of teacher learning: Interview at issue with Bruce Joyce. *Journal of Staff Development, 19*(4), 33–35.

Sparks, D. (2002). *Designing powerful professional development for teachers and principals.* Oxford, OH: National Staff Development Council. Available: http://www.nsdc.org/educatorindex.htm.

Sparks, D., & Hirsh, S. (1997). *A new vision for staff development.* Alexandria, VA: Association for Supervision and Curriculum Development.

Speck, M., & Knipe, C. (2001). *Why can't we get it right? Professional development in our schools.* Thousand Oaks, CA: Corwin.

Starratt, R. J. (1996). *Transforming educational administration: Meaning, community, and excellence.* New York: McGraw-Hill.

Stenvall, M. (2001). Balancing the calendar for year-round learning. *Principal, 80*(3), 18–20.

Stigler, J. W., & Hiebert, J. (1999). *The teaching gap: Best ideas from the world's teachers for improving education in the classroom.* New York: Free Press.

Thomas, G. W. (2003, May/June). In times of turmoil, great leaders emerge. *Leadership, 32*(5), 8–9.

Tyack, D., & Cuban, L. (1997). *Tinkering toward utopia: A century of public school reform.* Cambridge, MA: Harvard University Press.

U.S. Department of Education, Office of Elementary and Secondary Education. (2002). *Public Law print of PL 107-110, the No Child Left Behind Act of 2001.* Available: http://www.ed.gov/policy/elsec/leg/esea02/index.html.

Wenger, E. (1998). *Communities of practice.* New York: Cambridge University Press.

Wiggins, G., & McTighe, J. (1998). *Understanding by design*. Alexandria, VA: Association for Supervision and Curriculum Development.

Willis, S. (March, 2002). Creating a knowledge base for teaching: A conversation with James Stigler. *Educational Leadership, 59*(6), 6–11.

York-Barr, J., Sommers, W. A., Ghere, G. S., & Montie, J. (2001). *Reflective practice to improve schools*. Thousand Oaks, CA: Corwin.

Zepeda, S. (1999). *Staff development: Practices that promote leadership in learning communities*. Larchmont, NY: Eye on Education.

Index

Note: Page numbers in *italic* type refer to figures or tables.

**CORWIN
PRESS**

The Corwin Press logo—a raven striding across an open book—represents the union of courage and learning. Corwin Press is committed to improving education for all learners by publishing books and other professional development resources for those serving the field of K–12 education. By providing practical, hands-on materials, Corwin Press continues to carry out the promise of its motto: **"Helping Educators Do Their Work Better."**

Writing Process Revisited

Writing Process Revisited

Sharing Our Stories

Edited by

Donna Barnes
Mary Hurd School
North Berwick, Maine

Katherine Morgan
Oyster River High School
Durham, New Hampshire

Karen Weinhold
North Hampton Elementary School
North Hampton, New Hampshire

National Council of Teachers of English
1111 W. Kenyon Road, Urbana, Illinois 61801-1096

This book is dedicated to teachers at all grade levels who have struggled, as we have, in silence.

Staff Editor: Kurt Austin

Interior Design: Doug Burnett

Cover Design: Doug Burnett

This book was typeset in Futura and Garamond by Electronic Imaging. Typefaces used on the cover were University Roman, Avant Garde Medium, and Avant Garde Demi. The book was printed on 50 lb. offset by Bang Printing.

NCTE Stock Number: 28157-3050

Library of Congress Cataloging-in-Publication Data

Writing process revisited: sharing our stories/edited by Donna Barnes, Katherine Morgan, Karen Weinhold.
    p.   cm.
    Includes bibliographical references (p.) and index.
    ISBN 0-8141-2815-7 (pbk.)
    1. English language—Composition and exercises—Study and teaching—United States. I. Barnes, Donna, 1942– . II. Morgan, Katherine Redington, 1946–   III. Weinhold, Karen, 1944– .
    LB1576.W746 1997
    808' .042—dc21

97-25804
CIP

Contents

Acknowledgments

We want to thank Tom Newkirk for providing us with the inspiration for this book in his talk "Silences in Our Teaching Stories—What Do We Leave Out and Why?" We are indebted to Tom Romano, Lucy Calkins, Jane Hansen, Don Graves, Don Murray, Jane Kearns, and Nancie Atwell for their research and teaching in the field of writing process. We have not only sat in their classes, we have also read and reread their texts and learned the value of questioning our practices.

Introduction

Nothing is riskier than writing; nothing is scarier than writing; but nothing is as satisfying as a piece of writing that "works." Nothing, that is, except the teaching of writing. The purpose of this book is to explore the struggles, the risks, and the potential for failure that lurk just under the surface of teaching in a process-approach classroom. In a 1991 speech in Rochester, New York, Tom Newkirk called these struggles the "silences in our teaching stories—what we leave out and why." His description and his questions prompted us to consider the available literature about teaching writing and compare our own teaching stories with those that have been published (many of them written by University of New Hampshire professors), such as Nancie Atwell's *In the Middle*, Tom Romano's *Clearing the Way*, Don Graves's *Writing Teachers and Children at Work*, and Lucy Calkins's *The Art of Teaching Writing* (just to mention a few). We found that our experiences didn't always match theirs, and because of this difference we thought we had failed in our understanding or perhaps our implementation of writing-process theory.

Professionally, we teachers have existed in mute isolation. For years we've hidden behind closed doors, wringing our hands and wondering if there was something special in the water in New Hampshire. The three of us began to meet regularly to share our concerns, yet we felt as if we were just this side of sabotage. Leery of discussing our shortcomings, our "curriculum disabilities," even with each other, let alone with the experts who conduct and publish research on which we base our classroom practices, how can we hope to drive our future when we bury the present and deny the past? How do we open the floodgates and begin to talk to each other, and then to the larger community we serve? How do we learn to rely on our own experiences and instincts when the research of experts doesn't work in our classrooms? Instead of trying to dance a little faster, read more, attend more workshops, why not share these problems with other teachers?

We hope that reading the articles included here will raise at least as many questions as those with which we have struggled. The writers are all classroom teachers who are trying to implement writing-process approaches in their classrooms. Because of our perspectives and experiences as teachers, we speak to these issues in a way that experts in writing-process theory cannot. Our classrooms are our laboratories in which we carefully observe and thoughtfully reflect on the knowledge we gain from our daily interchanges. Because we are professionals who care deeply about our students, we are continually working to blend accepted theories in our field with productive, effective practices in our classrooms. We hope we have found the courage to weed out those practices which are not working, or to search for different approaches to make them work, while trying new ways based on what we know about learners and learning.

The book which has emerged is a collection of teachers' stories about teaching writing in which problems central to the writing process are discussed and tentative solutions sometimes suggested. We focus on how process instruction flounders because of particular circumstances or personal quirks or idiosyncrasies, not on the failure of writing process as a theory. Obviously we are all believers or we would have abandoned ship a long time ago! Candid questions are raised, but not always answered. In keeping with the idea that we wanted to open a dialogue, and mindful of the importance of reader response in both our own conference group and in our writing classes, we responded to each essay from the point of view of someone at a different grade level dealing with similar challenges. Our goal for this book is no less than removing the veil of silence which shrouds our classrooms and which keeps us from sharing the trials inherent in the nature of process teaching. This communication across grade levels is vital to our growth as teachers and for the evolution of writing process as a method of teaching.

We have been our own worst enemy, allowing just about anyone and everyone to diagnose our ills and to prescribe cures. For example, take the issue of time—how to balance equal amounts for different disciplines in self-contained classrooms, how to "cover" everything in departmentalized situations, how to determine focus in integration, how to allocate for the many components of process approach (drafting, revising, conferencing, proofreading, editing, publishing, etc.), and how to keep abreast of the current research and keep on top of the responses and assessments generated by the students' daily reading and writing. At different times, in different ways, each of the contributors has tangled with this overriding issue of time. Who knows better what works and what does not? Classroom teachers do. Yet where is our voice? Reformers see time as the panacea; keep the students in their classes for longer blocks of time, decrease the "free" time for teachers and students, extend the school year, and all will be right with the world!

But time is only one of the many topics discussed in this collection; the value of reflection, the particular challenges of the beginning process teacher, selecting curricula, fostering quality, the equal application of process strategies for both reading and writing, the ongoing "grammar" question, peer conferencing, and the sustaining of sanity, integrity, and enthusiasm are all tackled.

As editors and contributors, we envision an ongoing communication among reading and writing teachers and researchers in which an open and honest sharing of experiments, trials, successes, and perplexities could lead to important changes in how we teach and how we feel about ourselves as teachers and spokespersons for our profession. We need to speak out, confidently and with the conviction of our experience. The media will not be able to depict teachers as failures if teachers do not *feel* like failures.

Choose a chapter and read with both your head and your heart. Agree or disagree. Empathize, sympathize, or reject—but react! Then pick up your pen or keyboard and write to us. Share your stories, your puzzles and strategies. Help us to become better teachers by becoming better collaborators. Together we can lift the veil of silence and begin a dialogue which will shape the nature of writing process for the future.

1 Defining the Writing Process

Donna Barnes
Mary Hurd School
North Berwick, Maine

Katherine Morgan
Oyster River High School
Durham, New Hampshire

Karen Weinhold
North Hampton Elementary School
North Hampton, New Hampshire

Definition #1
Donna Barnes

For me the writing process is a lot like my life. I was born into a family and I grew and I grew. I was sheltered and nurtured those first few months and years. My mother and father talked to me, loved me, and showed me how to do things. They didn't yell at me or laugh at me when I made a mistake. I grew and learned; I practiced and imitated.

I was born into the writing process the summer I went to my first University of New Hampshire Writing Institute. Don Graves and Jane Hansen were my parents. Perhaps Don Graves's book *Writing: Teachers and Children at Work* (1983) was my godparent—the voice and philosophy that guided my thinking as I began to do some writing. The basic lesson I lived and learned that summer was that writing teachers *do* write. I heard it and repeated it and practiced it, but I didn't really get it.

Jane Hansen and Don Graves helped me through my infancy that summer. The reading lists and a clinic class helped me experience the writing process. I wrote and I wrote and I shared my writing daily with a small group of peers. This group, my conference group, were my playmates, my play group, during those early months and years. They helped me hear my writing, helped me find a voice, clarify my thoughts, revise my writing and move it toward a finished piece. The teacher helped me edit, and the class was my audience.

Yet when the course was over, so was my writing. I was born, but I was not growing strong. I was not writing daily. Hell, I wasn't writing at all. As a toddler I probably learned more in a short space of time than I will ever learn in a lifetime. Cripes! I learned to walk and talk and run and sing and write or scribble. How did I do this? By watching my mom and dad and relatives and friends; by trying out sounds, words, steps, and notes; by practicing over and over and over again.

My second-grade classroom in North Berwick, Maine, formed my toddler years in writing. With this class of students I did what Don Graves and Jane Hansen told me to do that summer at the University of New Hampshire. And I modeled what I learned with my peers in the clinic class.

My students and I learned together. We read and we wrote every single day. We wrote and wrote and wrote. If some event messed up our regular schedule, we rescheduled our writing time. They conferenced and I conferenced and we conferenced together. It was rough; it was not polished. I thought they were writing wonderful stories. Yet, as I think back and look back, there was a tremendous amount of garbage. Greg wrote, "I like baseball because we can run bases and run home runs. And I just hit a homerun." James wrote, "My pencil is bad. At worktime it pops out of my hand and I get in trouble. Sometimes it gathers up other pencils and makes a missile launcher. And shoots out at me!!!" T.J. seldom brought anything to completion. Jeremy only wrote meaningless drivel about aliens. I wrote a poem called "Why Can't I Write?" in a fit of frustration and sent it off to *Language Arts*.

I believed then and I still believe that kids of any age need models. They write and I write. They conference and I conference. They revise and I revise. They edit and I edit. The process is the same for all of us as we all work toward a finished piece of writing that we share together.

I spent five years teaching the second grade. Those were my childhood years. I practiced writing with the kids in class. I did very little writing out of class. I was a reader but not a writer.

As an adolescent, I was trying to find myself. Who was I, what did I want, where was I going? It was a confusing time. Nothing worked and everything worked. At times I knew I had the answers to everything, and at other times I cried in despair because I knew nothing. I began to doubt my mother and my father and my teachers. I could say with absolute assurance that I knew more than they did. It was a wonderful time and a horrible time.

My adolescent years in writing came the summer I returned to the University of New Hampshire for an advanced seminar in writing with

Maryellen Giacobbe. I am embarrassed now as I think about that summer. It seemed like the whole class was in the same adolescent frame of mind. It was an aloof and unfriendly class; Maryellen was trying to help us explore how people learn, and we resisted.

I now wish I had been more open and receptive to her thoughts and suggestions. As in life, I look back and regret many things I did as an adolescent. Maryellen wanted us to try to learn something we did not previously know, to explore and analyze what happened in that learning process. On some days I wanted her to tell me how people learn. And on other days *I* wanted to tell her how people learn. I wanted to write. I hated that class! I was confused and angry, but from that confusion and anger came a professional friendship with a fellow student and a new approach to teaching and learning. So perhaps I learned from that class in spite of my poor attitude.

My personal writing at this point was still disappointing. It was going nowhere. I only wrote in school when the students wrote—and lots of times I avoided that. Adolescence is long and traumatic, but thankfully it does end. With adulthood comes growing up and independence. As an adult, I am expected to make decisions and solve problems based on rational processes. As an adult, I am on my own, I can set a schedule that seems best for my needs and change it as I see fit. I am in charge of my own destiny. I make my own friends, seek my own employment, build my own family and . . . .

Adulthood came to my personal writing with Tom Romano in person and Tom Romano in *Clearing the Way* (1987) and with a conference group that began in 1988 and continues until this very day. This course with Tom Romano at the University of New Hampshire and this group affected my personal writing. These two circumstances made me a writer. In Tom's class I started writing for *me*. Up until that point I wrote because something was assigned or because I needed to be a model for students. With Tom I wrote a finished piece because I wanted to give my aunt and uncle a gift of writing for their twenty-fifth wedding anniversary. With Tom I wrote a book review for *The Jolly Postman*—a book I love. The review was published in *Read'em Cowboy,* the Wyoming Reading Association newsletter. With Tom Romano I became a writer and realized the importance of writing for real-life purposes.

Adulthood in the teaching of writing came to me from reading *Living Between the Lines* by Lucy Calkins. That book revolutionized my work with children. That book led me to New York City to Columbia University to a ten-day writing institute with Lucy Calkins. The book and the institute had an incredible impact. As Patricia MacLachlan said so well in *Baby*, "Life is not a straight line . . . sometimes we circle back to a past time. But we are not the same. We are changed forever" (108).

Calkins helped me understand exactly how to lead children away from their stories of aliens invading the city to writing that matters. So that now Erin writes, "Dear Benson, I wish there was some way to communicate with you, but I don't bark and you don't speak. So we can't communicate. But if we could I would want you to read this letter. I just wanted to say I think you're the best dog in the world. . . .You make the whole family's life shine with joy. You make us feel special and I think that we make your life special too." And Greg now writes of his grandfather, "My grandfather liked to fish because he was good at it. He fished at our camp on Lake Winnipesaukee. He liked camp so much we started to call him 'Grampa the Campa.' I think he liked camping so much because it made him feel so free." And Jordan writes, "I have to write. When I write I feel good. Writing is fun. I can tell how I feel on paper and not have to tell anybody just the paper in words. I think writing is a good way to help you release your emotions in a constructive way. Writing is good for your mind."

We all still write every day in school, but I think it is more legitimate writing. No one writes of Barbie going to Bermuda. Rachel writes a letter to the custodian asking for another coat hook to be installed, Michelle makes a card for her mom who is about to have a new baby, Greg writes about his grandfather who just died, and I write this because now I feel like a writer. I no longer write just in school; I write at home and in the car and in a cafe and wherever and whenever I feel like it.

So I reached adulthood in the teaching of writing and I continued to think and act as a writer. I was fortunate to meet two other people who felt the same way, Karen Weinhold and Kay Morgan. We decided to meet once a month in a cafe to share our reading and our writing. And we have continued to meet monthly for nine years! Nothing stops us. If a conflict arises, we reschedule our meetings. That is incredible, a nine-year conference group!

In our conference group we do what we will not allow our students to do. We always catch up on our lives—who is doing what, how they're doing it, whose child is happy or miserable, and why. We laugh, we cry, we carry on, AND we share our reading and writing.

Karen always has wonderful book titles to suggest to us. She used to work at the town library. She shared the chapter she contributed to Nancie Atwell's *Workshop I.* Kay and I listened with sadness as she shared the eulogy she wrote for her brother's funeral.

Kay edited a book of letters called *My Ever Dear Daughter, My Own Dear Mother*. She transcribed these letters from the originals she found in her grandmother's attic. She read us excerpts and listened to our feedback. Karen and I listened in horror as Kay shared some tense family moments.

I shared the poem published in *Language Arts*. No one could appreciate better than Kay and Karen my feelings when I saw the poem in print. They listened with empathy and sorrow as I went through the trying times of a messy divorce.

The three of us continue to meet, but now it's much more than once a month because our conference group has produced an offspring—this book. The idea of a book grew from our meetings. We suddenly realized we were all teachers of vastly different ages and grades, and yet we faced the same questions and concerns every day. It was always easy to share classroom stories when we were together—a second-grade teacher, a seventh-grade teacher, and a high school teacher.

We compared notes. Did we have peer conferences in our respective classrooms? Yes we did, but less and less frequently. Why was this so? Why were we uncomfortable when students were sharing life stories? Why did we feel this was off-task when we did the same thing at our meetings? Where did life stories fit? We actually asked each other, "Did conferences, peer conference, work?" We were all struggling with the conference question.

What else did we struggle with? Time, always a time crunch; assessment and self-assessment; mechanics; the implementation of a writing workshop classroom; feeling alone as a process teacher. Ah-ha—as we talked and brainstormed, we realized our concerns and worries were much the same. Thus, the idea of this book was born—all teachers from kindergarten to college face the same concerns and challenges. We needed to share this idea with others. So we solicited teachers from all grades to share their stories and struggles with us.

Dawn Boyer, our editor, urged us to include our definition of the writing process as part of the book. That would be easy—so we thought. We all came from the same writing background, University of New Hampshire courses and institutes. We read and reread the same professional books. We attended many of the same conferences, and when we didn't, we shared our notes and knowledge.

Our intent was to each write a definition of the writing process. We would then blend them together into one, taking the best of all three. We were amazed at the vastly different way each of us approached this statement of the writing process. Howard Gardner, with his theories of multiple intelligences, would probably smile as he read each of our definitions.

I took a linguistic approach to my definition. I wrote a poem—or perhaps the poem wrote itself:

Definition of Writing Process

First thing you do is get a notebook and a pen.
They need to fit you just right.
Then you write, and you write, and you
write some more.
You write fast
And you write slow.
You write in silence and
You write in bedlam.
You write at your desk
You write in your car.
You write in the cemetery and
You write at the mall.

You reread everything you wrote,
The garbage and the gems.
You laugh and you cry.
You're surprised and you're not.
You reread and you underline.
You reread and you take notes.
You reread and you highlight.
You talk to yourself and
you share parts with a friend.

You do everything you ask your students to do . . . .
They write; you write.
They reread; you reread.
They conference; you conference.
They question; you question.

You write and you write.
You find a seed and it begins to possess you.
You think about it as you shower.
You think about it as you drive to school.
You think about it as you eat lunch.
You dream about it.
You talk about it to anyone who will listen.
You share it with your friends.
You share it with your students.

You begin to wonder what to do with this seed.
You've grown it and grown it.
You've watered it and fertilized it.
Now, it is ready to bloom.

What will it look like
A letter, a poem, an essay, a short story,
A long story, a novel, a what?

You look at different forms,
You study them; you absorb them.
You question—what will this seed turn into?
You ask friends,
You ask students.
You listen—you experiment.
You make a decision.

Your seed moves out of the notebook.
Onto the paper.
It moves into the word processor,
Again it possesses you.
It won't go away.
You can't stop thinking about writing
Until it is done.
You finish.
You edit.
You give it to a friend to edit.
You rewrite and it is ready.
You share it in some way
A way that matters to you.

The writing process as it works for me!

Definition #2

Karen Weinhold

I looked at writing spatially, defining the writing process with a flowchart (see Figure 1). But I was not willing to live with a chart alone. I also submitted an outline:

What the Writing Process Teacher Has to Teach

   I. Process (steps leading to predetermined goal)

     A. Strategies

     B. Audience

     C. Purpose (to inform, entertain, persuade, enrich)

  II. Steps

     A. Generating an idea

     B. Drafting

     C. Conferencing

     D. Revising

    E. Proofreading
    F. Editing
    G. Publishing
III. Structure
    A. Sentence
    B. Paragraph
    C. Transitions
    D. Total Composition
IV. Language
    A. Vocabulary
    B. Grammar
    C. Mechanics
        1. spelling
        2. punctuation
        3. capitalization
    D. Usage
        1. tense
        2. agreement
 V. Techniques
    A. Drafting (paper, word processor)
    B. Conferencing
        1. self
        2. partner/peer
        3. small group
        4. large group
    C. Revising
    D. Proofreading
    E. Editing
VI. Ancillary Studies
    A. Research strategies
    B. Computing/typing/word processing
    C. Reference
    D. Publication

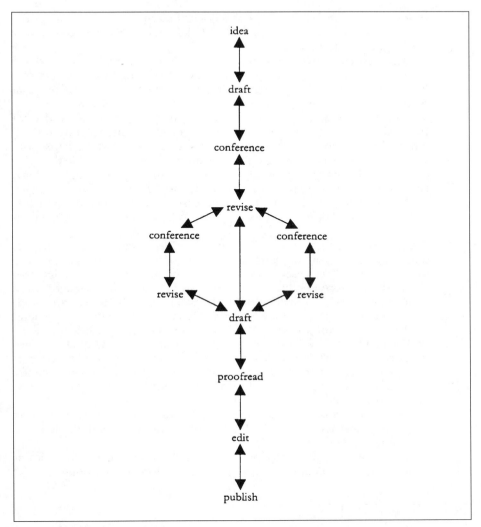

Figure 1. What Writing Process Looks Like

And I also included a narrative:

> Writing process involves a series of composing activities leading to an established goal, which may be an edited, finished piece of writing. These activities are teachable and definable and have a set of procedures or steps which, although not necessarily linear, can be followed in an alterable pattern.
>
> Writing means composing—forming ideas, expressing opinions, offering researched facts—by putting letters, words, sentences, and paragraphs together to form a meaningful (to the writer) whole. It is both an

observable and definable series of actions, though due to its recursive nature (a procedure that can repeat itself indefinitely), its patterns may vary from individual to individual.

The first step involves generating an idea from which to work—a focus, a seed, a theme. Many strategies exist for doing this, from external imposition to individual brainstorming; the preferred one is the one that works for each writer.

Step two requires the writer to put down on paper (or screen) what he or she initially knows or wants to say on the topic, creating for self what *is* known, and determining from this what to do next. Perhaps more research is needed, or refining/clarification of the original idea, or discarding, or interweaving, or any activity to gather more fodder. Perhaps enough has been generated to proceed to step three, conferencing.

Now the writer collaborates with at least one other person who reads or listens to the draft and offers suggestions, asks questions, and, in general, responds.

In step four, the writer may need to generate more material, delete, rearrange, refocus, all of which are considered *revising* strategies. Maybe the conference was not a viable one, and the author must seek another respondent before continuing. The author does not have to act on the critique of the reader/listener, only take what he or she deems appropriate for the piece. Trust or confidence in the conferee can be a factor here.

The middle components of writing process (conferencing and revising) thus involve constant *recursive* behaviors, during which the writer produces a *revised* draft, finds someone with whom to *conference,* performs some type of *revision* on the draft, and *conferences* again, until the writer is satisfied that the piece is now capable of effectively communicating the author's idea.

The next step involves proofreading (looking for errors in mechanics, usage, punctuation, etc.) and editing (fixing those errors), until the piece of writing meets the standards for written English.

The final step of writing process is publication, the sharing with at least one other person of the polished, finished piece of writing.

Definition #3
Katherine Morgan

My definition of the writing process took an intrapersonal approach, using a diary-like entry:

> I've always known that writing involved a process; that books didn't spring full-blown from the author's head. On the other hand, though I intuited that, I never translated it to my teaching of writing. In fact, I really don't think that I *taught* writing in my English classes. What I did was assign papers and assume that students would write them. After they were finished with a paper, I conducted the postmortem, pointing out all the places they should have said something differently, or in more depth, or more succinctly.

In 1983 I attended the New Hampshire Summer Writing Program at the University of New Hampshire, in which I actually experienced the writing process for the first time. I entered as a skeptic, but departed a believer, at least as far as my own writing was concerned. The teachers immersed us in our own writing and created a community of writers in which we learned to write, share, listen, provide supportive feedback, revise, edit, and finally "publish" our writing through group sharing and a publication at the end of the three weeks.

I wrote and wrote that summer, moving from personal narratives to personal narratives with a dash of fiction and finally to two children's stories, one of which was subsequently published in *Cricket* magazine. I learned that when I cared deeply about the topic, I might come close to crying when I shared it; I learned that the questions people asked me in conferences led me to think again about parts of my piece and then to revise them. I learned that not all ideas led to finished pieces; and finally I found out there were important differences between the writer and the critic in my head. Most important to me as a teacher, I learned what it was like to sit in the student's place and try to write.

I left the summer believing that I was a writer and that the writing process was the way to teach writing to students. I didn't need to assign papers anymore: I could let students choose topics and begin the process in a way that was likely to lead to a product which wouldn't require a postmortem by me. The writing process freed students to write and teachers to encourage and explain during the process instead of criticizing the end product.

One day in my Writing Workshop class, while students were writing and I was trying to write too, I realized that there was a remarkable similarity between the process of teaching and the process of writing. In order to define the writing process, I want to also define the teaching process as I experience it.

I find that I do a substantial amount of mental rehearsal for both teaching and writing. When I am not consciously directing that reflective process, my subconscious takes over for me. Then, usually in the moments before I fall asleep or just after I wake up, the plan for the day's class or the idea for revision of a piece of writing comes to me. As teachers, we know how critical time for planning is, and I believe that planning or "thinking" time is the first step in the writing process. Just as with teaching, time to reflect is important throughout the writing process.

At the high school level, we place a great deal of emphasis on knowledge of subject matter. Indeed, it would be impossible to be a good teacher in an unfamiliar field. Knowledge of your subject is also one of the key elements in a successful piece of writing. As teachers, we function best when we have control over our lesson plans and over curriculum decisions; as writers, we produce our best writing when we choose the topic.

When starting a piece of writing, I like to have a general plan for the whole piece. This is not to say that I have an outline set in stone; rather, I'm likely to have a brief list of brainstormed ideas or a concept web of ideas I'd like to include. One of the hallmarks of my general plan for a piece is that the plan is flexible. Don Murray suggests that we write in order to learn what we don't know about what we know. My lesson plans are the same. I map out the week, with as many specifics for a given day as I can muster, but I do so with the knowledge that the class may not get as far as I think on a particular day, or the students may generate an idea which leads to a new set of plans for the next day. Serendipity in teaching—the teachable moment—is like the sudden inspiration in writing.

At some point in teaching, and preferably early and often, sharing ideas with colleagues is important. Finding out what another teacher of ninth graders is doing, for example, is often helpful. We find many new ideas by talking to our colleagues. Peer conferencing in teaching is exactly like peer conferencing in the writing process. When we ask each other questions, whether in teaching or in writing, the outcome is a more refined idea or approach or a brand new idea or direction for thinking.

The goal of both teaching and writing is the communication of ideas. Words are the medium for communication, though in one case written and the other usually oral. Just as the writer shares responsibility for meaning with the reader, the teacher shares responsibility for learning with the student. Both parties are integral parts of the process if the goal is to be successfully attained.

A significant difference between the two processes occurs at what might be perceived as the end point of each. Presumably, in the writing process the end result is a final piece of writing; in teaching, I suppose the final product is the educated student. The end of the writing process leads to a tangible product, while the end of the teaching process is often not known to the teacher. In reality, a writer can keep revising a piece over and over, even after the piece is allegedly finished; in that sense the end product is never truly final. Although a teacher doesn't keep teaching the same student over and over, the student's education is an ongoing process which persists long after leaving a particular classroom. Like a piece of writing which may be revised, a student's ideas will grow and change as his or her education proceeds.

As I prepare again for a new year of teaching, after I have spent a summer of writing, I am reminded of the parallels between the two activities, and the conclusion that each is an art, not confined to a rigid set of rules, but more an evolving form that takes the shape of the individual who is the shaper: the teacher or the writer.

The three of us—so alike in our backgrounds and yet so different in our visualization of the definition of writing process. Yet each definition is exactly the same in the message it conveys. The writing process involves many steps, and though the steps may not be in the same order for everyone, the writing process always involves generating ideas, writing, drafting, reading, rereading, conferencing, revising, conferencing, editing, final drafting, proofreading, and sharing with an audience or publishing. Our means of delivery are different, but our message is identical!

2 A First-Draft Society: Self-Reflection and Slowing Down

Robert K. Griffith
Elementary Curriculum and Instructional Specialist
Newburyport, Massachusetts

Our students today lead such nonstop, crowded lives. Up in the morning, off to school, then band practice, gymnastics, horseback riding, intramurals—the list could go on and on. Children (and families) race from one activity to another with barely enough time to grab a quick bite at a fast-food drive-through. This living in the fast lane is reflected in entertainment options as well. Video games offer rapid-fire challenges requiring split-second decisions. Television programs present problems and neatly packaged solutions, all in just thirty minutes. TV problems are like microwave dinners—just wait a few minutes and they are done. Time is rarely spent on long, sustained activities. Calkins describes this as a "one-draft-only society" (*Art* 23).

Our school curricula are like this too. We "do" spelling for twelve minutes, math for forty minutes, social studies for thirty minutes, off to gym for forty-five minutes, fifteen minutes for sustained silent reading, a safety program assembly for twenty minutes. . . . Children's lives at school are hasty and fragmented.

Intercom announcements constantly disrupt the classroom. "Today's menu has been changed. Chef's choice will be today, not tomorrow, and tomorrow will be chicken." "Please send Bobby to the nurse. He forgot to take his medication again."

Children's lives are so blippy and fractured, lived in fast, compact time bites. Little time is taken in children's home or school lives for reflecting on what they are doing, much less on how well they are doing at any given activity. When I asked children in my classroom if they had done their best on particular pieces of work, they looked at me like I was crazy. "No, it's not really my best. But at least I finished it" was a familiar student response. The credo seems to be "Don't worry about how you do, just get it done and move on."

Thus, our students often come to us unaware of their strengths and weaknesses in the language arts, with no thoughts given to personal goals. As a consequence of this first-draft society, we as teachers are frequently faced with the dilemma of children's shallow writing and superficial responses to reading. Like many teachers, I have read children's sequels to *Nightmare on Elm Street,* blood and guts stories such as "G.I. Joe Meets the Terminator," "Little Princess" tales, and so on.

I wanted to help my students to slow down their lives, to thoughtfully consider their writing and reading. I wanted them to discover the strategies they were using that were successful and to recognize the areas each needed to work on. I wanted my students to set and strive toward personal reading and writing goals.

To try to accomplish this, I began asking my students about their writing strategies. Calkins wrote, "When students are asked to describe their writing processes, they often become aware of them for the first time. In anticipation of process conferences, children monitor their writing strategies and soon, they consciously revise those strategies" (*Art* 152). Not my students! They kept coming to process/reflection conferences with responses that demonstrated little self-awareness of their writing and reading strategies, strengths, weaknesses, or goals.

"How did you write this? What worked and didn't work?" I would ask in conferences.

"Gosh, Mr. G., I don't know. I just got my idea and wrote it."

"Ross, what did you try in this writing piece that you hadn't tried before?"

"I don't know. Nothing, I don't think. I just sort of wrote it. You know."

And that was the problem. Sometimes I knew, and sometimes I didn't. More important, my students didn't know what was working or not working for them. Thus, they had little, if any, insight into how to improve their writing. The big question was how I as the teacher could help them to develop this insight.

Could it be that these process/evaluation conferences used with such great success by Calkins, Atwell, and others weren't being conducted often enough in my classroom? I had been guiding conference discussions toward children's processes every couple of weeks. I decided to increase the frequency that the students and I discussed our writing and reading processes to once or twice a week. This helped a little in that students were a bit more able to describe their literacy processes, but still with little depth or thoughtfulness. I began to realize that for this self-reflection to be effective, it would have to become a continuing, regular part of the language arts workshop routine.

I was concerned that Graves, Calkins, and Atwell didn't talk much about the routines that they obviously appeared to use to help students become more reflective writers and readers. According to Robert Tierney, "There's a dearth of worthwhile pedagogical suggestions with respect to getting students involved in self-assessment" (5). Regardless, I realized that my students' lack of insight into their literary processes, reflected in their conference responses, illustrated the need for regular reflection activities. Additionally, as their teacher, I knew that I had a responsibility to be their guide and role model in reflective thinking.

I worried that these self-reflection activities might take too much time away from the students' writing and reading, thereby leading to even shallower writing and reading. At the same time, I found some helpful advice from Calkins which I tried to keep in mind as we began these activities. She advised, "If the activities are to be a forum for thinking about one's writing process, then they must become part of the backdrop of the workshop. If they are always changing, always new, they themselves become the focus of attention rather than a tool for focusing on something else" (*Art* 155). This helped me to see the importance of taking time to develop self-reflection routines that would become a natural part of the workshop fabric. It is important to note that these procedures are not all introduced at the same time. I begin slowly, first developing the routines of our writing and reading workshops. The following provides a brief overview of these workshops.

In my self-contained sixth-grade classroom, we read and write every day. As workshop routines are implemented, I model and participate in each activity and strategy that is introduced. I walk the students through each process, acting as a facilitator as they learn the procedures.

Writing workshop typically begins with a brief mini-lesson focused on some strategy or tip that children have shown a need for in their writing. At the beginning of the school year, I lead these short (five to eight minutes) lessons. Later in the year, as students become more confident and try out new strategies, they often request to plan and lead their own mini-lessons.

The mini-lesson is followed by sustained silent writing of approximately twenty minutes. Then, during the final twenty-five minutes or so of writing workshop, students conference with peers or with me, or continue to work on their writing pieces. Some students may be doing illustrations for a final piece, while others might be self-editing or peer-editing a rough draft.

Reading workshop time lasts about forty-five minutes. Groups of two to four students meet to read and discuss books they have chosen. One group may all be reading Patricia MacLachlan's *Journey,* while another reads *Missing May* by Cynthia Rylant. These groups, called Book Clubs, guide their own daily activities.

On one day, a Book Club may decide to independently read the next two chapters of its book. As students read, they jot down questions and ideas the book makes them think about. They also record any lines written by the author that stand out for them. The Book Club then meets the following day to discuss the chapters, using the questions and lines readers noticed as the starting point of their discussion. I often sit in on part of their discussion, as a facilitator at the beginning of the year and as more of a participant later in the year, as the students' group skills develop and mature.

Out of this conversation, students often choose to write a personal narrative inspired by a question raised during discussion of the book. For example, while reading *Journey,* Heather wrote a response to her question "How would I feel if my mother just up and left me one day?" Other times, Book Club members might draw a picture which makes connections between themselves and the book's theme or a main character.

During writing and reading time, I work hard at creating a classroom climate which is calm and relaxed. I model the difference between an "inside voice" and an "outside voice." We practice moving quietly from our desks to wherever a Book Club is meeting. I approach students and their writing pieces with respect, with an attitude of looking for what worked in what they've tried. I model thoughtful responses to books I'm reading, pondering aloud over how a book affects me and what it makes me think about. This modeling of slow, deliberate, quiet, thoughtful thinking and responding is one of the first things I do in a school year to begin helping students slow down and become more reflective.

As a class becomes comfortable with the preceding writing/reading workshop elements, I begin to introduce classroom routines, activities, and procedures for regularly engaging in self-reflection. As guides in determining when to implement these routines, I consider the students' maturity, preceding school year's experiences with a writing/reading workshop approach, and the class mixture of individual strengths and weaknesses. I have seldom used every one of the following procedures with a single group of students. Some classes have been ready for more of these routines than others.

The following sections more fully explain these self-reflection activities and procedures. They are generally described in the order in which they are introduced in the classroom.

Daily

Mary is talking with Melissa about what she is going to do today in reading/writing workshop: "Well, yesterday my Book Club began this really neat book called *The Pinballs.* Today we're going to try to read the next two chapters. They're pretty short. I think in writing I'll bring my writer's notebook [see Calkins, *Living*] to a conference to try to find seed ideas for a writing project. Want to conference with me?" As Mary talks, she jots down these plans on her daily workshop schedule (see Figure 1).

In making her plans, Mary has needed to reflect upon what she has already done and decide what she is going to try to accomplish this day. This process of assessing where she stands at the moment as well as setting goals for what she will do next occurs each day. Mary, Melissa, and the other students use the daily workshop schedule to record their reading and writing plans. This committing to paper of daily, self-selected activities places responsibility, choice, and ownership in the students' hands. It helps the children to slow down and think about their reading and writing. Further, the students must be aware of what they have already accomplished and decide what they should do next in order to achieve their goals.

At the close of each morning's workshop, Mary and the other students think about how they have done with their daily goals. On their workshop schedule, they place a check plus (✓+) if they feel they've accomplished their goal completely, a check (✓) if they made good progress, and an asterisk (*) to indicate a goal they feel they need to continue working on. This daily self-evaluation leads to further reflection on what has been accomplished, as well as identifying areas in which further attention is needed.

Weekly

As weekly self-reflection is introduced, students have been deeply immersed in their own reading and writing for several weeks. The students begin to make a weekly self-reflection record in the form of a checklist. This checklist grows out of a series of teacher-led mini-lessons on what strong readers and writers do as they read and write.

After this mini-lessons series concludes, I call the class to a circle in front of our chart stand. The children gather, greeting one another as they find a seat on the floor. Once the group is settled, I begin.

"Okay, class. You have been readers and writers for many years. Based on your past experiences, as well as on our recent mini-lessons, I'd like to have us brainstorm what we think strong writers and readers do. The more aware we are of what they do, the more able we are to

Figure 1. Daily Workshop Schedule

Weekly Schedule of: Mary				Figure 1
Monday	Tuesday	Wednesday	Thursday	Friday
Writing: Write in Writers Notebook	Writing: Seed conference	Writing: Focus on Whale Watching	Writing: continue draft →	Writing: continue draft
How I Did = √+	How I Did = √+	How I Did = ✳	How I Did = √+	How I Did = √
Reading: Begin Pinballs	Reading: Read Pinballs chapters 2+3	Reading: Read Pinballs chapters 4+5	Reading: Reading conference	Reading: Write in reading Journal
How I Did = √+	How I Did = √+	How I Did = √+		

What do strong writers do?
- Write a lot, every day.
- Like to write. They choose to write during their free time.
- Write about things, people, or places they care about.
- Choose their words carefully to set a mood.
- Try new things.
- Share their writing with other people, and try out their suggestions.
- Really care about their writing.
- They write poems, books, magazine articles, etc.
- Show their writing to different people.
- Write pieces that make sense, that others can understand and follow.
- Write thoughtfully, showing or getting across their feelings and ideas.
- Edit their writing, after they've worked on their ideas.
- Change their writing sometimes when they get good suggestions.
- Meet with other writers.

What do strong readers do?
- Buy books.
- Read in their free time.
- Like to read.
- Can feel the feelings of the book's characters.
- Pick good books.
- Try out suggestions if someone says a book is good.
- Think about what they're reading.
- Share what they're reading with others.
- Know things to do if they don't understand something.
- Reread sometimes.
- Use other words as clues when they don't know an important word.

Figure 2. Examples of Students' Brainstormed Ideas of What Strong Readers and Writers Do

improve our own reading and writing strategies. Who would like to lead this?"

Heather and Stephen volunteer to call on people and serve as recorders, and the brainstorming session begins.

Darcey offers, "Good writers care about what they write about. They write thoughtfully." Heather records this on the chart.

Stephen calls on T.J. "Strong writers take their time editing their final drafts. They try to find their own mistakes, and know who to ask for help."

Class members continue to contribute their ideas (see Figure 2 for brainstorming examples).

As our discussion continues, we take time to clarify our meanings. "Jenny, what do you mean by 'good writers set a mood'?"

"Well, some writers set a mood in their writing. Like some stories make me feel calm and quiet, and other pieces get me excited or tensed up."

"How do you think they do that?"

"I think it's mostly because of the words and scenes they use. Like Cynthia Rylant in *Night in the Country*. She uses words that make me feel peaceful, like with the animals sleeping, and the way she describes the quiet sounds of the night."

Class discussion continues in this vein. Eventually we reach consensus on a number of strategies and actions used by strong writers and readers. We next make a weekly self-reflection checklist (see Figure 3) following a procedure similar to the above.

Each week, the children take time during reading/writing workshop to fill out this self-reflection checklist. They also jot down any interesting observations they may have regarding their reading and writing. For example, Mary recently noticed that "Some of the stories I've written really sound like real books. A lot of people like them, and when they say they like them it makes me feel good because I've worked hard and done good on what I did."

In addition to using the weekly self-reflection checklist, students analyze their current writing pieces. On the backs of their writer's notebooks, children add to and update two lists: Things I Can Do Well in Writing, and Things I Need to Work On in Writing. These comments are quite specific. Josh has listed that he's "doing a good job of describing characters" and that he needs to "work on using quotation marks correctly." Brooke says she is "writing leads that grab the reader" and that she wants to "make some of my stories funnier."

Also weekly, the children write in their language arts journals. Language arts journals are one way, among many, of having students respond and think about their reading, writing, listening, and speaking. The students brainstormed a list of potential language arts journal topics and questions which are posted in the room (see Figure 4). Children can either choose one of these or write on their own language-related ideas.

Often these written responses are reflective in nature. Listen to what Meg has to say in her language arts journal about how she is changing as a reader: "At the beginning of the year, I used to read books that were kind of easy for me, but now I'm reading books that are just right, and some are kind of challenging. I'm also sticking to books a lot better. Like in the first quarter I dropped quite a few books, but this quarter I

I choose to write, and stick with my writing					I choose to read, and stick with my reading				
I share my writing w/others in conferences					I share my reading w/others in conferences				
My writing is thoughtful and makes sense					I understand what I read				
I try new strategies with my writing pieces					I know and use strategies when I get confused				
I edit final drafts carefully					I make connections between books and myself				
Other things I've noticed about my writing:					Other things I've noticed about my reading:				
Key: 5 = Excellent progress 4 = Making good progress 3 = Working toward, making some progress 2 = Not progressing as much as I'd like to 1 = Not attempting, making very little, if any, progress									

Figure 3. Weekly Self-Reflection Checklist

haven't dropped a book yet. I take more time at choosing books I'm sure I'll be interested in. Like if the book has a character that's like me, or if there's a problem that I can relate to."

I respond to children's entries in short letters back to them in their journals. To Meg, I wrote, "You've definitely been thinking about your reading! I've noticed that your reading habits have changed, also. I can remember when you read almost all of the Peggy Parish books. Now you're reading books that are more challenging for you, like *The Fledgling*.

Writing:
- How can I tell the difference between a "good" topic and a "bad" topic?
- What do I do when I'm "stuck?"
- How do I know when to make changes in my writing piece? How do I decide?
- Why do I write? What does it do for me?
- How is writing like reading? How is it different?

Reading:
- How do I choose a book? What gets me interested in a book?
- Am I a good reader? How do I know?
- What makes a good reader? What things does a good reader do?
- Why do I read? What does it do for me?
- What do I do when I have problems reading a section of something?

Listening:
- What kinds of things catch my attention so much that I have to listen?
- When I'm listening really closely to something, why don't all the other little noises around me bother me?
- How is listening like reading? Or like speaking, or writing?
- Am I a good listener? How do I know?
- Did anyone have to teach me how to listen? How did I become able to listen?

Speaking:
- How do I think I learned to talk?
- Are there ways of talking without saying anything? If so, how do people do it? How do they learn it?
- Why do some people talk a lot, while others don't say much?
- How would I feel if I couldn't talk?
- Why do people sometimes forget what they were going to say?

Figure 4. Language Arts Journal Topics and Questions

You are choosing books more carefully now! I think that's great. What do you think caused these changes?"

In my return letters I just try to respond honestly to what the students have said. I also typically (though not always) ask a question which will cause the children to think a bit more deeply about what they have written. These journals are one record of students' increasing awareness of their language arts processes.

Biweekly

"What is my best piece so far? What makes it the best? What did I do on this piece that I haven't tried before? How can I show how much the book

Tuck Everlasting affected me?" These are some of the questions Mike is considering as he chooses representative samples of his writing and reading for his portfolio. Portfolios are collections of students' writing pieces, including notes, webs, drafts, and published pieces, as well as reading lists, reading journal letters, and other artifacts that are representative of all of the processes and products involved in the students' reading and writing (see Farr; Rief, "Finding").

About every two weeks, my students and I review and update our portfolios. Items for the portfolios are selected by both the students and myself. Occasionally, parents will add materials as well, such as lists of books read aloud at home. The students' portfolios, as well as my own, are kept in the classroom and are easily accessible.

I use portfolios to help children document their development and growth. Portfolios provide a more complete picture of students than do isolated pieces taken out of context or standardized tests, with their emphasis on one correct answer to each question. Thinking, problem solving, being able to use a variety of strategies, and tracing students' change and growth over time can easily be demonstrated through a portfolio.

Periodically, about every four to five weeks, I hold a portfolio conference with each student.

"Kristen, what do you think your portfolio shows about you as a writer?"

"I think it shows a lot. If you look at my writing pieces from the beginning of the year, you can see how short they were. Also, I wasn't really writing about things I think about, or care about. Like in this first piece, I wrote about an elf living in my closet. How silly! I can't believe I wrote that!

"Now, look at what I've written recently. I feel really proud of this piece about my grandfather. It's pretty good. I tried to make scenes showing Grampa and I doing things together, like when we go fishing. I think it comes across how much we love each other, and like being together. Same thing with this one about watching my dad at hockey practice.

"Also, notice how many spelling mistakes I had in my elf story. And that was in my final piece! I'm still not the best speller, but at least now I can find most of my mistakes and fix them."

Kristen has become aware of her processes and products. She is able to see concrete evidence of her growth and changes. Her self-awareness in turn leads to positive self-esteem ("I feel really proud") and further growth.

As portfolio conferences continue, I talk with the students about favorite pieces in their portfolios, what new strategies and reading genres they are trying, and how the items are indicative of their growth as readers and writers. I keep track of our conversations through short notes I jot to myself in a language arts notebook. This notebook has one section for each student. As we conference throughout the year, an anecdotal record of students' changes and growth emerges.

Linda Rief sums up the place of portfolios so well. "Portfolios become the evidence for what we value in our classrooms. The act of putting together a portfolio is a reflective act in itself, as students choose what to put in there and why. That reflection on where they've been, where they are now, and how they got there, is what real learning is all about" (*Seeking* 145).

Quarterly

In our school system, progress reports are sent home on a quarterly basis. The language arts component of our progress report is shown in Figure 5.

As an educator, I realize that the above progress report does not give parents a clear, contextual picture of their child's learning. However, the original progress report used in this school system for many years simply listed the subject area of language arts and then used a letter grade from A to F to indicate a child's performance. Implementing a change from the traditional grade card to the progress report shown in Figure 5 was a long, hard-fought battle.

It has been quite helpful to me as a teacher to have this type of progress report, rather than one with grades from A to F. A colleague and I developed this progress report in a manner similar to the way the students developed their weekly self-reflection checklist. We first brainstormed the behaviors of good readers and writers. We then clarified and revised our ideas. Next we checked to make sure the listed behaviors were actually observable in some way in a classroom setting.

We then made an observation checklist based on the progress report (see Figure 6). I have a checklist for each student in my language arts notebook. As I conference with children and observe them working, I write short notes or just use the key to keep track of children's progress.

About two weeks before a quarter ends, I hold progress conferences with the students. The class and I first brainstorm some questions we would like to discuss which will help us to assess the growth that has taken place over the last nine weeks. These questions vary somewhat from quarter to quarter, yet always focus on three areas: changes and growth (i.e., How have you changed as a reader/writer? Why?), trying out

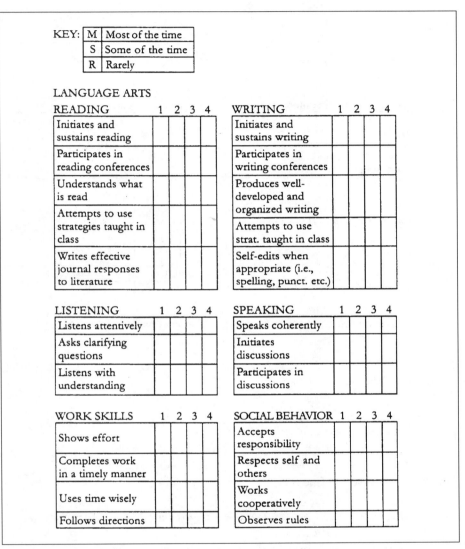

Figure 5. Quarterly Progress Report, Language Arts Component

new strategies (i.e., What new things have you attempted? How did they turn out?), and accomplishments (i.e., What are you proudest of? Why?).

The children next prepare themselves for their conferences. Caileen, Julie, and Audrey sit quietly, jotting down important thoughts which they want to remember to bring up in their conferences. Nick and Roy spread their portfolio items out on the carpet in the reading center, sharing favorite pieces and discussing new writing strategies they have been trying.

Writing					Reading				
Initiates/sustains writing					Initiates/sustains reading				
Participates in writing conferences					Participates in reading conferences				
Produces well-developed and organized writing					Understands what is read				
Attempts to use strats. taught in class					Attempts to use strats. taught in class				
Self-edits when approp.					Writes effective journal responses				
Other observations:					Other observations:				

Writing and Reading Observations
Key: 5 = Excellent progress
        4 = Making good progress
        3 = Working toward, making some progress
        2 = Not progressing as much as I'd like to
        1 = Not attempting, making very little, if any, progress

Figure 6. Observation Checklist

Jacob and Justin conference together, discussing their responses to the questions I will ask them.

Then, the week before the quarter ends, I hold a self-assessment conference with each child. We talk about their peaks and valleys, attempts and successes over the past nine weeks. Portfolios are reviewed and discussed. Each conference culminates with the child setting personal reading and writing goals for the coming quarter. The next quarter-ending conference with each child begins with a discussion of the progress that has been made toward these goals.

During Mary's third-quarter conference, her growing confidence as a writer was reflected in one of her goals: "I want to try writing some poetry. I've been reading a lot of poetry, but I've never tried writing it before. So I'm going to give it a try during this last nine weeks!" (See Figure 7 for other examples of goals set by past students.)

These quarter-end conferences serve many important functions. They acknowledge the importance of the students' control and owner-ship of their literacy processes. They reinforce the notion that students are to be responsible for their own progress, as well as for assessing this progress. Assessment is viewed as an opportunity to acknowledge and celebrate achievements, as well as for identifying further goals to work toward. Self-assessment conferences help students to reflect on where they have been, as well as setting further direction for where they want to go.

I take the children's observations and self-assessments into serious consideration as I fill out their progress reports. In most cases, my obser-vations closely mirror those of the students. I hope that some school year in the future the children and I can fill out their progress reports collaboratively and indicate this to the parents. At the moment, the com-munity in which I teach is not ready to accept this degree of student ownership. Perhaps one day, however!

Yearly

As the school year draws to a close, the students and I wrap up loose ends. Reading and writing lists are updated. Portfolios are reorganized one last time. Final self-assessment conferences are held. Plans are made on what to try to read and write over the summer.

The end of the school year is a time of both sadness and celebra-tion: sadness because our learning community is dispersing in various directions; celebration because of all we have accomplished and become together. The last days of school are filled with rememberings; rememberings of favorite books and characters (who could ever forget Gilly Hopkins? Or Anastasia? Or Winnie Foster?); of touching writing pieces (Jenny's story "Divorced," Mary's "If I Were Only Bigger"); and of work-shop time spent together. The children and I sift through our portfolios, notebooks, and lists. We retrace the processes and products of the past nine months. We are aware of what we once were, revel in where we are now, and look forward to what we may become.

Closing Thoughts and New Directions

Through these many self-reflection activities and procedures, my stu-dents have been able to slow down their lives, at least their literary

- Read at least 4 magazines
- Keep making predictions as I read
- Share a book in whole group sharing
- Read at least 2 nonfiction books
- Do an interview project over a book
- Read an adventure book by David Budbill, Bill Wallace, or Gary Paulsen
- Stay on task and not get distracted by what other people are doing
- Keep my Reading Record up to date
- Try one new sharing way
- Make my journal letters as thoughtful as they *used* to be
- Do a play over a book I've read
- Remember to always use capitals and periods
- Write and publish at least two pieces
- Stay on topic in all my stories
- Do self-reflection once a week
- Write a fiction story that sounds true
- Learn to use commas correctly
- Start using indented paragraphs
- Plan a mini-lesson to teach to the class
- Edit finished pieces much faster
- Try to write a poem
- Listen to some author tapes to find out about how they write
- Write *more*

Figure 7. Examples of Goals Set by Students

lives. They are aware of their many strengths, work thoughtfully on their weaknesses, and use a variety of strategies to achieve their goals.

This slowing down has led to insightful, meaningful writing. Two examples in particular stand out. Mary wrote "Bigger Is Better," in which she explored her conflicting feelings on the advantages and disadvantages of growing up, of maturing from childhood to adolescence. Summer wrote a piece, "My Beautiful Family," which showed the various ways love and caring are expressed in her family. Rarely now do the children write fictional fantasy pieces which go on forever with no real point or ending.

Reading has taken on new meaning for the students as well. While Josh was reading Lloyd Alexander's five-volume *Chronicles of Prydain*, he was struck by the similarities between himself and Taran, the main character: "Taran's a lot like me! He worries about not being brave enough.

I feel that way sometimes, too. But like Taran, I still try new things." Josh went on to explore this insight in great depth in his language arts journal.

With this increasing self-awareness, my students are strengthening their metacognitive skills as well. The distinction between cognition and metacognition is an important one and needs to be made. Briefly, cognition refers to using knowledge which one has acquired, and is characterized by remembering, comprehending, focusing, and processing information. Metacognition refers to a person's awareness and understanding of that knowledge. A key element in metacognition is a conscious attempt to control one's thought processes. The value of thinking about thinking has been stressed since Dewey's important studies on reflective thinking. Metacognitive activities (see Griffith, "Metacognition") are now having a greater impact on my students' reading comprehension, thanks, I believe, to their increased participation in self-reflection procedures.

Now that my students are thoughtfully considering their writing and reading, and are discovering the strategies that are successful for them, we are looking for ways to apply this process of slowing down and self-assessing to the rest of our curriculum. In classroom discussions, the children have raised some important and stimulating questions, including, "How can we become more aware of our strategies in math? What goals do we have for ourselves in social studies and science? How do we reach these goals? How will we know, and show, that we have reached our goals? Shouldn't we have portfolios in every subject? Are there ways that other subjects go together like reading and writing do?"

That's the wonderful thing about learning: it's a lifelong process. New challenges lead to new discoveries, which in turn lead to more new questions and challenges. As teachers, we must provide the time for this questioning to occur. We must slow down children's classroom lives and help them to become involved in this lifelong process.

Works Cited

Alexander, Lloyd. *The High King*. New York: Holt, 1968.

———. *Taran Wanderer*. New York: Holt, 1967.

———. *The Castle of Llyr*. New York: Holt, 1966.

———. *The Black Cauldron*. New York: Holt, 1965.

———. *The Book of Three*. New York: Holt, 1964.

Babbitt, Natalie. *Tuck Everlasting*. New York: Farrar, 1975.

Calkins, Lucy M. *The Art of Teaching Writing*. Portsmouth, NH: Heinemann, 1986.

———. *Living Between the Lines*. Portsmouth, NH: Heinemann, 1991.

Dewey, John. *How We Think*. New York: Heath, 1910.

Farr, Roger. "Portfolio Assessment." *The Reading Teacher* (Dec. 1989): 264–65.

Griffith, Robert. "Metacognition: What Reading Teachers Can Do." *Ohio Reading Teacher* 21.2 (1987): 33–39.

Lowry, Lois. *Anastasia Krupnik*. New York: Dell Yearling, 1979.

Paterson, Katherine. *The Great Gilly Hopkins*. New York: Thomas Y. Crowell, 1978.

Rief, Linda. "Finding the Value in Evaluation: Self-Assessment in a Middle School Classroom." *Educational Leadership* 47.6 (1990): 24–29.

———. *Seeking Diversity: Language Arts with Adolescents*. Portsmouth, NH: Heinemann, 1992.

Tierney, Robert J., M.A. Carter, and L.E. Desai. *Portfolio Assessment in the Reading-Writing Classroom*. Norwood, MA: Christopher-Gordon Publishers, Inc., 1991.

Response
Karen Weinhold

Nodding vigorously in total empathy with the description of the lives of students today, teachers will chuckle and despair reading through this piece. Restructuring to "middle school concept," creating block scheduling, and building interdisciplinary units through teaming have all helped to reduce the fragmentation, but not enough. Trying to develop equality among disciplines, particularly unified arts, seems to be complicating scheduling. Teachers think they'd like longer, uninterrupted blocks of time like Bob has in his self-contained elementary classroom, but are they sure? How does he deal with difficult behaviors over extended periods? Having longer periods might mean not meeting every class daily, revamping not just the curriculum but also the schedule. In his self-contained room, how does he ensure that all subjects get equal time by the end of the week—or does he?

This chapter will prompt teachers to start thinking about why they've been doing things the way they have for so long. How do students learn most effectively in time blocks? What do teachers do to help students adjust to a more sustained time period since they are quite used to the "cha-cha-cha" day now? What are each teacher's goals for the coming year? Reading this article will make everyone slow down, reflect, and engage in some metacognitive activities of their own!

Teachers will want to try many of the strategies and tools Bob suggests here. Already I use dialogue journals with the eighth graders, focused primarily on "packing their suitcases" for high school. Teachers may worry that they will not be able to keep up with all the "stuff," such as the daily workshop schedules and self-reflection checklists. Even though these are student-generated, it's easy to become overwhelmed with too many records; teachers don't need any more guilt-inducing paraphernalia. Teachers need to adapt forms and records to meet their needs and their students' needs. Would it be more cumbersome if there was more than one class to juggle? Teachers need some reassurance that they're not creating a monster before they dive into this.

3 Ring the Bell and Run

Kate Belavitch
Exeter Adult Literacy Program
Exeter, New Hampshire

Beginnings

I passed Maria's preschool classroom, stopped short and backed up. Inside, Maria sat in a chair surrounded by preschoolers. They read their morning greeting off the word pocket chart—in Spanish. I watched for a few minutes and saw the students thoroughly absorbed in Maria and what they were doing.

"Welcome!" Maria greeted me, and I walked into the classroom. "Can we greet Miss Belavitch in Spanish?" she inquired of the four-year-olds. "Hola," resounded throughout the room. "Stay as long as you like," Maria said. She returned to her students.

I taught the second grade, but since I had a few spare moments, I decided that I would browse around. Right away, I liked what I saw. As a first-year teacher with a degree in history, I had no concept of whole language, cooperative learning, or process writing. However, I felt the enthusiasm, the action, and the intense involvement of the students as I wandered around miniature tables and chairs. Maria read to the students in a corner filled with a large chair, mats, and books. It looked snug and inviting.

A long table loaded with sand and toys sat waiting for playful hands. Colorful baskets overflowed with overcoats, boas, old skirts, shirts, and aprons. Busy students played, surrounded by bookcases overflowing with soft, plush blocks, huge wooden blocks, and interlocking blocks. In the back by Maria's desk, slots were labeled with each student's name. Inside were many different papers and a folder. The room looked well lived-in and loved.

Next to Maria's desk was a floor-to-ceiling closet stuffed with books, magazines, pamphlets, and folders. I leaned closer and read titles like *How to Read to Young Students* and *Writing in the Classroom*; this must be Maria's reference collection. I made up my mind: I would be spending some time with this woman.

As it turned out, I was taking a class after school and had to walk to the subway once a week with Maria. We started off at a jog. For a slight, petite fortysomething, Maria had me panting to keep up.

"I just wanted to ask you how you got started with all that stuff in your classroom." Maria smiled and began to explain the usage of the bright blue pocket chart. I hadn't planned on walking the *nine* New York avenues to my uptown subway, but I couldn't break away from Maria's running monologue—and I didn't want to. I didn't even have to ask questions. She just kept explaining, as if she knew what I wanted to learn.

The next day, I went right to Maria. "Here," she said. Into my hands she thrust a pile of books, articles, and magazines. Thus began my introduction to process and whole language. In this pile were books by Donald Graves and Nancie Atwell, a copy of *The Reading Teacher*, a reading-conference pamphlet that featured Lucy Calkins as guest speaker. I began my journey toward discovery with a newfound mentor.

I spent this first year listening, reading, observing, and absorbing details. I attended whole language workshops and took classes on implementing writing in the classroom. My second-grade students worked on their writing in groups and alone. Together we edited for spelling, discussed illustration and revision, and put final work on large poster board or in paper-covered books. We constructed our own ABC book and presented it to the first grade. I loved what I was doing with the second graders, but Nancie Atwell's *In the Middle* became such a catalyst for me that I, too, wanted a class of young adolescents who would create meaningful prose, fraught with expectant anger, hope, anxiety, ambition, fear, and playfulness: all the things you find in students just learning about life.

I approached my principal in April and told him I would like the position of middle grades English teacher. I knew I would be responsible for teaching grammar and computers as well as writing, but it was the writing I was interested in teaching. All year long I had been reading about writing process and writing workshops; I knew what I wanted in a writing classroom. I wanted the writing class to develop so that I would be able to share my love for the written word and learn from the students as they wrote their pieces. Together we would discover our writing abilities and make all our experiences, wishes, hopes, dreams, and fantasy creations come alive on paper.

I launched into the summer with great enthusiasm. Three whole months to develop teaching strategies and plans for my writing class. I met many new teachers that summer at the University of New Hampshire while attending a class on computers. I listened to their ideas and advice. I was fortunate to meet Karen Weinhold, who plied me with folders filled with story starters and biographical information on young adult authors. I was on a first-name basis with the librarians in my town. Almost every day I would stop in to pick up books by Gary Paulsen and S.E. Hinton, and not to forget the classics, I reread *Adventures of Huckleberry Finn, The Secret Garden, Romeo and Juliet,* and Poe's poetry and short stories.

I imagined a writing classroom. Each student would have a permanent writing folder kept in the room for final papers. Each student would also have a working folder. Inside, students would keep all their drafts and three permanent sheets titled My Ideas, What I Want to Know, and What I Need to Know, an idea taken from Atwell's *In the Middle.* Students would keep a list of topics on the idea sheet; the second sheet would be for students to write down any questions they had about grammar, structure, or any problems they had, to ask during conferences. The last sheet would be something new they learned during the conferences that they could work on while they were writing. I was diligently following Atwell's book and I planned on conferences with the students while they were writing. I would take the last five minutes of class for group discussion. Throughout this summer I read many other authors on writing process, including Linda Rief and Tom Newkirk. Their ideas and case studies, along with the structure of Atwell's *In the Middle,* continued to be my main source of guidance.

My excitement grew as I envisioned an active class writing, creating, and sharing. We would become great friends as our mutual love for literature and writing would bridge the gap between teacher and student. This bond was to be the greatest asset of the classroom. By fostering an environment of creativity and freedom, I would spark in the students a desire to produce excellent work.

I, too, would be writing and keeping a journal about each of the 120 students. In this journal I would record my comments to each student; I would make contact with each writer. My journal would also be an invaluable tool to track an individual's progress and give me information when it came time to give grades. I would also use status sheets to track students' writing. I would have a legal pad with each student's name, all 120. At the start of each class, I would call names and they would tell me their status. I would know if they had started a new piece, were editing, doing another draft, or needed a conference. This would ensure that all students were working.

Nancie Atwell also spoke of meeting with each student at the end of the term to discuss an appropriate grade for the semester. I wanted to do this also. It would give me and my students a chance to discuss our expectations and set goals for the next term. This I thought very important. Communication would facilitate better understanding and give the students the encouragement needed to succeed.

I did not plan to grade the students' writing but to edit their work as they gave it to me. I expected each student to write each day. They might not hand something in every day, but they would develop an idea or just an opening paragraph. Whatever they came up with, they would continue the next day. I hoped for at least a rough draft of a story from each student at the end of the week. Students would confer with peers or with me about their drafts, which they would edit themselves and revise for details or other additions. Next, they would give me their work. I, too, would edit the work for grammar and punctuation. I would make comments to the student regarding clarity, or ask the student to expand an idea or delete an area. I would make a brief comment in my journal with regard to the student's topic, difficulties, and strengths. I would hand papers back on Monday and the process would begin again.

I believed I could accomplish this task over the weekend; I needed my other nights to correct tests and homework for my grammar classes. If students completed work during the week, I would make their work a priority to read so that we could conference the next day. I did not want the students to wait for their writing or interrupt their work in any way. We would discuss my questions and editing marks and talk about where the piece would go next.

I planned on using mini-lessons to teach those things that would meet the students' needs. For example, if they seemed interested in poetry, I would plan a lesson to introduce different styles and forms. I didn't set up any structure for myself; I thought everything would fall into place. I didn't think it necessary to develop a strategy for when to teach a mini-lesson. I had no plans to deal with the student who wouldn't write; I did not expect this to happen in this writing process classroom. Writing was a creative process; my teaching of this subject would be creative too. We would create the classroom as we went along. Atwell's book shows a smooth-running class where everything fits into place, a class the students look forward to each day. Mine would be too.

Day One

Naturally, I had the jitters. But then, this was only my second year, and I assured myself that they would pass after the first five minutes. By last period I accepted that the jitters were not leaving. These students were such, such—*adolescents,* quite unlike the second graders I had taught. I was not greeted with the awe and wonder, excitement, or enthusiasm I had anticipated. I spent most of my time explaining how free writing explores and develops everyday experiences, that they all had great potential to take these experiences and generate exciting pieces of writing. My first class was the only class of eighth graders I would have this year. Twenty-seven students entered at 8:35. Each period was to be thirty-three minutes long, so I began right away.

"Good morning. I'm Kate Belavitch, and this morning I want to talk about writing. You will be meeting me in here for grammar at 11:30 and downstairs on Monday and Friday afternoons for computer instruction, but every day at 8:30 we will be conducting a writing workshop. I expect everyone to come prepared with their working folders, which we'll hand out later, a favorite pen or pencil, and a willingness to sit down and write."

"You mean we can write in pencil?"

"Yes. If that is what is most comfortable for you, then by all means, write in pencil. Writing is a very personal thing. I write only with a cheap, blue ballpoint. Never red or black, just blue. And it has to be one of those that just glides over the paper. As soon as I feel it run out of ink, I throw it out and crack open a new pen."

"You mean I can write in red if I want to?"

"Yes, but my point is, that you want to feel free to express yourself. If you are going to write about your innermost thoughts or feelings, if you want to create a vivid picture of your visit to Europe or a fantasy fiction delight about a cruise in the islands, a fantastic murder mystery, or a true-life comedy show from your evening dinner table, you need to be able to express yourself freely." (Why did I keep saying this?) "Basically, I don't want minor things like the color of your pen or whether you use pencil or crayon to inhibit your thoughts. It is important just to jot down your ideas. Also, your first draft is just that—a draft. You can focus on spelling, punctuation, and sentence structure later. You will be able to go back and make revisions. Have you ever had a dream that seemed so real? A great story, almost lifelike, you felt you were actually there, but when you woke up, you couldn't even remember the first thing about it?" (I spoke on like this for the rest of the period. I was really warming to my subject.)

"Do you see these areas labeled 'Conference Corner'? You can meet here to discuss your writing. Sometimes it helps to read your work aloud to another person. When someone shares his or her writing, you need to listen carefully and think about how your responses will help that person. As we get started, we will share our writing. We will work on responding to other writers' work. It helps to hear and see other people's writing. Often, we gain ideas for our own writing by reading. Books, magazines, the newspaper, and your peers' work will all contribute to your ability to choose and develop your topics."

I walked around the room talking about what pleasure I have from spending time just writing down my own thoughts and ideas. Before I knew it, this class was over. Before they left I told them, "There is no homework tonight except for this: I want you to think about what you would like to write about. Writing doesn't just happen as soon as you sit down with your pen and paper. Each day, you need to be thinking about how your actions, joys, disappointments, and successes can be written down. Will you write about breaking curfew from your point of view or your mother's? Will your piece be serious or funny? This is your job to be prepared for this class. See you later in computer lab."

Just about every class went the same. I followed the same pattern, hoping my nerves wouldn't cause me to miss any valuable instructions. My sixth graders were the least vocal of the students, and I noticed they jotted down in their homework pads my assignment, whereas I guess the others had just committed it to memory or memory loss. Tomorrow we would lay the foundation by outlining the writing workshop, and maybe even get a chance to write.

Day Two

"There is only one rule in my classroom: you must write while you are here." My opening statement was greeted with whoops and cheers, and I smiled back. Rapport was established—we would be friends. I was off to a great start. "Not bad," I thought, as I handed everyone permanent writing folders. The students marked them with their names and placed them into the file cabinet.

Next, the students received their working folders and three sheets of papers which were marked My Ideas, Things I Know, Things I Ought to Know. We passed the stapler around so there would be no chance of misplacing these sheets. I explained all the sheets, and there were no questions. I had forgotten to mention a few things the day before, and I wanted to draw their attention to writing contests and the idea I had for a literary magazine. I had a bulletin board posted with all kinds of writing contests. I told the students they were welcome to peruse this first and perhaps choose one of these contests as a jumping-off point for their writing. We read the contests aloud, and I explained the directions. I told the students, if they chose to enter a contest, they would need to focus their energy right away so as to meet the deadline. I saw some of the kids perk up at the mention of the writing contests. I accomplished a goal by trying to reach out to those who might need a competitive spark to start them off.

Also, on my desk I had two file slots. They were labeled Work to Return and Work to Be Edited. I told the students they should hand in at least one piece of writing a week, not necessarily a completed piece, but perhaps the first draft they had revised, or it could be the beginning of a story. I felt that maybe I would not have a chance to see each student every day, but if they handed in something to me, I would know what they were working on and could focus my direction toward a particular student the next day. "Okay, okay, let's get moving and get on to the good stuff." Uh-oh, at this point there were about five minutes left in my thirty-three minute period. I realized we wouldn't have a full period to write, so I spoke with the students about reading to them at the end of class. I had expected to do this at the end of my grammar class, but what better way to spend the last five minutes of this class? My eighth graders chose *The Outsiders*. One of the seventh grades chose a book one of the students was reading, my other seventh grade wanted *To Kill a Mockingbird,* and my sixth grade chose *The Cat Ate My Gymsuit.*

Day Three

"Today is the day we write," I said with a smile. They all grinned back and I sat down with a sheet of paper. I put my head down, bit the end of my pencil, and began to write. The words flowed easily as I wrote about my first-day jitters. My students would get a kick out of hearing how silly I had been, how they had made me nervous and how I desperately wanted them to respond with enthusiasm for my class. I could hear mild chatter around me, but I didn't want to disturb them. I wanted the students to find their own way. It was a chance for me to see how they would approach this new style of classroom. Anyway, I wanted to be a good example, so I continued writing and let the students settle into their own writing.

I was so absorbed that when I glanced at my watch I realized ten minutes had flown by. Reluctantly, I put my pencil down and looked up. Thirty-two faces gazed back at me with blank looks. I smiled sheepishly and slowly stood up. As I walked over to the nearest student, all eyes followed me. "So, what have you written?" I asked casually. Slowly, the head turned, and I looked into clear brown eyes. The eyes glanced down at the paper and I followed her gaze to an empty sheet. Panic!!! Not her, me! "Keep thinking," I encouraged and moved on to the next student. First I looked at the paper—blank. "No ideas?" I queried. A slow negative nod was my response. "Okay, guys, remember yesterday when I told you that you need to use your own lives and experiences to draw ideas? And you need to come prepared to write?" A few nods. "So? Okay. Start with this morning. What happened? David?" (I know, a cheap shot on my part to call on someone who hasn't raised his hand. But I was getting nowhere and I needed them to be involved.)

"I got up."

"Good. Then what happened?"

"I ate breakfast."

"What did you eat?"

"Toast."

"Good, David. But can you tell me anything about the toast. How did it smell? Did you make it? Was it burnt, or undercooked and slightly soft in the middle? White, wheat, rye, pumpernickel, what kind? Did you use butter, jam, peanut butter?"

"It was just toast, Miss B. I don't usually get that excited about it." Laughter from the rest of the class.

"Well, what do you get excited about, David?"

"Not school." OK, where do I go with this?

"Great! You have plenty of material to write a piece. Be creative. What is it that makes school unexciting? Maybe write something that happened one day and school became exciting. Imagine that school was always exciting." (Rolling eyes all around.) "Just imagine," I said. "What would a typical day be like? See? Now let's start again."

Not the uplifting, motivating dialogue I had hoped for, but at least it was a starting point. Eyes looked heavenward for encouragement, and I did see some pencils reach some paper. The last ten minutes of class I spent wandering around and having mini David-like conversations with those students who still needed to get going. Tomorrow was another day.

Day Four

The first thing I noticed was that my writing corner was completely cleaned out—empty. It looked like a ghost town for writing implements. A few lone papers fluttered over the shelves, and scattered pens and marker tops that had escaped grabbing hands rolled like tumbleweeds over a dusty prairie. It was a pathetic sight. I had no more pens, all my loose-leaf paper had disappeared, even the plastic canister holding the markers was gone.

"Listen guys," I began, "if you use material from the writing corner, please return it. I have four other classes who would like fresh paper and markers to work on illustrations. Please be considerate of your classmates."

What happened here? When I set up this area, I used Nancie Atwell's book as a guide. At the beginning of the chapter titled "Getting Ready" there is a beautiful picture of her material center. It is a clean and neatly organized bookshelf. Piles of paper stand at attention, not one piece is astray. I mean the stacks are so neat I got the impression that her students must gently push the piles back into place after taking their sheet. Post-it notes and pads of scrap sit in small compartments, and a filled, yes, *filled* container of pencils stands upright, and you just know each one has a pointy tip. No returns made here without first being re-sharpened for the next student. There is also a tidy little tray containing glue, paper clips, white-out, and a tape dispenser. The inside of my *own* desk wasn't this organized. Also in the picture were stacks of books, lined up so you can actually read the titles on the jackets. The caption under the picture reads, "Keith borrows a resource book from the materials center" (52). The key word here is *borrows,* since it implies the book will be returned.

My kids were kleptos. The writing material corner soon became a disastrous pile of scrap and a few lone dictionaries. I doled out loose-leaf paper for finals, and pretty soon it became a prerequisite to bring your own extra writing implements as my personal stash gradually disappeared. But this was only one aspect of the classroom; not everything could be a carbon copy of Atwell's book. I wouldn't let it deter me from my main objective—producing students who write.

One day, I decided we would try to fit in a group share at the end of class. The students settled down, and we began to write. Again I started writing with the class for the first five minutes and then I began to move around the room. I had had a difficult time conferring with the students the day before, so I reread Atwell's chapter on conferences. All this reliance on one book may seem ridiculous, but I had it in my mind that this was the prototype reading/writing process classroom. My classroom was going to be a relatively good copy. I copied down the half page of open-ended questions so I would be fully prepared. I wasn't quite sure about what I was doing, and I was a bit timid in my actions. I approached my first student. I memorized the first five prompts, figuring I didn't want to look like I was reading from a guide. By number five, I thought, they should find something they wanted to write about.

"So, Anne, stuck for a topic?"

"Yeah, what am I supposed to write about?" (Eureka! A child in need of help with a topic, and me prepared with my handy-dandy list of topic-guiding questions.)

"What did you do this past weekend?"

"Nothing. I was grounded, so I couldn't go out."

"So this made you unhappy and maybe angry. This would be a good topic."

"Nah, I just vegged, watching TV. I really don't want to relive that situation." I guess this would eliminate a paper on her family and friends, so . . . .

"What about a pet?"

"I don't have any."

"OK. What do you like the most? Something you own or do, or what do you dislike the most?"

"My brother."

"Good." I think. "Why don't you write about your brother."

"OK." Ah, success.

I had quite a few encounters similar to my conference with Anne. I was a bit nervous as I continued approaching students struggling for topics. I was not quite sure how to react to their questions, but armed with my folder and trusty written prompts, I had something with which to get started. I know the kids felt awkward, as did I, but we were just starting out, and I knew soon things would come together.

It was a pleasure to come across someone who was writing. Very often, this was the student who had extracurricular activities after school. Many were writing pieces on swimming, baseball, hockey, or piano lessons. I noticed a similarity in most of these pieces: they almost all began, "I like to . . . ." Clearly, we could use a mini-lesson on writing leads. My lesson plan for tomorrow hatched. I was absorbed in following the students and helping them get started when suddenly I noticed we had only three minutes left. Hastily I called out to them to stop their writing. "Would anyone like to tell us or read to us something they have written?" No response. "Would anyone like to share just their opening paragraph?" Again, no response. I volunteered to read what I wrote. It was a short paragraph about my morning. That morning had been somewhat of a disaster: a pipe burst in my bathroom, flooding my hall. It was funny and some of the kids laughed and then the bell rang. Another day without group share, but I was happy with the progress made in the classroom.

Day Five

On this day, I decided to begin with a lesson. I wanted the students to understand what it means to grab your reader. Nothing beats example, so I chose to share with the kids the opening lines of Natalie Babbitt's *Tuck Everlasting*. Babbitt's tale begins, "The first week of August hangs at the very top of summer, the top of the live-long year, like the highest seat of a Ferris wheel when it pauses in its turning." The rest of the opening paragraph paints a picture of August so vividly that we feel feverish from heat just from reading. We discussed the use of simile and brainstormed some on the blackboard. I spoke to the students about using specifics and the importance of showing and not telling. I truly enjoyed this lesson.

Because I was not the reading teacher, we didn't have a class set of paperbacks and we did no reading together except when I read to the students. This was a major obstacle in my room. I believe reading literature is important in order to draw examples and ideas for your own writing. The students spent their time in reading class reading aloud and answering questions for homework. They hated it and they were bored. Whenever I brought up the subject of reading, they groaned. However, when I pulled out these opening paragraphs and the kids really listened, something else happened. I didn't ask them what Babbitt meant in her lead and we didn't analyze her use of words, but after this lesson I began to see pieces that had more description and thought. During our conferences we spoke about how we could change a sentence to "show" rather than tell.

My first month progressed much like the first week. I smiled and cajoled, laughed and encouraged, but the kids didn't seem to do much writing, or not as much as I hoped. I expected the students to be constantly writing, revising, editing. Some students spent whole class periods trying to find a topic. I felt discouraged when they spent the whole period thinking and not writing. This was truly a month of discovery. I worked on implementing many aspects of the process classroom. I felt positive that once we became acclimated to the process environment, writing would begin.

Self-Reflections

We were well into October, and many of the students still experienced difficulty with beginning writing or they abandoned papers shortly after they started. Out of 120 students, I had roughly twenty-five from whom I had seen no writing at all. It was at this point that I began to evaluate some of the things I was doing. First, keeping a journal for 120 students was completely idealistic. Idealistic is being kind; I was an idiot!

In the beginning, the majority of students were writing nothing. Hour after hour, each night I wrote in my journal expectations for each student and what we would discuss tomorrow. This left me exactly no time to work on mini-lessons or attend to more pressing matters, such as the lack of student writing for me to read.

Looking back, I can't believe I kept the journal for this long. I kept a separate journal for each of my five classes. I lugged them back and forth to home, outside for lunch duty, down to lunch, but they never accomplished what I intended. I wanted them to be a running record of the students' work and progress. However, I was using valuable time in an area that was not supporting my needs in the classroom. My journal was devoted exclusively to those kids who were writing; I had nothing to write about the others. This was when I abandoned my journal. It was not a wise use of my time.

Something else I abandoned to create more structured direction was the class status sheet. This, too, I had thought would be a good way for me to see at a glance what my students were working on. I couldn't implement this the first week because we barely got into writing, but by week two, I was armed and ready with my legal pad. I explained to the kids that I would call their names and they could respond with new piece (and name their topic), second draft, third draft, etc., final, revision, or conference. This last one would enable me to set up my time to meet with those who needed to work on their pieces.

"Status please. Zach?"

"Um, I'm looking for something to write about."

"OK, just say new piece and you don't have a title yet."

"Um, new piece and I don't have a title yet." Now we were moving. "Max?"

"Second draft."

"On what, Max?"

"I wrote this science fiction thing."

"Did I read it?"

"No, but I gave it to Jason to read."

"Well, I'd like to see it, Max, before you move on."

"Um, conference?"

"Good, see you in a bit. Bridget?"

"Revision. I'm working on my second draft using your editing marks and some of my own ideas for changes."

"Great, Bridget, I'm looking forward to seeing your next draft."

So, with thirty-three-minute periods, how prudent was this? It was so tedious for the other students who were waiting and distracting to those who wanted to get started. Also, the lingo was not making it. Some kids would retort, "I don't know, second or third, I can't remember."

With my workload from computers and grammar, I needed my extra time to spend preparing mini-lessons for my struggling writers. The students who were writing had begun to occupy most of my time. I worked with them in conference, we edited together, read aloud their writing, and their work flourished. I needed to concentrate on why the others were not writing as much. There needed to be some individual instruction. The size of my classes—32, 28, 29, and 27—made my task even more challenging. A lot of the assessment tools I was trying to implement, such as journal tracking of the students and meeting with each child every day, proved impossible. I needed much more structure to succeed in creating writers. I didn't want to start assigning topics because it went against the very teaching of process. However, in hindsight, topic assignments would have given me a grasp of the students' capabilities and a starting point from which to work. I finally devoted a full class period to discussing topic searching. The kids were still having a difficult time finding material, and I needed to reach the kids who did not write anything. I also could not ignore those who were bravely plugging along and getting their thoughts on paper. They needed to learn how to hone these first simple ideas, to make their writing readable and exciting.

Almost daily, I read to the students. I also read aloud my own writing, but this modeling was not enough. We talked about our own lives, drawing topics from events, people, and places that we knew personally. My students came from a wide spectrum of ethnic groups. I asked many to talk briefly about their country of origin, holiday celebrations, language, or difficulties acclimating to a new culture. They began to see that their own lives provided an immense body of topics. On the board, we webbed ideas from one broad topic.

My students rarely spoke to each other about their writing. Only a few students who worked very well together talked about their writing and actually read it to each other. However, the majority of my students, when left to their own devices, didn't use conference time to discuss writing.

My sixth-grade class was an exception. They used their conference time to discuss their writing, collaborate, or search for topics. They also sought me out more than the other students. My sixth graders worked lying down on the floor, or at their desks. They watched the writing contest board and entered quite a few. Zach received an honorable mention for his essay on Martin Luther King. Bridget and I attended an awards ceremony in honor of her poem espousing water conservation. These students also experimented with many different forms of writing. To what do I attribute this? I think I had quite a few advantages in the sixth grade. This was my homeroom. We had a rapport that comes from sharing extra time, attending assemblies together, and taking field trips. I also read more to this class than any other. We finished two novels, read countless short stories and a few plays from *Read* magazine, and while we had no organized group share, I read much more of their work aloud in class.

I gave each of the different classes a lesson on editing marks. This I think was one of my greatest accomplishments. As I went around the room conferring with students, I read their pieces and placed editing marks on their papers. The students asked, What does this mean? I copied the marks on their Things I Need to Know papers and explained the marks. I didn't want to inundate them with a lot of information at once, so I gave them one mark at a time as it was used. Soon I realized that this was taking a lot of my time. I decided to put all the marks on an overhead and list what they were. Then I put up some sample writing and showed how to edit the piece. The students all copied the marks on the board into their folder. Editing is a good way to ensure that the students are reading what they have written. Too often I would get papers that had words missing in the middle of the sentence and I knew that they could not have read over their piece. They thought just to write, hand it in, and they were done.

Once into November, everyone's patience began to wear thin. Those students who were still struggling with topic searching began to lose interest in class. Soon the conference corners became havens for these students. They would study for the next class, get a jump on their homework, or just socialize. I became a transit cop trying to reach those who were working and pushing the other students around the room to get them to work and keep them from distracting others. I was completely annoyed by now. I had at least eight students in each class from whom I had received no work.

On average, I had about three pieces from most of my students and they were nothing to gloat about. I was not only discouraged, but I was also beginning to dread my writing period. There was a serious gap between what the students were doing and what I wanted them to do. There was also a serious breakdown in communication. I was trying to pry writing from reluctant writers.

Assessment

It was around the end of this month that my principal approached me about grades for writing. I was given so much freedom with this class, that I had just assumed my method of assessment would be . . . actually, I had not truly thought of formal assessment. I thought the student portfolios would be representations of work in progress and the individual goals included in the portfolio would go home. I was taken aback when my principal told me I needed to give grades such as 96 or 87. How could I possibly do this when I had not graded their writing? My principal thought I was nuts.

"I need grades for the students in order to determine their standing in the class. It is especially important for the eighth graders. We average their grades to determine valedictorian." (This was when I first became aware of the true politics of grades!)

"But writing is subjective," I argued, "I can't put a number grade on their ideas. I want the students to feel free to express themselves without worrying how I am going to pass judgment." His idea was not to grade their writing for content but to grade it based on expectations I set for them. He suggested I use grammar, punctuation, and editing skills as well as the amount of work each child produced as criteria for my grades. We also came to a compromise: I would give the students letter grades. I could lump them into the A, B, or C categories.

This was how I came to devise the quota system. I had no set guidelines and the students had no set objective. I decided to tell them that they would have to do a minimum of ten pieces of writing (drafts with at least two finals) in order to obtain a B. An A would be the result of producing high quality work, writing every class, taking risks by trying new styles and genres, and self-improvement. There was enough time before grades closed (six weeks) to produce at least four new pieces of writing. That made at least one draft and two pieces that were completed to final form. I set this as an objective for the end of the first term. I had records of the kids' writing and I showed the principal the difference between an A and a C in my writing class. The student earning an A had worked at least two pieces to a final draft. They were diligent in class and wrote during the whole period. The child who would be earning a C had two or three different drafts, was struggling to work a topic to completion, and needed to spend more class time practicing writing. The majority of grades given out the first term were C's. I met with all 120 students to determine grades. I had an idea in my mind what each student would receive, but I didn't have anything in writing before I met with the student. I thought our conference would be collaborative and the resulting grade would be satisfactory to us both. I first met with the seventh graders. This particular class was receiving mostly C's and I figured they would expect this because they failed to meet the quota criteria.

I first met with Jacob. My conversation began this way: "Let's take a look at what you have in your portfolio and read some things together. Why don't you tell me what is your favorite piece." Jake chose a two-paragraph story about a monster. It was written as a draft and was not self-edited. It had my editing marks on it, and the piece was dated in September. "This is the first thing I did and I like it the best."

"Well, why exactly, Jake?"

"It's funny."

Well, I hadn't found the piece particularly amusing and wasn't quite sure it was meant to be a comedy, but it was his writing, so I figured he knew best. Jake had four more pieces of writing dated for the months of September and October.

"What kind of a grade do you think you deserve for this, Jake?"

"An A." Not a question but a statement.

"Um, you didn't meet the quota criteria, Jake, and most of your work was done in September and October. You have not done anything for the month of November."

"Oh, yes I did, but you lost them."

"I lost them?"

"Yes. I handed them in but you never gave them back." At this point I went over to my desk and looked through the pieces I had not edited. There was nothing here. Next I looked at the work to be handed back and there was nothing in this pile as well.

"There doesn't seem to be anything here, Jake. I don't recall seeing any of your work. Why don't you describe a piece to me and maybe I'll remember it if I read it."

"I wrote them so long ago I can't remember them."

"Jake, I don't know what to tell you. Look in your folder again, but I can't grade you on work I haven't seen."

"So what is my grade?"

"Considering you didn't reach the quota and none of your pieces were completed to a final, I can't give you more than a C." I thought this was generous.

"What! I'm an A student! C'mon, gimme a B at least." Wait a minute. I'm the teacher and this is the student. He can't be serious.

"Do you really think this is fair, Jake? What about the student who wrote eight pieces and did two finals?"

"Can't you give him an A?"

"No, Jake, I can't. There are rules and they need to be followed. If you got five problems wrong on a math test and the person next to you got ten wrong, would you want them to receive the same grade?" All I received for this was a roll of the eyes and a very reluctant, "I guess not."

"So, I get a C, right?"

"For this term, Jake, but we can set goals for the next semester. What do you think you might want to accomplish?"

"I'm gonna write ten pieces so I can get an A."

"Great, Jake, I know you can do it."

I thought this conversation would be unique, but I had many similar ones with other students. Those who received a B or an A were extremely happy. In fact, those who received a B had the clearest set of objectives and the strongest determination to achieve an A for the following term.

I felt like I had conceded a point by setting up this quota. I didn't want the kids to be forced to write; it was supposed to happen naturally. However, once the quota had been established, I noticed a perceptible change in the classroom. Grades had been given in December and many of the students were disappointed. Once the quota was set up, it provided a guideline which the students could work toward.

Beginning Again

The following semester began with everyone starting anew. By this time many of the kinks were worked out. I longed to have meaningful conferences with the students, and in the first semester they had been few and far between. Now that more of my students were writing, we had more to converse about. It was during this semester that I found conferences to be invaluable. They gave me a chance to see the writer at work. I was able to help individuals over trouble spots. We would just chat and maybe share a laugh about what they were writing or discuss where they could go next.

I often stopped to check on Elizabeth and Hannah. Sometimes they would wave me by because they were writing intensely and could not be disturbed. Other times I had to interrupt them because they would get into loud arguments about their writing. They collaborated and were in the middle of doing their own rendition of *The Pigman*. These two were an interesting contrast of styles. Elizabeth wrote long, descriptive poems about love, nature, and life. Hannah was the next Barbara Taylor Bradford. When she wasn't working with Elizabeth, she was deep into her book (which reached Chapter 8 or 9, I lost track) and the steamy romance of the two main characters.

I found my conferences to last sometimes five to ten minutes with a student. It took me quite some time to learn how to navigate the classroom and make myself available to everyone. Naturally, those students who wrote a lot constantly called out to me and approached me with their work.

I felt overwhelmed by the number of kids in a classroom. Often after school I made a list for myself of the students with whom I had not conferenced that day. I tried to reach these students the following day. I wasn't using the journal system any more, but I did have some idea of who needed my help. Also, when I was with these writers, I made notations on their writing or in their folders so I knew what skill they were working on. I also made brief notes for myself about the goal I had for each of them. For kids who were writing a lot, I made notations for them to try a different genre. For others, it was to work on sequence, scene or plot development, or correct use of punctuation in dialogue. My grade conferences at the end of the second semester were quite different from the ones I had in December. The students had writing to show me and together we could establish realistic goals for the next term. Most of my writers earned A's and B's this semester. But more important than the grades, they worked hard to develop a personal objective for their writing.

A New Year

From my experiences in this class, I have learned what I need, what I want to accomplish, and what I would do differently. I need to define my goals, for myself and then for the students. I want the students to write, but I want them to enjoy what they are doing as well. I'm still a little timid about letting them have free rein, so I think I would implement the quota system right from the beginning. This may not be the best way to go, but I think it would give me more confidence to know that I would at least have a base upon which to build.

Each child would still get a permanent folder as well as a working folder, but I would not use idea sheets or conference sheets. Nor would I try to keep track of 120 students in a journal format.

I would outline a set of mini-lessons that I want to teach. I would have them totally prepared and give myself a time frame in which to teach them. The second day would be a mini-lesson on brainstorming. We would spend the rest of the class time brainstorming topics and ideas.

I would share some of my writing and model a personal narrative. I think for many new writers, it is much easier to write about a familiar subject. I would also stress and model the idea of the students being aware of the events in their lives, their actions and reactions. I would want them to think constantly about what they would write the next day. And, I would not want them to limit themselves to writing just in the class. I would assign structured homework, sometimes a working idea for a dialogue, or a revision of their work done from a different perspective, or even a reflection on someone's piece.

I found that we never had enough time to share our writing. I shared or modeled a lot for my sixth-grade class and often asked the students if they would read something they wrote to the class. The significance of shared writing showed in the amount of work produced by this class, as well as the quality of it. However, thirty-three-minute periods with almost thirty kids a class made sharing an impossibility. I also had a hard time letting go of valuable writing time. Yet sharing helps in so many ways. Students gain new writing ideas from each other and, more important, they learn to listen and critique the writing of others. I would definitely establish a listening session. If I were pressed for class time, I would set up each Friday as a listening class. I would want everyone to share during this time. I would also like to ask volunteers (maybe just one each Friday) to put their work on the overhead projector and we would discuss how we would edit the piece for style, clarity, or structure.

I would want to teach some sort of reading with the writing. Even if I were in a system that kept the two subjects separate, I would somehow incorporate short stories, poetry, mystery, and other genres into the writing class. It is also important to share what we are reading. As writers, we can learn how to use foreshadowing or flashback just from reading or listening to different authors. It would be ideal to have classtime to allow for shared reading, silent reading, or book discussions.

I continued my own education, pursuing a graduate degree as a reading specialist. I also continued my own personal writing and reading. Both of these things continue to contribute to my ever-expanding knowledge of how best to teach adolescents to write.

Works Cited

Atwell, Nancie. *In the Middle: Writing, Reading, and Learning with Adolescents*. Portsmouth, NH: Heinemann, 1987.

Babbitt, Natalie. *Tuck Everlasting*. New York: Farrar, 1975.

Newkirk, Thomas, and Nancie Atwell. *Understanding Writing*. Portsmouth: Heinemann, 1987.

Rief, Linda. *Seeking Diversity: Language Arts with Adolescents*. Portsmouth: Heinemann, 1991.

Response
Kay Morgan

This chapter takes teachers back to the energy, enthusiasm, and almost revolutionary fervor they experienced when they first discovered the writing process.

The fact that Kate was a new teacher and that after only one year she was trying both a new grade level and a new approach shows the dramatic impact this method had on her.

Perhaps one of the stunning aspects of the writing process approach is that teachers instinctively know it is the "right" way to teach writing. It offers the opportunity for student-directed learning; it offers the opportunity for individualized learning; it offers the opportunity to focus on critical thinking skills and develop a community of learners who learn from each other, not just from the teacher. Further, the writing process provides collaborative and cooperative learning occasions which help build student self-esteem and reduce the competitive atmosphere which has dominated classrooms for too long. Given all these pluses, wherein lie the difficulties? Are the difficulties insurmountable?

One of the areas Kate identifies as a big problem for her is one all teachers experience, and that is the issue of TIME. Whether it is time enough for conferences with each student who is ready for one; or time enough for all-group sharing; or time enough to prepare the necessary mini-lesson; or time enough to read all the drafts before the next day's class, all teachers struggle to stretch the minutes in a class period or the hours in a day to meet the most basic requirements of a process-oriented, student-centered classroom.

Assessment is another area loaded with potential problems. Kate's journal-keeping turned into a nightmare and had to be abandoned. How does a teacher arrive at a final grade if he or she isn't grading drafts? What do teachers do with 120 portfolios of final, polished pieces at the end of the marking period? Don't grades actually run counter to the whole process approach? What do teachers try to grade, the process or the product? Where is the student involvement in the assessment process?

As the days went by, Kate's struggle with students who didn't seem to turn into the magical community of writers she expected and hoped for speaks to the heart of this book. How many veteran teachers struggle each year or each day with some aspect of the process that doesn't quite go the way they thought or were taught it would? How they deal with that struggle—or *whether* they deal with it or decide they are failures—is central to their mental health as teachers and central to the continuing success of teaching writing through the process approach. Kate's experience, candor and confusion, bravery and idealism which she identifies as bordering on idiocy, remind me of the necessity to try to approach each year with the enthusiasm of the first-year teacher, seasoned by the reality that certain aspects of the process work better than others, and that teachers needn't view themselves as failures when some things just plain don't work.

4 "ThiiNG I Do'T, WoT To FGeT"

Michelle Toch
Carlisle Elementary School
Carlisle, Massachusetts

'm ready to publish this!" By mid-January these words haunted me. Not that I didn't want all twenty of my first graders to be prolific writers; I just didn't want to have to publish every word they wrote.

My writing program, right from its launch on the first day of school, took off with the children. They loved to write and often chose to write at every opportunity they had. My young novelists just burst to retell the events of their latest birthday party, their trip to Grandma's, or their new bike that didn't come with training wheels. After many mini-lessons, conferences, and discussions about publication, they were ready to turn their pieces of wide-lined paper, upon which they had drawn precious Crayola illustrations accompanied by a few words (written in all capitals, with no punctuation, and in invented spelling), into printed masterpieces with all the conventions that come with publication. From then on, I spent every moment of every writers' workshop in authors' circles and editing conferences. I spent all of my free time after school typing and printing and laminating and binding. I didn't want to discourage the children from wanting to publish. They were learning conventions and developing as writers, but I felt completely overwhelmed. As much as I loved teaching process writing, all I could think was "Calgon, take me away!"

By the time February rolled around, I became so far behind in publishing the children's stories that I feared they would start to boycott writers' workshop. Caught up in the motions of writing, conferring, revising, and editing, they had become noticeably less vested in their writing. Most of their writing was uninspired, and many of the students were topic-jumping because they couldn't get hooked into a story that really excited them. Their pieces primarily recounted a series of events. Particularly popular were stories about school, written in an almost *This Is Your Life* style.

Though I knew that for some students this style was appropriate, I felt I could expect more sophisticated pieces from others. I spent many hours thinking about the modeling I did for them, the kinds of questions and comments we gave each other about our writing, and the literature we shared and discussed. We then spent a lot of time talking about how important it was for an author to imbue a piece of writing with thoughts and feelings. As a result, they began to put more of themselves into their writing, but the problem still remained that their motivation was primarily external, and they weren't writing about anything for which they had particularly strong thoughts or feelings. They didn't seem to be able to choose topics which could capture themselves, let alone an audience.

This all changed after one particularly fateful February vacation. I took the time to read Lucy Calkins's *Living Between the Lines*. Calkins devotes many pages in her book to getting children in touch with the things in their lives which leave indelible impressions and having them record these into notebooks. Through the use of writers' notebooks, writers are able to capture on paper thoughts, events, impressions, phrases—whatever strikes them. These entries chronicle significance in a writer's life—entries that may serve as rehearsal for a story, entries that may some day be used directly in a piece of writing.

Several ideas in her book struck me, particularly the understanding that literacy permeates life, and the need to have a place to write about life in scraps of time and thought. Here is where writing becomes inseparable from living. Having read this, it occurred to me that what the children really needed was validation of their lives. With the understanding that the things which happened in their lives were valued, they would see the meaning in writing about them. I had spent my time with them trying to get them to infuse their stories with thoughts and feelings when what they really needed to do was take important thoughts or feelings and weave them into a story. When children realize this purpose of their notebooks, as Calkins comments, children lead more "wide-awake" lives (42).

After reading Calkins's book, I was eager to begin to keep a notebook of my own. One day during vacation, I took a break from my love of the snow to venture out and enjoy an unseasonably warm day. Since I live so close to Walden Pond, I decided this would be the perfect place to spend such a day. It was quiet, with only a few other people out in the early morning "spring." As I walked around the pond and through the wooded path, I suddenly became acutely aware of the sound the snow made under my feet, and I realized that even on this warm, spring-like day, I was still enjoying winter. I couldn't wait to get home to write it all down in my notebook:

> I love to hear the sound of the crunching snow under my feet! Today I went to Walden Pond for the first time this year. There was still a lot of snow on the ground, and although the sun was strong and warm, the air still had a crispness to it—a comfort that it was still winter. The pond was still frozen, and many ventured out to walk on it—I, however, chose to walk around it. There were many beautiful things to see, but what appealed most to my senses was the crunching of the snow.

I thought about my experience a little more, and wrote again:

> Crunching Snow—It's so loud! It reminds me of a particular night in college when, as I walked across campus in the snow, I suddenly became keenly aware of that crunching! I think Jane Yolen has written about that crunching in *Owl Moon*. I'll have to check.
>
> Yes, she has! "Our feet crunched over the crisp snow and little gray footprints followed us." Wow—That's poetry!

Throughout vacation I continued to collect snippets of my life which I planned to share with the children. I included some poems I wrote, some favorite quotes, an incident which enraged me while I was waiting in line at a local store, things I wondered about—anything that struck me. I found myself leading a "wide-awake" life.

That first morning back I was anxious for the children to share my newfound passion for writing and especially anxious to get them all started in notebooks of their own. We discussed becoming aware of our senses while doing ordinary things. At this point I shared with them my Walden Pond entry, emphasizing the pleasure the sound of the crunching snow had brought me. I told them this experience was so special to me that I didn't ever want to forget it, so I wrote it down. I then read my second entry, explaining I felt I had more to say. I wanted them to see that you could write about a particular topic in more than one way. As I told them this, I had my notebook with me and I held it close to my heart; I wanted them to see how treasured it is because it holds the things that are most special to me, the things I don't ever want to forget.

Hoping they were catching on, I asked if they had ever been doing something and suddenly realized it was something they didn't ever want to forget. The responses I got were varied and didn't always hit the target I was aiming for, but every hand enthusiastically went up. I realized I had found validation for their experiences. Krystina shared that one day, while she was playing at her toy sink (she also included a detailed description of how the faucets actually work), she suddenly noticed a bug crawling on the wall. Not that I *don't* think this bug may somehow have had an impact on Krystina's life, but I think she was thinking more along the lines of "suddenly noticed" rather than "didn't ever want to forget." After a little refocusing, Suzanne shared with us that when she moved to Carlisle she had mixed feelings. On moving day that mix was anger and sadness when she suddenly realized that she didn't know into which house she was moving. We sympathetically discussed Suzanne's experience and talked about how this was a very strong memory for her, one she's not likely to forget. Barrett shared an experience from preschool when he was not allowed onto a model trolley car because he was too small. Laura kicked off the dead pet theme by telling us about her pet turtle that died when she was "three or five or six or something." Noah had us all near tears when he told us of his late dog, Klondike, and how he can still feel how soft his fur was.

We sat and listened and empathized with all who shared. I then told them I was going to give each of them a notebook like mine in which they could save these cherished memories. They immediately broke into choruses of cheers and were eager to get started. Before I sent them to their tables to get writing, I asked each of them to say what their first entry would be about. I wanted to get a handle on what would be happening, and I wanted them to hear a variety of possible entries.

We also talked about an important "rule" for our notebook time, a "rule" which I believe has really contributed to the success of our new project: We would write in silence. They were used to using "quiet, inside voices" and restricting their conversations to "writing conversations," but working in silence would be new for them. I felt very uncomfortable with this at first. I thought I would be somehow taking away ownership and community from them (a sin among writing process teachers). Calkins writes about exactly this feeling, and she made me feel much more comfortable, helping me to understand that I would be doing what is best for the children and for me. I believe *they* needed silence to be able to focus completely on these entries which were of such importance to them. I believe *I* needed the silence to process all that was happening with this project and to be able to confer effectively with children. Surprisingly, there weren't any objections; they were so eager to write down their special memories, they weren't interested in chatting. So, off they went, many of them skipping back to their tables. They all got right to work. I didn't hear any "I have nothing to write about," "I'm tired of writing. Isn't it time for snack yet?," or "I've just been scribbling while I think about what I'm going to write next." I circulated around the room to be sure everyone was comfortably on task, and then I sat down to write in my notebook as well.

They had stayed so focused I felt guilty for interrupting them for snack and recess. As soon as the children went out to recess, I couldn't wait to read the results of their morning endeavors. Reading through their entries I smiled a lot and made a mental note to talk the next day about opening their generic blue notebooks in the right direction. Another mental note I made was "WOW!" I was amazed at the emotional charge in their entries. They wrote using language and feelings they hadn't used when writing their stories.

On day two of our adventure, I again read more of my notebook, trying to model different kinds of entries. I then gave the children time to finish entries from the previous day and then time to decorate their notebooks. We again discussed the importance of these keepsakes and how to decorate them with things that would make them uniquely beautiful. Once ornamented with color and symbols of the things the children love, these notebooks were even more precious, and I could still actually read most of the names which were written on the front covers. Jaret, who apparently wanted to feel a little more ownership over his notebook, chose to cross out where I wrote his name and wrote it again in his own writing. He then wrote in large black-marker letters, "ThiiNG I Do'T, WoT To FGeT" [Things I Don't Want to Forget].

Their entries varied as much in style as they varied in content. One child wrote in a rather stream-of-consciousness style, writing a little bit about various things which impact her.

> I love my butterfly P.J.'s. I've slept with them since I was one. And my pillow, too. I made Pillow myself. I love both of them. I like Pillar, too. My favorite singing group is the Beatles. I love their music. I like the way they look, too. I remember when Veronica gave me a seal. I named it Jessica (Jessica the person is my cousin!) I had a terrible cold. I was very sick. I cried a lot. My mom said I had the flu, but I didn't think so. I said I didn't.

Some entries were about new accomplishments:

> It was Saturday. I went to Ballet. My teacher said, "If you work hard, you may be a real ballerina some day." I danced until it was time to go home.

> I went to Roller Kingdom. I felt bad because I couldn't go fast, and then felt good because I could go fast. Yes! I was proud of myself. I could go faster than Bobby and my friends.

> I learned how to tie my shoes. I was very happy that I could tie my shoes.

I was pleased to see that Rose had related one of her entries to literature:

> My birthday is soon. My birthday is March 11. I'm turning 7. We are
> getting ready for my birthday. It reminds me of when I read a book.
> It was called *Angelina's Birthday Surprise*. I really, really loved it.
> I'm happy.

Some entries captured moments in time:

> I once was driving in the car. My Daddy stopped. I said, "Why did
> you stop?" My Daddy said, "I see a rainbow." Johnny said, "Wow!
> That is neat-o." I said, "I can see it, too." "Yes," said my Daddy.

> I wrote a letter to my cousin. I miss her a lot. I hoped I could see
> her again.

> I thought: I would have a pet, and I would be happy.

Some children seemed to be trying to work through some personal issues
in their entries.

> I was five years old. My Dad said, "You have to move to a new
> school." I didn't want to go, but I went anyway. When I got there,
> there were lots of children to make friends with, but I was afraid to
> talk to them. My teacher was nice, but I wasn't sure later in the
> year.

> Me and my brother love each other, but sometimes we get in
> fights, but I still love him, but I don't think he does.

> I hate my little sister. She's a lunatic. She pulls my hair and hits me,
> but I don't hit her back. I go and tell my Mom and Dad. She has to
> go to her room. She's mean, but I still love her.

> We are building a new house. My parents are planning out the
> house with the architect and with the carpenter. We haven't fin-
> ished planning out the house. Mom and Dad want our opinion so
> they can build the house so me and Amy are happy in it.

After they had a few opportunities to work on entries, I wanted
them to begin to hear each other's thoughts. The low number of children
who wanted to share their entries surprised and disappointed me at first.
During our regular authors' circles, they usually begged for more time to
share. When I asked why they were so reluctant, Mandy replied, "Because they're so private." In retrospect I realize this was a sign of success;
the children were writing about topics which held strong meanings for
them. However, I still tried encouraging them to share, reminding them
how helpful it can be to hear what others are thinking. I took the few
volunteers I could muster up, discussed their entries enthusiastically, and
deluged them with sincere thanks for sharing. As the children developed
more of a repertoire of entries and saw how helpful sharing was for all of

us (and how much appreciation and encouragement they were getting from me), they became more eager to share their work.

At the end of the first week, I tried having them get into small groups of about four children to each read their notebooks in their entirety. I was attempting a couple of different things. First, I wanted to create a more intimate and safe setting in which they could share, and second, I wanted to take a stab at what Calkins refers to as "reflecting and adding rings of meaning." She explains this as having the children look for common threads which run through their entries, and the meanings those threads may hold. I wasn't sure how the children would do with this; I wasn't sure they even *had* any threads running through their writing. Even so, they did very well conferring with one another, although I could tell they were having difficulty giving authentic feedback; they weren't quite sure of how to respond to these cathartic glimpses into one another's lives. Some of the feedback was as dry as "good writing," and some was as expressive as, "I like the way you explained how old you were, or people might say 'How old were you?'" or "I really like the way you spent time on this entry, telling us all the details." Some was as impressive as "Why did you choose to include that in your notebook?"

In fascination, I watched them confer. Some of the children paired up and exchanged notebooks while others conducted a mini authors' circle. One group of three boys listened to each other's entries and then noticed they all wrote about a pet dog, but each wrote with a different emotion. "Stuart's was exciting and violent when he wrote about the fight his dog got into, Noah's was sad when he wrote about that his dog died, and mine [Deven] was happy when I wrote about how I was thinking and hoping to get a new dog!" Even though that thread had been pulled through a few different notebooks, I was delighted they had found it. This was how we ended the first week of our new excursion. Not bad, I thought.

Over the weekend I took their notebooks home to read and respond to. I really wanted to validate what they wrote and decided to write them letters commenting and reflecting on their entries. I remember taking a course in graduate school with Don Graves in which over the course of the semester I compiled a "notebook" of my own. This was actually more of a portfolio of things which I felt represented the different aspects of who I was. The highlight of that semester was getting my notebook back from him with a letter enclosed. Knowing that he had looked at my notebook and took the time to write down his thoughts was tremendously confirming. I remember feeling uplifted, inspired, and honored. I wanted to give my students those same feelings as they began their second week of this excursion. It was easy responding to them as "gluey valentines" (as Calkins calls it), and they were overjoyed reading their letters on Monday morning.

The next week I tried to share my notebook with them every day, showing them the way my thoughts were flowing and developing. I wanted them to see many different ways in which to write in a notebook, hoping that my entries didn't sound too contrived. I also strongly encouraged children who experimented in their notebooks to share as well. I was really taken aback at how these modeling occasions influenced the children. I had written one entry wondering about honeycomb:

> I wonder why bees build honeycomb in hexagons. The shape tessellates well (we have just finished studying tessellations in math) and provides efficient storage space for honey, but why not a square, or a triangle, or an octagon? A hexagon does provide more area than a square or a triangle, but then an octagon would provide even more. I wonder if I could find the answer, or is this just another wonder of nature? (I like the way I used the word wonder in two different ways.)

The next day one child wrote an entry wondering about how flowers grow:

> I want to learn how to plant. I don't know how to plant a carrot or a flower, and want to learn.

After our seed and plant study, she went back and changed the entry:

> I want to learn how to plant. I don't know how to plant a carrot. Now I do do do do do do do!

I also shared an entry in which I wrote favorite lines from books, but had no takers on that one. Then I shared with them that I like to use my notebook to work on poems, trying out words and images, and the next day Mandy had done the same in her notebook:

> I like to make poems like:

> Friends are here to help you
> when you are in trouble
> and when you are feeling blue.

These few responses delighted me, since most of the children seemed to be of the conviction that their notebook was a journal. I think for many at this age level, it's the easiest type of entry to write.

In an effort to get them to think of their notebooks as a place to craft a story, I wanted them to do some "re-visioning." I wanted them to "re-see" their thoughts and feelings and take revision further to find the insights that come from re-thinking a piece. Some of the children did this by writing about one particular topic several times in their notebooks. I showed them how I did this in my own notebook in writing about snow several times. I explained to them that was probably because winter and snow are things for which I have very strong feelings, and somewhere inside of me, there was probably a story about snow waiting to be written. I asked the children who did more than one entry on a particular subject why they felt they did so. Without getting overly introspective, they gave reasons similar to mine—they felt they had more to say. "I wasn't done talking about it," or "I forgot to tell about which songs we sang" (referring to an entry about a concert they had been in).

I wanted them all to have a shot at revising an entry. I'm still not quite sure if this was a mistake or not. I learned from conferring on their previous stories that revision at this level of development was very difficult, and was usually limited to adding in a sentence or two to whichever page had some space. I thought, though, that perhaps some of them were ready for more sophisticated types of amendment. While some children copied their entry verbatim onto a new page (all the while thinking I was crazy because they had already written the entry once), others simply added on to the end of their first entry. Although this wasn't what I had in mind for revision, it did get them to add more details, thoughts, and feelings.

So, just like Henny Penny, we went along, and we went along, and we went along, but we weren't trying to get to the king—we were trying to get to publication. Thus came the launch into writing a story from their notebooks. It was an almost spiritual experience. I read to them *I'm in Charge of Celebrations* by Byrd Baylor, but beforehand I told them I wanted them to think about why the author may have decided to write this story. They were really mesmerized by the text. At the end, there was a moment of complete silence during which we were all savoring what we had just experienced. Then their hands started to shoot up.

"I know why you read that to us! Because she used a notebook too!"

"Yes, I noticed that too," I said. "How did the character in this book use her notebook?"

"Just like us! She used it to write down the things she doesn't ever want to forget!"

I gave them a few moments to process that one. "As I was reading this story, you were thinking about why the author may have written this book. What are some of your ideas?"

"She wanted to show that she uses a notebook."

"She wanted to tell about her celebrations."

"She wanted to tell us about the desert and the animals and what she does."

Unable to hold back my smile I said, "I think I agree with all those reasons, and I think she gave us a clue about her purpose in the beginning of the story when she's asked if she ever gets lonely living in the desert. I think she wrote the story as a kind of answer. What do you think?"

I was answered with affirmative nods. "I think she must have had some pretty strong feelings about the desert for her to be able to write such a beautiful story." More nods. "Let's take a look at a couple of other books, some old favorites."

They were exuberant when they saw the books I had: *Seven Blind Mice* by Ed Young, *Sarah Morton's Day* by Kate Waters, and *Owl Moon* by Jane Yolen. The children adored these books each time they read them. I asked them for their thoughts about the authors' purposes, and they came up with terrific ideas. One of them even noticed, "Jane Yolen's given us a clue about her purpose in her dedication!" Yolen wrote, "For my husband, David, who took all of our children owling." They decided Yolen wrote the book because going owling created a special memory for her. They also thought she wanted to write about what you do when you go owling. The discussion then moved toward how special a memory it was for her, and how that helped her to write such a wonderful story. "I agree," someone chimed in, "it's a masterpiece!"

"That it is," I answered. "Do you think if Jane Yolen keeps a notebook, she has an entry about owling?"

"She's probably written about it about a million times!" Again the refrain of nods.

"I agree." I then posed the questions, "Do you think each time she wrote about owling she wrote the same things? Do you think she used her notebook to experiment with and practice her story before she sat down to write it?"

"Yeah, like, one time she probably wrote about seeing the owl and her thoughts and feelings about that, and then the next time maybe she wrote about that you have to be quiet, and then the next time maybe she wrote about how cold it was, and then maybe she wrote about it a bunch more times, and then she wrote her story."

I hoped they were starting to see where I was headed. "Look what happens when you have a really strong feeling about something, and you have a strong reason for writing about it, and you try writing it in different ways, and you include lots of thoughts and feelings. You come up with a masterpiece! You could do that! This masterpiece has even won a gold Caldecott!"

They all gasped at the climax. Barrett, however, didn't seem to buy what I was trying to sell. "But a Caldecott is given for the illustrations, and Jane Yolen wrote the words."

"You're absolutely right, Barrett, but John Schoenherr wouldn't have been able to do his beautiful, award-winning illustrations if Jane Yolen hadn't first written beautiful words." He bought that. On that note we were ready to sow the seeds our notebooks gave us.

These notebooks had a significant impact on the development of three particular writers in the class, Noah, Brittney, and Deven. Here I will share selections from their notebooks, and how they made the transition into stories.

Noah was a member of the Dead Pet Society. There were several children in the class who chose to write about the passing of a dear pet. This was understandable considering the impact it seemed to have on them. Noah's notebook included the following:

My Dog

I liked to pet my dog! He reminds me of my other dog named Kodiak. I was sad when my dog Klondike have died because of he had a broken leg, and he was blind when Klondike was alive. I loved him, and he was very soft! He was born blind, and when he was blind he ran into a wall and broke his leg! My Dad was sad when we took Klondike to the vet to kill him.

My Bunny Rabbit

My bunny rabbit was fast! I chased him around a lot to pet him because he's so soft! But once he got out of his cage and the dog ate him. I was very sad. My Mom was sad, too.

My Bunny Rabbit

I waited long, but when my Mom told me that Kodi ate my bunny rabbit, I was sad. So was my Dad, too. So was my Mom, too. So was my brother, too. My Mom and Dad and brother were mad at Kodiak. So was I.

My Duck

I used to have a duck. My Mom always feeds my duck and always puts a lock on so robbers can't get him. My duck always stays in a metal cage so a different animal can't eat him, but one day a raccoon came and jiggled the lock and it fell off of the cage and the raccoon opened the door and went inside the cage and ate my duck.

After conferring with him on his entries, I learned that Noah had some very vivid memories of finding out about his rabbit's death that he hadn't included in his notebook. Even though we talked about the other entries, he kept coming back to his entries about his rabbit. I was over-joyed to see Noah's rings of meaning. He discovered his masterpiece waiting to be written, and I agreed with that insight.

Noah spent a lot of time on this piece, writing and illustrating very carefully. He would frequently update me on his progress, including a prediction about how many more pages it would take him until he finished. When he did finish, he was beaming with pride and alacrity to share his masterpiece with me and with his peers. His story had a most surprising (and upsetting) ending for most of the children who didn't already know the outcome. His peers were left speechless, but Noah was grinning from ear to ear, eager to take questions and comments. This had been a very meaningful experience for him, both as a writer and as a little boy trying to get over the sudden loss of a dear pet.

My Bunny Rabbit

-dedicated to my bunny rabbit because it's about him-

I got a bunny rabbit in 1991. We named him Jezabel. He was cute! Everybody loved him! We gave my duck cage to my bunny rabbit! My bunny rabbit liked his cage a lot! When it's Spring, we let him out of his cage so he can run around! We played with my bunny rabbit a lot! I got worn out! When it's Winter, we put him in the basement!! Sometimes I bring him up a big huge rock. One day when my Mom was feeding my rabbit, he jumped out of his cage, and my dog ate him. I was sad when my dog ate my bunny rabbit. Me and my brother waited a very long time for my Mom to come in. She told me about my dog ate my rabbit. Everybody was mad at Kodiak.

About the Author/Illustrator:

Noah lives in Massachusetts. He got the idea of the story because his rabbit really did get eaten up.

Brittney was a writer who came into first grade very unsure of herself. Because she was so quiet and reserved, it was challenging for me to find ways to connect with her. These entries gave me glimpses into her life which allowed me to interact with her meaningfully and help her to feel more confident. As a writer who struggled with stories, often spending her time only on illustrations, she surprised me with her comfort with and understanding of notebook writing. Brittney's notebook includes entries like the following:

I had some new fish. I don't have fish now. They died. I felt bad. I had different colored fish. The black fish had black babies. I was happy, but Kurt was lucky. I was sad because I thought Kurt was lucky. It wasn't fair that he got fish [that had babies].

Although she had many succinct and meaningful entries which could lead her into a story, we chose this entry as her seed. This entry elicited the strongest feelings in her, and we both agreed this would make a great story. Her style was to get right to the task at hand and get it done quickly. After meeting about her story several times to get it focused and to be sure that all the information she wanted to include was included, she had a piece to be proud of.

When We Got Fish

-dedicated to my Mom and Dad-

We got in the car. We were going to buy fish. We drove to the fish store. We were there. We got out of the car. We went in the fish store. I picked out the red and the blue fish. My brother got black fish. We got out of the fish store. We went back to the house. We got home. We got in the house. We put the fish in the tank. We were watching and watching. We were watching the fish. The black ones had black babies. It wasn't fair that Kurt's black fish had babies.

About the Author/Illustrator:

I live in Carlisle. I got that feeling because I like my fish.

Although Brittney didn't show her pride as evidently as Noah, I did catch a rare smile when her book was completed. This piece was a great risk for her; she revealed true emotion in her writing. I suspect Brittney's notebook provided for her a purpose for writing that was not in place for her before. She felt she could write freely without feeling overwhelmed and pressured to produce a story. Brittney confirms how far learning and "mastery of skills" advance when children are engaged and interested in their learning. This was authentic for Brittney; she saw a clear purpose for written language—she had something important to say. As a result Brittney displayed her knowledge of story, including detail, control of time, purpose, setting, and even a little suspense. Until this point I had no real gauge of her development as a writer.

Deven was my most reluctant writer. I don't think this was due to any lack of ability or misunderstanding of expectations, but merely because he found it far more interesting to draw graphic pictures of incidents from video games. He filled his writing folder with reams of these pictures, without a blessed word written on any one of them. During our conferences he would quickly push aside his pictures and explain that he was still thinking of something to write about. Just when I'd think we had come up with a working plan, our time would be up, and I didn't seem to be able to check in with him enough to be sure he was on task—or more specifically, on our agreed-upon task.

From the very start of our notebook project, Deven seemed to tap into a source of emotion and meaning in his life which he kept very private. He was a writer who would make an entry in his notebook of perhaps only a sentence, but that sentence would be so full of feeling that I often was surprised at how insightful he could be in so few words. His very first entry launched one of the most affective and effective pieces in the room.

I thought: I would have a pet and I would be happy.

He then left that thought for a while and wrote about a few other topics before returning to it; he was still very reluctant to discuss the emotions behind it. Then he returned to writing about a pet—one pet in particular.

I like my dog Gretchen. I was very sad when she died. I miss her. I cried. I really miss her a lot.
I miss my dog.

After many attempts to get to the story behind these entries, he finally talked about his dog's death, and I learned he had some very vivid memories of this. As he was conveying the details, I could see the tears welling up in his eyes. We both agreed there was a masterpiece here waiting to be written. This time he stayed with it:

My Dog

-dedicated to Pete and Howie because they're my two favorite friends, and I have other friends in my class, too-

I had my puppy. I was happy. My puppy was named Gretchen. She was a Golden Retriever. I liked her so much. She was a nice dog. My puppy has died a long time ago. Now she is 99. That day she went to heaven. We got our new puppy. We named her Samantha. She was a Yellow Lab. I play fetch with her. That night I had a dream. I dreamed about Gretchen. She looked at me. She licked my face. I woke up. We took a picture with Samantha.

About the Author/Illustrator:

I miss Gretchen a lot, because she died. I cried when she died. My mom said we should get a new dog.

This finished piece brought tears to my eyes and to his mother's eyes when he shared it. I had never before seen him so invested in anything, or so proud of what he had accomplished. As with Brittney, I wasn't able to get an accurate picture of Deven's learning until this piece. He still needed my help in keeping his writing moving, but he was able to get right into his piece each day and stick with it enthusiastically. This was truly progress!

So far in their chosen stories the children have continued to include more detail and more thoughts and feelings than they had in their previous writing. I find them really vested in their pieces, staying with them for longer periods of time, and they seem to be very impressed with the work they are producing—true masterpieces. They have also gained an enhanced appreciation of authors and their works; they now read as writers!

Undertaking this project has been a tremendous learning experience for me. As I think about this I am reminded of words written by Don Graves: "If children are to cross that threshold and demonstrate a higher quality of literate engagement than we have seen before, teachers' literacy will have to change as well" (*Discover* 123). I have always felt my teaching is more powerful when I dive into learning with my students. It has not always been easy, though. I feel I have taken an enormous risk in my teaching by trying something as new as this. Many times I can recall myself thinking about the words that so moved Georgia Heard in her book *For the Good of the Earth and Sun*: "Here is the deep water." Sometimes I wasn't sure what I was getting into. I found comfort once again between the covers of her book. She, too, writes about using a notebook, and the need to begin any piece of writing with a feeling, not just a topic.

This reassures me as I discover notebook writing didn't spark all of my students' interest as I had fantasized it would. Not surprisingly, some students didn't buy into the idea of using notebooks. Don Graves once again helped me here: "In a class of thirty, there will *always be three to five children* with whom *no teacher* relates as well as hoped. This doesn't mean the teacher dismisses the children as hopeless; the search continues" (*Writing* 145). And so my search continues. As responsible educators we try to seek out ways of connecting with everyone. I'm just taking comfort in knowing I have connected this year with some with whom I'm not sure I would have connected had we not tried this experiment.

I did realize, however, that publication was not actually what my initial struggle was about. It was in fact an evident symptom of the ailment "Uninspired Writers Syndrome." Fortunately, in my search to simplify publication, I found a way to tap into their little souls and give them a medium for expression that none of us had found before. Unfortunately, as educators there's always *something* we're longing to improve and refine, and I haven't yet done all my improving and refining. I'm still struggling with the management of time during my writers' workshops. My goals are to discipline myself to hold more succinct conferences and to discipline the children to take more of an active role in the conferences. Letting go of these reins has not always been easy.

I would also like the children to have more opportunities to share their work with one another and to respond in more meaningful ways. I would like to try a completely different model of response; rather than having the children give each other questions and comments, I'd like them to reflect what they hear and understand from their peers' writing. I want to train the listener, not just the writer. Just as they have learned to appreciate their reading as writers, I think they will be better able to write with an audience in mind after having had more meaningful and active experiences as audience members.

I have also begun to re-examine my understanding of "publication." I now look at it more broadly, as making print accessible to an audience. With this in mind I will look to using posters, dramatizations, letters, audiotapes, songs, anthologies, and other presentations as some of the options of publication available. Hopefully this will alleviate some of the publication anxiety we were all feeling.

Through keeping a notebook of my own and a record of our experiences in the classroom, I have moved closer to being the individual and the educator I aspire to be. I will continue to keep a notebook of my own, and I look forward to introducing new classes of first graders to these precious tools in the years to come.

This entry to my notebook expresses my experience eloquently:

> It is one of the most beautiful compensations of this life that no man can sincerely try to help another without helping himself.
>
> —Ralph Waldo Emerson

Works Cited

Baylor, Byrd. *I'm in Charge of Celebrations*. New York: Scribner, 1986.

Butler, Andrea, and Jane Turbill. *Towards a Reading-Writing Classroom*. Australia: Primary English Teaching Association, 1987.

Calkins, Lucy McCormick. *The Art of Teaching Writing*. Portsmouth, NH: Heinemann, 1986.

———. *Living Between the Lines*. Portsmouth, NH: Heinemann, 1991.

Graves, Donald, H. *Discover Your Own Literacy*. Portsmouth, NH: Heinemann, 1990.

————. *Writing: Teachers and Children at Work*. Portsmouth, NH: Heinemann, 1983.

Heard, Georgia. *For the Good of the Earth and Sun*. Portsmouth, NH: Heinemann, 1989.

Waters, Kate. *Sarah Morton's Day*. New York: Scholastic, 1989.

Yolen, Jane. *Owl Moon*. New York: Philomel Books, 1987.

Young, Ed. *Seven Blind Mice*. New York: Scholastic, 1992.

Response
Donna Barnes

Teachers everywhere, and not just language arts teachers, need to do what Michelle did during that "fateful February vacation": take the time to read *Living Between the Lines*. It is an inspiration. It is a new and profound way to view students' learning and peoples' learning and living. Since reading that book, I have filled fifteen notebooks. This book prompted me to go to New York to take the Summer Writing Institute at Columbia Teachers College which, by the way, was even better than the book.

Michelle, at the end of her chapter, says, "I have always felt that my teaching is more powerful when I dive into learning with my students." So often teachers are afraid to be learners with their students. Too often teachers feel inadequate if they don't know ALL the answers. Michelle took us on a trip through her philosophy. She showed us how to help children become more vested in their writing by modeling again and again with her own writing. She showed us a community all learning together. She painted the picture. For all language arts teachers the landscape is the same, with the figures in the foreground different. I agree with Michelle completely that writing workshop time needs to include a chunk of silence. Again, teachers are fearful of silence and often want to fill the space with talk. I need silence to think, to reflect, to gather language, and to write. My students, whether six years old or sixty, always welcomed silent writing time.

It is amazing how similar all these struggles are. "I'm ready to publish this!" Those words make all language arts teachers cringe. They all feel and understand this dilemma. It's important to present writing to an audience, but it's also unrealistic to think every word one writes is fit to print. Teachers need to find a way to help students understand this without deflating their writing ego. Many teachers are able to find a parent volunteer to help publish children's writing. These days it is even easier since many parents have access to a computer.

Michelle discussed the reading of *I'm in Charge of Celebrations* and what happened as a result of Baylor's book. She read it with first graders. I used this book with a multi-age classroom of nine- to eleven-year-olds. I read the book and instead of discussing it, closed the book. Emotional energy filled the silence as ALL members of the community opened their notebooks and wrote.

Michelle showed how notebooks made a difference for four of her students. That is an important reminder for all teachers that they will not reach 100 percent of the students. And perhaps that is okay. Teachers need to remind themselves constantly to celebrate the children for whom they've made a difference and not beat themselves up when they don't reach some children. Sometimes teachers are making a difference with a student but it is not immediately apparent.

The case of Kate comes immediately to my mind. Kate was a fourth-grade student who never ever wrote anything except horse stories. Her notebooks were filled with horse descriptions and fabricated stories about horses. She included no feelings or thoughts. All her horse writing was surface writing.

Her fifth-grade year, however, was remarkable. Her writing was outstanding. Her topics varied from family to friendship, to herself and her impressions of the world. Horses played a minor role in her writing. All the mini-lessons, strategies, peer sharing, conferencing, editing, and final drafting paid off for Kate—but it was not obvious until the following year.

Teachers must never give up or dismiss a student. They must always try to reach students, even those who seem reluctant.

5 Seeking Equilibrium

Katherine Morgan

I glance at the clock and my heart sinks as I see 9:00 p.m. flashing relentlessly from its red face. The stack of drafts on the table by my chair still numbers seven—at least an hour and a half of reading to go. The dilemma which faces me on Sunday nights sits beside me once again. "Well," I mutter to myself, "I can either finish these drafts, or I can spend the time from now till ll:00 planning the writing class for the week." As I ponder the possibilities, I feel frustration, almost anger rising in me. What the heck, I think, I shouldn't have to be crafting plans for the week in Writing Workshop anyway. Shouldn't I just turn the kids loose to write? After all, their interests should drive the course and their writing, not my prescriptions. I think about Don Graves, at the University of New Hampshire, his eyes twinkling as he wrote, "Pass out the lined paper, as well as a small piece of newsprint to go with it. The newsprint sheet is to jot down titles or subjects the children might write about. Take a sheet for yourself as well, and after the paper has been passed out, mention that you are going to put down the topics you will write about with them" (12). Has he dealt with high school students, I wonder? He mentions older students, who "often want to know what topics you expect . . . many will need weeks or months to be convinced you seriously wish to know what they have to offer" (19). That sounds more like my twenty-five high school sophomores, but where does that leave me in my eighteen-week Writing Workshop?

Turning to Tom Romano for guidance in his book *Clearing the Way*, I read, "In any writing class, then, the first and constant order of business is to enable all students to establish and develop their individual voices. Teachers must cut them loose the first day. Let them write in any form they choose. But make sure they write and sustain that writing long enough to rev up their voices" (7). The clock now says 9:10, and I compromise with myself and the writing gurus of the world by deciding to finish reading the drafts and have the kids spend Monday in conferences with me and with each other about those same drafts. Planning for the week will have to wait for tomorrow's prep period, or tomorrow night, or never.

This struggle that I have every Sunday night, and often during the week, actually begins before the semester ever starts. Each semester I re-examine the course, which is one of two required courses students take in our English curriculum. I ask myself what my obligations are to these students, and to their parents and the school board which complains that we don't teach grammar and basic skills. What *should* be in the writing curriculum at the high school level?

As I discuss this question with myself each year, several aspects of my personality and background shape my response. Since all of us bring both personal and pedagogical baggage into our teaching, I think that what influences me may also, although in different ways, affect other teachers.

I am a Libra, and not only do I see both sides of every question, I also see both the pluses and minuses of each approach, method, and technique. I want harmony in my classroom and I want a balance between students and teacher as "owners" of the space and directors of the action which takes place in the writing workshop each day. This may sound like hocus pocus, but I know that this aspect of my personality is a decisive factor in the struggle I experience in the teaching of writing.

Second, I've been teaching for over twenty years. I don't think age is the issue, but I do know that my first English teaching experience took place in a room where I was "in charge" and had every minute of each class planned out. A red spiral notebook was my planbook, and in it I wrote careful notes about each reading assignment, made sure to include what the literary critics had said, and listed questions I would ask in class. In 1970, when I began teaching English in a small independent school, the hot educational philosophers advocated a more child-centered approach, and the inquiry method was just about as far as I stretched my pedagogy. I started teaching *Hamlet* by asking the class of seniors, "What do you know about Shakespeare?" Pretty dangerous stuff. I wish now I had asked them, "What do you know about murder?," "What do you know about incest?," "What do you know about being a young adult agonizing over life's choices?"

In that first English class, however, when Kathy, Betsy, and Helen complained about not having enough freedom to choose what they were reading, writing, and discussing, I listened carefully, and fearing total rebellion, abandoned my plans and let them do a large unit of independent study. This was my first experience in individualizing and in a conference approach to teaching and, in retrospect, the experience was rewarding. Student interest in the course revived, and I enjoyed the variety of the experience as well as the challenge of overseeing such a diverse classroom. Student work included a group studying and performing Millay's *Aria da Capo* and a group reading bestsellers (including

Everything You Always Wanted to Know about Sex but Were Afraid to Ask, obviously not one of my selections) and trying to decide what qualities of a book led to bestsellerdom. In addition, individuals carried out in-depth reading projects, such as Helen's study of the revolutionary writer Franz Fanon, and some tackled creative and reflective writing: Vicki writing a play which she later produced for the whole school, and Pat writing about her brother's death from leukemia and the subsequent breakup of her family.

I might have learned more from that experience, but the next year I was back to the lecture mode. Lucy Calkins believes that "success, even partial success, can be dangerous. It sucks you in. You end up not wanting to deviate from what you've been doing" (32). I wish that had been my realization at the time of the experimental independent study, but teaching was too new, and I was too fresh out of college to make the transition from a teacher-centered to a student-centered pedagogy. As I was learning to parent that year in the way I had been parented, I was still teaching in the way I had been taught. I was uneasy, though, as I recalled the minor mutiny in my classroom the year before, and I was uneasy because the balance was tipped so far toward me and so away from the students. On the other hand, I reasoned (the Libra in me) I had learned successfully in the "old method," and I was both a competent reader and writer, so was it necessary to change my approach?

From the distance of time, I now realize that after a college education in the traditional mode I was perhaps competent, but far from realizing my potential as either a reader or a writer. I ran to the critics for an interpretation of the books I read and taught, and I could write a good research paper which synthesized many other people's ideas but was short on my own. I had never written reflectively or responsively about *anything*, and certainly had never plumbed my own thinking in my mode as a passive recipient of knowledge.

Twenty-plus years have passed, and my ninth graders are working in groups sharing their responses to a piece of professional writing and formulating questions to ask each other when the whole group reconvenes. I circulate among the groups, realizing how I have relinquished control over this learning experience. The noise level rises a bit and Kristi, a bright, dark-haired girl, says (shouts), "I know what this class is, Ms. M., it's organized chaos." I smile weakly and respond, "I hope the emphasis is on *organized*." I have had less trouble moving toward a student-centered approach with my ninth graders, I think because there is a curriculum which provides a framework for what we do.

My problem in developing the Writing Workshop class stems not only from my own personal and pedagogical baggage but also from the constraints of community and school board expectations. Our students, who are involved in writing process from the elementary grades, historically have done poorly on standardized tests where they have to identify a particular error, place a punctuation mark, or choose the best sentence. On the other hand, they turn out brilliant pieces of writing which, when the process is carried through the editing phase, are remarkably error-free. It is difficult to explain this apparent paradox to the world at large. Each time we are faced with accountability to the school board, we are forced to explain why teaching grammar doesn't necessarily translate to improved writing. I hear myself at Open House trying to play to those parent/school board concerns by talking a lot about how, at the high school level, we focus much more on the editing phase of the writing process; how this necessitates the teaching of punctuation and usage. Who am I kidding? I know that the teaching of skills in context which I try to do as part of the writing process is not the repetitive skill and drill they have in mind.

Add to the local pressure the steady barrage of news stories decrying the current state of education and in particular the appalling lack of basic literacy skills among high school graduates, and any self-respecting English teacher becomes nervous. Who can ignore *A Nation at Risk*? Who can ignore the fact that students have stopped using apostrophes except in "it's" when they want to show possession? Perversely, I believe the question should be "How *can* I focus on the important work I'm doing which allows students to develop as readers and writers who think for themselves and struggle to express those thoughts?!" Who can argue with a course in which students come up with the ideas and motivation for learning?

The Writing Workshop should operate as an individualized learning experience for students. It would make no sense in this situation to say to my group of heterogeneously mixed students, "OK, now we're all going to study gerund phrases, whether you need to or not." I couldn't agree more with Tom Clark (writing in his essay "How to Completely Individualize a Writing Program"): "When you individualize, there are precious few generalizations you can make that apply to all students in a class" (52). Students' need for grammar seems to fall at one extreme or the other: Students who can't write complete sentences at one end and gifted writers who are eager to fine-tune their writing and who seek variety in their mode of expression at the other end. In order to meet the divergent "basic skills" needs of the twenty-five students in the class, I either need to create small-group mini-lessons or individual mini-lessons. Now let's look at exactly what that means, and keep in mind the stack of papers at my elbow on Sunday through Saturday nights. I already teach four different preparations and five classes, which means I have to keep up with reading and writing assignments and create plans in four different areas every day. If within the Writing Workshop class I needed to create small-group or, worse yet, individual lessons on any sort of regular basis, I would have to stay up twenty-four hours a day, and I would *still* be behind.

Typically I address individual problems in a conference format, but I'm never satisfied with the overall results of this approach, partly because I'm never able to be systematic about following up on these conferences with additional skills work, and partly because it's too easy to let the skills issue slide when there are more interesting questions to address in conference with a student, questions like, "How did you feel when you heard the news of your friend's suicide?", "What happened after you were arrested?", or "What else can you say about the defects in the school administration?" The net effect, then, is that I feel as if I have failed when at the end of the semester I still see certain errors appearing in student work and realize that I should have done more. Devoted as I am to the process approach, I think some students need repeated experience (do I dare mention the word drill?) in order to overcome certain technical problems. At the high school level, what should the grammar/usage curriculum include, and are mini-lessons and skills-in-context the best way to teach that curriculum?

The question of curriculum, however, goes far beyond the issue of grammar and usage. Should adolescents have the freedom to determine the direction of their semester of Writing Workshop? Should I let Sarah write poetry all semester? Should I let Ray write only science fiction/fantasy? What about the kids who don't want to write anything? What limits or direction should I impose or suggest? How can I challenge the students to take risks and grow as writers while at the same time allowing and encouraging them to pursue their interests? How can I "surround the children with literature" as Graves suggests (65) when their reading levels are so varied? These issues, in addition to basic skills needs, are the ones which perplex, challenge, and frustrate me.

Students leave no doubt about what the limits, or lack thereof, should be in Writing Workshop. After I asked them to evaluate the curriculum, Josh wrote, "I liked the free-writing the best, obviously it's much easier to write about what you care about, not something the teacher tells you to do." He then went on to say, "The most important piece of writing which we did this year in my opinion is the point of view one. A strong point of view is important to have in today's world and being able to write it into a piece which expresses your thoughts might prove to be useful." His analysis interests me because the point-of-view piece he thought was so important was one which I assigned, not a freewrite.

Tim said, "The most memorable part of this year was the free-writing because that is where I put out the piece which I thought was my best. I wrote a piece called 'The Buck' which came pretty easily and when I free write I tend to be able to find ideas for pieces more readily."

Bonny, more concerned, I think, with pleasing me, wrote, "We did a lot of different styles of writing in this class and all of those can probably be used somewhere. I really liked the way how we started a lot of different pieces, then did rough drafts of some and had choices on which ones we wanted to finish. This made it a lot easier to produce one good piece of writing than if we had had to polish specific ones." But even Bonny couldn't keep from expressing the majority opinion: "I personally liked free writing the best. It gives you a chance to develop and improve the type of writing you are best at and also are interested in rather than ones that you know you will probably never use again." Though these evaluations reinforce the importance of student choice in the writing process, they also argue for some direction. But how much?

Ideally, I would like to say to students as they begin Writing Workshop, "I'm going to give you the gift of fifty minutes each day to sit and write. You may write whatever you want; a polished piece will be due every so often; conferences will take place when you need one; have a nice semester!" Experience suggests that perhaps five out of twenty-five students would welcome this opportunity, but they are the students who are already the writers. The other twenty would return a blank stare and begin the litany: "I don't know what to write"; "I don't like to write"; "I can't write in school." The ensuing struggle might ultimately produce some excellent student writing, but it might not, so I have so far been unwilling to take this risk.

Anything beyond simply guiding students to topic choice begins to impose a curriculum and undermines the assumption that student motivation to write is directly connected with their freedom to choose topics and genres. When this freedom is taken away, is anything gained which can counterbalance the potential loss of motivation? I suppose the answer to this question has to do with the *extent* to which the teacher imposes a curriculum and a structure in the class. In seeking some kind of equilibrium in the writing curriculum, I try to alternate freewrites with assigned genres; hence, everyone has the opportunity to exercise his or her creative will at the same time each has to try new forms of writing. Although I require certain "genres" such as literary analysis or persuasive writing, I never impose topics within genres. Individuals develop their own set of topics, then through a period of all-class sharing, we learn from each other and expand our own ideas for topics.

Jen, a sophomore in Writing Workshop, affirmed my belief that requiring certain genres was not a subversion of the writing process when she wrote in the preface to her final portfolio, "Overall this year I feel I improved tremendously as a writer. I learned how to write so many different forms of writing and had fun doing it. I became a stronger writer by learning when to use quotes effectively and how not to bore a reader. I'm glad I took this class because it brought out a writer in me I never knew I had." Jen was a "good student" who conscientiously tried everything. Tess, a free spirit and a girl who always spoke her mind frankly, wrote different responses to my first request for critique of the curriculum and then in her portfolio preface. Her comments at the end of the semester help me believe that what I implemented for a curriculum was actually all right. At the end of the first quarter, which she failed, Tess wrote:

> I hate to say it but I didn't pick up any skills during this class. I expected free writing, sharing, learning about expressing ourselves in written words, poetry, things that flowed. Instead I suffered the same plight I wanted to avoid getting caught up in the techniques of a piece rather than the expression. Being forced to write about something we didn't like doesn't really discipline us[;] you don't learn skills if you don't like the task at hand.

At the end of the semester, in her portfolio, exercising the free choice she believed she had been denied, she wrote:

> I believe we were to write up a commentary for each of the pieces of writing to go in our portfolio but for my purpose I have decided to write one for all the pieces. I did not pick these because they got good grades but because after 4 1/2 months in a class I produced some very personal stories, poems and drafts. I would have submitted maybe even more but finally I decided between these four. "Boyfriends" is the least personal but I did like the comparison [I think she meant analogy] and the comparison and contrast in it. I enjoyed writing a definition that I could include my boyfriend in and I even enjoyed bad-mouthing my x! [This piece was the assigned essay which had to include three techniques: definition, analogy, and comparison/contrast.] "Death" I had fun with. I could define something in a very personal manner. No right or wrong. No bible to argue with, no dictionary to argue with. It was just my belief. I think to me the definition pieces that we did were

> some of the funnest. You have no limits, because they are opinion only there is no right or wrong answer, no disagreement and it's easy to write an opinion[;] it is a lot easier than writing stories you have to think about and make up. I did a good job expressing myself in this piece it is about me and my religious beliefs, that is how it made it into my portfolio.

Her other two pieces were freewrites. Do I believe the Tess at the end of first quarter who had wanted to do only freewrites? Or do I believe the Tess in her portfolio who liked two of the essay techniques I assigned? Her evaluation again seems to suggest that some level of teacher-imposed curriculum helped her to stretch as a writer.

Even my limited structure of alternating a required form with a freewrite leads to the imposition of certain deadlines so that we all move to the next piece at the same time. At this point I become uncomfortable that the balance shifts too much toward my authority and away from individual student needs. Some students need more time than others; some are virtually first draft/final draft writers. I'm flexible about deadlines, but I'm afraid that without them, some students will never complete a draft. With deadlines, I worry that I rush students too much and therefore receive pieces of writing that are not as fully developed as they might be. Jeff spoke to this concern in his evaluation of the curriculum, "It's all good kinds of writing that we did but sometimes we get rushed to hand in a piece of writing. I think we should be allowed to hand in a certain number of pieces every couple of weeks so we won't feel so rushed." So, even if "it's all good kinds of writing" in my Writing Workshop, how do I move students from one kind of writing to another and still meet their individual deadline needs?

Don Murray, in a course I took at the University of New Hampshire, always said "Writing should be fun." By extension, I think teaching writing should be fun, and not fraught with the amount of worrying I do over whether or not I'm doing it right! If I could keep in mind that there is no better way to learn to write than by writing, then my goal should be to have students writing every day, and working with each other and with me to express themselves in clear, direct, correct prose. It shouldn't matter whether they achieve this goal through writing literary analysis or personal narrative. Although I know that some of my uneasiness is the result of my personal makeup in addition to my history as a teacher and a learner, I think that in some ways, I have evolved as a teacher in a system that has remained static. Where we should conceive of writing at the secondary level as a continuing process of discovery for the student, it is, instead, the handmaid of analytical response and the need to produce written answers to teacher-devised questions. Does this sound familiar? If you are over forty, this is the way you learned to read and write.

I'm currently teaching an Advanced Writing course to ten juniors and seniors, and I finally had the courage to base the course on their expectations. These students are all WRITERS, and it was no surprise to me that they want fifty minutes to write each day, unfettered by genre expectations of mine. I have finally been able to say, "Welcome to the writing workshop; my gift to you is fifty minutes to write." We set goals individually each Monday, and so far student output has far exceeded goals in most cases. I write while they write, as I try to do, but less successfully, in Writing Workshop. I share my writing on Fridays when we all share something from our week of writing. We are a true community of writers.

What is it that prevents me from transferring this experience to the required Writing Workshop class? Is it just a question of my having the courage to try this more open-ended approach? I think not. I have finally decided that given who I am, I must operate within a framework that works for me and enables me to deal with ever larger writing classes (this year twenty-eight students) and the increasing number of students with unusual behavioral and social needs. It verges on the absurd to use a conference approach with this many students, and reading and commenting on drafts from the whole class on any given night is a virtual impossibility. Topic choice remains within the genre I select. In many ways, however, I am no closer to knowing what should comprise the curriculum of the Writing Workshop, and I am angry that I can't simply begin the semester by asking the students at the beginning of class, "What do you know about writing?" and "What would you *like* to know about writing?"

In the meantime, it's the first day of the new semester and students in Writing Workshop are creating lists of topics on which they are authorities as the first step toward several pieces of writing. I haven't yet cracked the curriculum barrier and I feel the leap is farther away than ever. In classes larger than twenty students, the "organized chaos" which characterizes the student-centered classroom would, I believe, become total chaos in the writing workshop where each student pursued his or her individualized curriculum, all the way from topic and genre choice through the issue of basic skills needs. As class sizes increase, teachers may have no choice but to implement more direction and more structure in order to maintain some semblance of order in the room and sanity for themselves.

Trying desperately to hold onto Graves's and Romano's theories and keep a balance in curriculum, a balanced sense of authority over decision-making in the room, and my own inner balance, I wander around the circle of desks, stopping to chat here and there with students who seem to be having trouble thinking of anything to write about. Although now I seem to have plenty of thoughts, I can identify with students who think they have none. I glance at the door every now and then, wondering if an administrator or stray school board member may look into my room and wonder if I'm teaching. After the all-group sharing of topics, which takes the rest of the period, I ask students to write the opening paragraph of their personal narrative for homework. Matt asks, "Is it all right to write a poem instead of a personal narrative?" I roll my eyes and nod in the affirmative. Writing Workshop has begun again. I ask myself before I go in for day number two, "What do I know about teaching writing?"

Works Cited

Calkins, Lucy M. *Living Between the Lines*. Portsmouth, NH: Heinemann, 1991.

Clark, Tom. "How to Completely Individualize a Writing Program." *To Compose: Teaching Writing in the High School*. Ed. Tom Newkirk. Portsmouth, NH: Heinemann, 1986.

Graves, Donald. *Writing: Teachers and Children at Work*. Portsmouth, NH: Heinemann, 1983.

Romano, Tom. *Clearing the Way: Working with Teenage Writers*. Portsmouth, NH: Heinemann, 1987.

Response
Karen Weinhold

All teachers identify with this Sunday-night struggle. Even though we may teach at a different grade level, the issues seem to be identical. Most English teachers don't have the luxury of an advanced writing class, but most of their "English" classes are heterogeneously grouped and definitely span both the skill and developmental spectrums!

My chief dilemma is, how do students acquire the freedom to write in whatever genre they choose if they've never explored what those choices might be through curricula instruction? How would any student recognize that a particular topic might best be expressed through a persuasive essay, a sonnet, or a one-act play, if not familiar with them? Are they supposed to innately know these structures and functions even though they may not know the exact labels? Were they supposed to learn them through reading them in the literature strand of "English" class? If so, how is the reading curriculum structured? Philosophically, shouldn't freedom of choice extend to both disciplines? Do teachers introduce genres to individuals or small groups? Do teachers guide some students, or provide a smorgasbord of appropriate genres to others and assign specific forms to others? Logistically that would be difficult, and would ensure disciplinary difficulties with the nonparticipating students. Is the answer mini-lessons on the various genres? Has anyone out there figured this out?

So, teachers not only empathize with the issues raised here but also raise even more! All teachers love it when a student knows just which genre to use, but that is rare. Most of the seventh graders I work with have written picture books, alphabet books, personal narratives, and rhyming poems. Most would continue to write just these forms if not urged, lured, tricked, whatever, into experimenting with others. Current practice supports belief in a student-centered classroom, but we all wrestle daily with the practical and academic constraints of how to achieve it. In order to provide freedom of choice, the participants must be informed about the options—and therein lies the rub!

6 Beyond Reading and Writing: Realizing Each Child's Potential

Tony Beaumier
York Middle School, York, Maine

"It is not so important where we are, but rather in what direction we are headed."

—Goethe

"In times of change learners inherit the Earth, while the learned find themselves beautifully equipped to deal with a world that no longer exists."

—Hoffer

For those of us who are immersed in the world of children, reading and writing can depend on two things: constant discoveries and new directions as a result of those discoveries. As I discover more about my students and how they learn, I adapt what I do in the classroom to correspond with that new information.

One important discovery involved trust. I adapted my writing program this year when I realized that I trusted my students as readers but not as writers. In reading, except for one or two teacher-selected class novels and two small-group novels where four to five students come together to read and discuss a common work, students select their own reading materials. But in writing I picked the genres and set the schedules they would write in. I was in charge. I set the agenda and the deadlines. I made kids dependent on me to lead them. They were not real writers.

There was an inconsistency in what I did in writing and reading. In reading I was not concerned that each child read one mystery, one biography, one historical fiction, and one poetry book. Perhaps such a structured approach would make them well-rounded readers, but I would be telling them what to read—and I would not want to do that. At the risk of turning kids off to reading by making them read a genre they do not like or are not ready for, I expose them to many different genres through book talks, read-aloud books, author studies, and individual conferences. I expose them to the different genres and then I let them read what they choose. Occasionally I nudge, but usually I don't have to. It sounds silly for me to assign mysteries to everyone for three weeks, then biographies for two weeks, then historical fiction for four weeks, then . . . . Yet that is exactly what I did in writing.

When I used our reading time to go over basal workbooks and various skills, I was in control. This is what I thought was important. I knew the independent reading was important too, but I didn't feel it was important enough to block a significant amount of class time to it every day. With class time so precious, I reasoned that students could read at home independently. Kids had to get those skills in class. But after reading hundreds of empty or poorly written reading-journal entries and coming away from one too many conferences where I suspected or was flat-out told that the student wasn't reading, I realized the majority of the students weren't reading at home. Whether because of after-school sports, written homework that had to be handed in, computer games, television, or just hanging out with friends, reading for a half hour was not a priority for most. I knew there had to be another way. It wasn't until I actually observed whole language classrooms where most of the reading time was spent having students read that I began to trust my students, myself, and the power of literature.

In those whole language classrooms that I observed in Stratham, New Hampshire, I saw third- and sixth-grade students immersed in books, talking about books, and writing about books. I watched and listened, amazed, as the teachers and students asked provocative questions and teachers facilitated students' reading conference groups. Students chose their own books, read at their own pace, kept reading journals to set personal goals, explored their thoughts and interpretations of their books, recorded progress and reactions, and talked intelligently about their books. I remember feeling envious of those classes. These students were real readers. The teachers trusted their students to let them take control of a large portion of their own reading materials. Students would, with guidance, choose what to read, when to read, and how much to read. Personal responses and reactions to literature were encouraged.

It was at this point I knew that for my students to become real readers, readers who would explore authors and genres and develop individual literary tastes and habits, I had to trust them—trust that they would read and develop as readers. I had to trust myself, trust that I would be able to organize a classroom and facilitate the progress of fifty students reading fifty different novels. And finally I had to trust the power of literature, real literature—literature that would captivate and mesmerize students as no basal anthology could ever hope to. Seeing the kind of stimulating and passionate literary environment in Stratham convinced me that I had found a better way.

To immerse students in reading, I had to provide time in class for them to read. Half of our forty-five-minute reading period is now reserved for silent sustained reading. Most of that time I can be found reading with my students. I find that my participation sets a definite tone. Students follow a good example. Occasionally I'll read an adult book, but usually I'm reading adolescent literature. Where once I would have felt guilty sitting on the rug alongside my students immersed in a book, I now acknowledge it is the basis of everything else I do. Too often students never see anyone in their lives reading. Often we, the teachers, are the only models of reading and writing that children have today. Not enough educators understand this. Reading along with students is how I become versed in what the students are reading.

It is important for me to be able to communicate with students about the books they're reading and recommend books I think certain students would enjoy. About halfway into the silent reading block, I'll quietly get up and wander about the room observing who is reading what. Sometimes I'll quietly ask a student how a book is coming, where a student is in his or her reading, why the student chose the book, or what has been a favorite part so far, or I'll ask a student for a prediction. We spend the other half of the period conferring, looking at reading-writing connections, sharing books, and writing a weekly one-page journal entry about what we have read. Conferring may be one-on-one or in a small group. I keep a record of all conferences on a conference sheet for each child (see Figure 1). Each student keeps a reading progress sheet (see Figure 2), recording the number of pages read during silent reading and at home. I ask that each child read thirty minutes at home. Not every child reads at home, but most do and I contribute that to the time spent reading in class. When I tell students that silent reading time is up, most groan and beg for five more minutes. Many students read at home because they get hooked on a book at school. I will usually view the progress sheet while conferring. In a conference I may ask what is happening where the reader is in the book, about the main plot of the story, about the reaction of the reader to the story, about what the reader thinks will happen next, or something about the writer's style or intent.

Figure 1. Reading Conference Sheet

Reading Conference Sheet

Name _____
Group _____ Section _____
Trimester _____

Weekly Date	Book Title	Page On	Reading 1/2 hour nightly?	Conference Comments (circle)		Classroom Observation
week of:			yes some no	comprehension: details: interest: high level responses: other:_____	strong OK weak strong OK weak strong OK weak strong OK weak _____	
week of:			yes some no	comprehension: details: interest: high level responses: other:_____	strong OK weak strong OK weak strong OK weak strong OK weak _____	
week of:			yes some no	comprehension: details: interest: high level responses: other:_____	strong OK weak strong OK weak strong OK weak strong OK weak _____	

January

Reading Progress Sheet

Name: _____

Pages

Date	Title	Author	Class Begin	Class End	Home Begin	Home End
Thurs., Jan.4						
Fri., Jan.5						
weekend						
			weekly	total		
Mon., Jan.8						
Tues., Jan.9						
Wed., Jan.10						
Thurs., Jan.11						
Fri., Jan.12						
Weekend						
			weekly	total		
Mon., Jan.15						
Tues, Jan.16						
Wed., Jan.17						
Thurs., Jan.18						
Fri., Jan.19						
weekend						
			weekly	total		
Mon., Jan.22						
Tues., Jan.23						
Wed., Jan.24						
Thurs., Jan.25						
Fri., Jan.26						
Weekend						
			weekly	total		
Mon., Jan.29						
Tues., Jan.30						
Wed., Jan.31						
			weekly	total		

Total pages read this month: _____

What was your reading goal this month?

_____

Did you achieve it? Why or why not?

_____

What will your reading goal be for next month?

_____

Figure 2. Reading Progress Sheet

I have also noticed that more students are bringing in their own books from home to read. This means that students are building personal libraries. They're spending their own money (or asking others to spend money) on books for themselves. For example, one student this year enjoyed my personal copy of Brian Jacques's *Redwall* so much that he went out and bought the hardcover sequel when he found out I didn't have it. He later found another novel in the series in the public library and checked it out. I see more reading being done at home now because students want to continue the reading they start in class. Our music teacher commented that during the last few years, she has noticed that students automatically take their paperback books from their book bags and begin reading when they finish a test or their work early. Many parents have also commented that their children read independently at home for the first time. Most important, I can sense the difference in my students myself. They eagerly look forward to their reading time and on an occasion when we don't have silent reading, students do express disappointment. My students have become readers.

In writing I did not have such luck. My students came to sixth grade with the notion that writing was just "stories." For most of them writing meant creating one fiction piece after another. The genres these students will need to be able to write in their lives will include more than simply fiction. I wanted them to take chances and explore the multitude of other genres, but most did not know any other genre well enough to pursue it on their own. Often students would finish one story and complain about having to start another. I would give them suggestions: a poem, a chapter book on a topic they knew about, a mini-mystery, etc. They would often say they did not know how to write those things. I would give them samples and talk about strategies. Some decided it would be easier to just write another story and gave up, while a few tried and came up with some good writing. But most of them, I felt, were floundering.

I remember having a number of students over the course of several weeks hand in poems that were written on lined paper with margins. The first line was indented and they wrote to the edge of the page for every line as if they were writing a story, as in this child's poem:

I Wish

I wish I was a cat. They get to lay around like they are king. They eat all they want, they sleep all they want. They can go outside or inside whenever they want. I wish I could be a cat.

With most there were no similes or metaphors or thought-out line breaks, and if the poem was rhymed, the rhyme often took control of the poem instead of enhancing it. I had just assumed that my sixth-grade students knew different genres. Now I realized they did not. One year I spent a little over a month reading, writing, and sharing poetry. Everyone wrote and read poems. I was amazed at the results. We even published a small booklet of our poems. The poem below, by April, is indicative of the quality:

Jungle Fever

Birds fly into the night
They can sense the spirits near
You can hear the hearts beating
like the drums of the Indian tribes

The vibrations drive fear into their hearts
He walks through the town
He is the Arabian Sheik
The snake falls into the basket
and his tamer stops his flute
No more singing—none at all
Not even the ritual
The tiger stops in his tracks
They are afraid of him

The waves crash on the shore
The young man struggles
to be free
The dawn before he was chosen
The heat of the African desert hurts
They come from the jungle
with a beast
He cries out in pain
He has no life

Later they praise the god
They sing
and play
an instrument
They are still on the beach
and the gulls cry
In the distance the waterfall whispers
like the quiet humming of the church choir
and the sacrifice is complete.

I was convinced that in order to have students produce quality writing, I needed to present more genre studies and assignments. My takeover happened slowly over the course of several years, doing a poetry unit here and a research paper there, but by last year I had pretty much taken over the whole writing program. We started with poetry for four weeks, then we moved on to persuasive essays for five weeks, then the short story for three weeks, then the research paper . . . you get the picture. I let them have choice within the genres, but the writing program became mine, not ours. I told them what to write and when to write it. I wanted to feel accountable for what the students were learning. While the enthusiasm for reading soared, writing time became something less than a period we looked forward to. I especially dreaded having seventy pieces of similar writing to evaluate all at the same time when a certain "genre piece" was due. I knew something was wrong. How could I get my students to know different genres and write as enthusiastically as they read?

Last summer I did much reading, writing, listening, and discussing during a reading-writing program at the University of New Hampshire. It was the combination of a number of things that helped me discover what was missing from my writing program:

> When Jane Hansen, professor at the University of New Hampshire and author of *When Writers Read,* introduced Don Graves, former professor at the University of New Hampshire and author of *Writing: Teachers and Children at Work,* at a talk given during the above-mentioned program, she said, "Don's work goes beyond reading and writing. It is about his belief in each child's potential." I knew I was seeing each child's potential in reading. Many students chose challenging books that far exceeded their "reading abilities." Given the freedom of time and choice, most students took off in reading. Beyond reading, I also saw students develop personal interests: student hunters and naturalists enjoyed Jean George's survival adventure books, sports fans devoured biographies of famous athletes, two students whose fathers are EMTs read nonfiction 911 stories, students interested in World War II read Yolen's and Lowry's historical fiction, and those interested in preadolescent issues enjoyed books by Judy Blume. I knew I had to do something different in writing to realize each child's potential in this area.

> An NCTE report ("Report of the Secondary Strand," in *The English Coalition Conference: Democracy Through Language*) outlined several findings about today's secondary students. One was a resistance to "mass production" education, where all students do the same thing in rows and never feel that they have an individual voice. The report stresses the importance of students' "need to feel individually important and identifiable within society, and therefore responsible to it" (19). I can't imagine feeling individually important when I'm being told what, when, and how to write. For students to truly develop personal identities, they must be given the freedom of topic choice. Exposure to different genres and instruction in those genres should take place, but the choice of

pursuing those genres should be left to the individual student. I'm thinking of a time frame in writing that is similar to reading—half the period reserved for silent (or quiet) writing and the other half for sharing, conferring, and exposure and instruction.

Linda Rief, author of *Seeking Diversity* and summer instructor at the University of New Hampshire, said that she teaches the essay genre every few years because she feels guilty that she normally doesn't. After reading the first few student papers, she remembers WHY she doesn't. I, too, know what it is like to read seventy pieces of writing that are similar. I can sense the forced interest, the lack of commitment. Students should be exploring their *own* ideas, interests, and feelings—not mine. Only in this manner will writing be real and purposeful for students.

Parents magazine runs a series of columns, "As They Grow," with each focusing on an age-level issue. I always read the column that corresponds with my young daughter's age, but I also read the column that deals with eleven- to thirteen-year-old children to better understand the children I work with. The April 1991 column was titled "Looking Good" and included four photos of the same girl doing different things with her hair. The caption under the photos read, "In trying out new hairstyles, youngsters are trying on new selves." The article goes on to say that "this is a period of trying on new identities and new behaviors. These changes are reflected in a youngster's work, play, and personal grooming habits as she/he struggles with the question, who am I?"

I don't think the struggle for identity is ever more prevalent than in the preadolescent years. The emotions of a middle school child are intense and ever changing. While students yearn to carve out an identity that is unique and personal, they also feel a need to conform. (I clearly remember a few years back when nearly half the sixth-grade boys wore white socks with a particular brand of sandals.) While some students would welcome the thoughtlessness and safety of being assigned topics, we must encourage and support the risks and challenges students encounter when breaking away from what is safe and easy.

Don Murray, former professor at the University of New Hampshire, suggests that we should seek diversity, not proficient mediocrity, in writing. I became aware that we should also seek diversity in students—encouraging them to be who they are and to work hard at becoming who they want to be—instead of conforming to peer-pressure-set standards and a writing program that denies students the opportunity to write about the things that interest them and are important to them.

Last summer in that writing program, Linda Rief asked us to respond to the question, "What do I value most about what students can do by the time they leave my classroom?" I wrote:

> It is the sense of the students seeing themselves as readers. We spend time reading, choosing books, writing and conferring about books, keeping track of progress, and setting goals. I believe my students do see themselves as readers by the time they leave the sixth grade.

I did *not* feel they saw themselves as writers. Most would admit they enjoyed reading more than writing.

This year I gave the majority of choice back to the writers, as I had for the readers. Instead of requiring students to write in specific genres for most of the year, I began exposing them to different genres and gave students the option of writing in them. Whereas before I just expected them to know different genres, I realize now through my own classroom experience how important the reading-writing connection is. A writing classroom where there is little or no connection to literature becomes a "writing ghetto." Students' writing can be greatly enhanced when they read examples of a genre before they write it. It helps to read with a writer's eye—and that should be where classroom instruction is centered, looking at examples and options and leaving it at that. Barry Lane, in his book *After THE END: Teaching and Learning Creative Revision*, writes, "Writers who lose their voices are often blindly following an outline or laundry-list form (e.g., the five paragraph essay, the research paper, the biography)" (160). When we tell students "how" to write in a particular genre, we rob them of their voices. To ask each student to produce a piece in every genre presented is to take control of the writing program. It is to not trust in yourself as a teacher or your students as writers. It takes away choice from the students and stops them from creating an identity of themselves as writers and as people. I want students to carve identities of themselves as writers as they do as readers.

When I think of reading and past students, I can make instant connections: Josh and Jeff and the Terry Brooks fantasy novels, Molly and the Cynthia Voigt books, Jeremy and the Redwall books, Beth and her goal to read every book that Roald Dahl had written, Heather and Justin and the John Bellairs books, Marcy and World War II books, Steve and any biography or fact book dealing with sports . . . I could go on. The point is that my students had reading identities. When I thought of writing and students, I could not make those same connections. When I ask seventy students to write a persuasive essay and teach them how, they do all sound the same. My students must have felt that "mass production" education in my classroom.

This year I made a major change in my writing program. I decided to structure it similarly to the reading program where there were blocks of time set aside for silent writing, conferring, and sharing. Other than a few assigned pieces (the science fair report and individual nonfiction chapters for a class book on the Maya Indians), students chose their own writing genres. The only requirements were to produce four pages of new or revised writing every week, which I stamped (an idea I got from Linda Rief), and to bring at least nine pages of writing to final draft each quarter. These nine pages could be several short pieces, one piece, or part of a long piece. This was to set expectations, ensure productivity, and give me a system of recording progress.

The *Parents* magazine article states that children this age are searching for who they are. This is where what happens in a classroom, complete with choice, goes beyond reading and writing. Kids could realize their potential in our reading class. They were given the time and freedom of choice to select the books they wanted. Some students needed an occasional nudge or extra bit of guidance, but for the most part the drive came from within themselves. Last year students were not realizing their potential in our writing class because I was limiting them by making them write what I felt was important and giving them a schedule in which to do it. When kids see themselves as poets or as readers of Mildred Taylor books, as experts on a certain topic so that they can write about what they know and live, they are creating their own identities. They are given the opportunity and freedom to break out of mass production education and realize their individual strengths and differences. They are allowed to realize their own potential, to try on new selves. I am encouraging diversity in students—not just in reading and writing.

This year certain students gained new identities. Beth became the Roald Dahl expert. She was given the time to read every Dahl book written. Students went to her when they wanted to get an opinion of a particular Dahl book before they read it. We all looked forward to her latest writing piece that was a take-off of one of our favorite Dahl books. David was the war expert. He knew all about the history of World War II and about the fighter planes that became so important in that war. His father was a pilot, and with his help he proudly gave a forty-five-minute presentation, complete with detailed chalk-drawn maps on the blackboard, to each of my reading classes that were reading *Friedrich,* a novel about the Holocaust by Hans Peter Richter. He went on to create a lengthy historical fiction piece about a World War II fighter bomber.

I was amazed at how many genres were explored this year. Why did I see such an improvement in writing? I think it had to do with several things:

1. Connecting reading and writing much more than I did before (it helps that I teach the same class both reading and writing). This is probably the single most important factor. Allowing choice without this support is meaningless. Students flounder aimlessly. I realize this is what happened in my classroom. Students need good models to aspire to and learn from and they need to see the endless possibilities of the many genres and formats that are out there. I want to expose them to as much as I can so that students have more ideas for writing pieces and projects than they could ever hope to accomplish. I still occasionally hear a student lament about not having anything to write, but it is much less frequent, and often it only takes a few reminders or suggestions of things that we have read or that someone else has written to get the student going again.

2. Requiring a certain number of pages to be written or revised every week and providing time in class. These strategies keep every student productive and they help me to better keep track of progress. For me the best way to overcome writer's block is to just write. Just as readers need to read, I believe that students need to write on a regular basis to become writers. When students have expectations and deadlines, they're more apt to jump in. It also makes record keeping manageable for me. I can monitor progress of those students who are soaring as well as of those who may need a nudge or some extra guidance. I initially questioned this policy because it doesn't mesh with what I did in reading—I wouldn't think of giving a page requirement for reading. Below I share what happened when I did experiment with page requirements in writing at the end of this year and why I decided to resume them for next year.

3. Allowing choice. Jane Hansen, in *When Writers Read*, writes, "Children would cease to view themselves as writers if we told them they could no longer choose their own topics" (122). I have gone full circle with this. In looking back, I think much of it had to do with my lack of understanding with the reading-writing connection. In not having the same classes for reading and writing, I tended to separate the two processes. I now realize the two cannot be separated. Whereas before I blamed the lack of progress in writing on the writing process

and choice, I now realize that my room had become a "writing ghetto," as I refer to above. Bringing literature into the writing class is not only valid, it is essential. I see now that choice does work when I weave it into writing with literature as models and inspiration. Having an understanding of who each child is through interest surveys and conversations allows me to suggest literature and writing topics based on individual interests.

At the end of this year I am pleased with the changes I have made. This year I got to know my students as readers and writers and got to know them better personally as well. I learned that students can create and share those identities only when given the time and opportunity to do so. I learned many things this year and am planning several adaptations to next year's program based on my experiences. I still, however, have several things I am uncertain about.

For example, some students had no trouble writing four pages and often wrote more. But for other students, four pages per week proved to be a little overwhelming. Several students said they felt pressured by the four-page requirement and said they could not spend the time they needed to make careful revisions, do research, etc. During third quarter, after discussing it with my class, we decided to do away with weekly page requirements and let them work at their own pace. The result: the amount of writing and the productivity level in writing workshop went way down. Clearly, most students needed the page requirement. Professional writers have (and I suspect many will say need) deadlines, so I do not feel unfair about requiring them of students. I will try three pages at the beginning of next year and maybe move it back up to four at the middle of the year.

I am still unsure of how to deal with final draft pages. At the beginning of the year I asked students to bring nine rough draft pages to final draft per quarter. I had a system worked out where students would write and confer with peers or me and when they were comfortable with their draft, they would hand it to me to take home, where I would read it and make comments on content and editing for a conference the next day. To prevent students from waiting until the end of the quarter to hand in most or all of the nine pages, I asked each student to have at least three pages (they could have been one piece or part of a longer piece) in final draft every three weeks, a quarter being nine weeks. What happened was that most students did not hand in their first three pages until the end of the three-week period (and most students handed in more than three pages).

I was up until two or three in the morning those first deadline nights reading rough drafts and making comments. During second quarter we talked about this problem and decided that it would be better to only have a mid-quarter and end-of-quarter deadline for final draft pages. My hope was that drafts would trickle in a few at a time. Once again, I got most rough draft pages on the day of the deadline. With seventy students we are talking 250–300 pages of writing. This time I decided not to stay up until early morning and did not get drafts back for several days. I was getting so bogged down with reading drafts and making comments, I did not have time to write myself or to do much quality planning. Was I asking my students to produce too much? During third quarter I decided to do away with all deadlines and page requirements. But that is when I saw the productivity level go way down. This leads me to wonder why students will take off independently with reading but are still unwilling (at least to bring pieces to final draft), for the most part, to do so in writing.

My students had some interesting comments when I asked them about these things. They said that choice was more important in reading than in writing because with reading if a book was assigned and they didn't like it, there was nothing they could do other than suffer through it. In writing, even if they were assigned a genre they didn't like, they still had control over their actual piece and could try to make it fun and interesting. They were in complete agreement over choice in reading, but a little divided when it came to writing. Some students said they wanted complete choice, while others said they liked having genres assigned because it opened up new genres for them that they wouldn't have normally explored. In coming to a compromise, students suggested presenting genres in class on a monthly basis and giving them the option of writing in a specific genre or not.

I have a lot of decisions to make before the fall. How will I handle conferences? Some teachers have verbal conferences about a piece of writing and do not actually see the written piece until it is in final draft. For me, waiting until the final draft is like doing an autopsy. I feel I really learn about where a child is at and can be most helpful with my comments when I take the rough draft home to read carefully on my own (with an attached comment sheet filled out by the author and a peer— see Figure 3) before I confer with the student the next day. It is also the only way I can manage conferences timewise in class. I can not have a five-minute conference in class and feel like I have done more than scratch the surface. Yet if I took the 10–15 minutes I needed, I would never get to everyone. This leaves me with a number of thoughts for next year:

1. Look again at reading. I do not have a schedule requiring each student to read a certain number of books or pages per week like

Editing Sheet   #4

Self:
name: _____ Section: _____ Date: _____
title of your Piece: _____ Genre: _____
What is Your Piece about? _____
_____
_____

What would you like help on / comments on? _____
_____

Is Your Piece written with :   Paragraphs   Yes   no   If no, go back
      (circle answers)   complete sentences   Yes no   and correct
                               correct dialogue   Yes no   now.

• •

Small Group Share :
    Share your piece in small group at the conference table.
(No more than 5 Pages) fill in below during feedback:
What the listeners felt was strong:
    1. _____
    2. _____
Questions / Suggestions / Comments they had:
    1. _____
    2. _____
    3. _____

• •

Revision (re·vision = to see again) 
How have you revised Your rough draft to make
it better? Think of both content changes
(added more description, cleared up a confusing Part, etc.) as well as
mechanical changes (spelling, Paragraphs, commas, etc.) List Your specific
revisions below:
    1. _____
    2. _____
    3. _____

• •

Teacher :   Conference Topics :
comments: _____   1. _____
_____   2. _____
_____   3. _____
_____   4. _____
_____
_____

Figure 3. Editing Sheet

I do in writing. Do I really need it in writing? Some students complained about the four pages but others said it was helpful in getting them started. They knew they had to fulfill the minimum—and then got so involved in their writing they went on to write more than four pages. Should I make a page requirement in reading? My first reaction is to think not. Why do I have conflicting feelings about this idea in reading and writing?

2. Am I being too much of a perfectionist? Do I need to read every rough draft that is brought to final draft? As a teacher, I feel I know each child's strengths and weaknesses when I do. But to do it and do it well as I am doing now takes more time than I can give. Should I have fewer than nine pages of final draft writing due per quarter? Should students hand in only part of the nine pages to be teacher-conferred? What about peer editing? Every piece needs to be peer edited before I see it, but so many things get overlooked when peer edited. Should I spend more time training students to peer edit? And will I be able to adequately assess students' abilities when I look at rough drafts less and confer less?

3. Finally, I realize that I need to write more for myself and for my students. I mentioned above that my reading with the students is the basis of everything else I do in reading class. This kind of involvement should probably occur with writing also. I don't write enough with my students. Writing, like reading, takes time, but whereas in reading I can start and stop a book in class and continue it at home before bed, my writing tends to stay in the briefcase. With an active family of my own and piles of schoolwork already, I have very little energy or time left to write at home. Good writing is hard work. I want to write with my students, but how much can I realistically write and bring to final draft when I only write for ten minutes at the most? I seem more pressed for time in writing class than in reading.

One of the most exciting aspects of teaching is the opportunity to constantly improve. As I find answers and solutions to the concerns above, they will be replaced by new ones. It is this struggle that is the challenge of teaching. At the end of a writing workshop several years ago, Jane Hansen shared with our group a piece of writing by Lao-tzu that she identified with (quoted in Hansen 4). It is about what makes a good leader, and those of us in that group realized that Jane was that kind of leader. It describes the kind of leader I became in our reading classes—and the kind of leader I am becoming in our writing class.

A leader is best
When people barely know that he exist,
Not so good when people obey and acclaim him,
Worse when they despise him.
Fail to honor people
They fail to honor you.

But of a good leader, who talks little,
When his work is done, his aim fulfilled,
They will say,
"We did this ourselves."

Works Cited

Atwell, Nancie. *In the Middle: Writing, Reading, and Learning with Adolescents.* Upper Montclair, NJ: Boynton/Cook, 1987.

Calkins, Lucy M. *The Art of Teaching Writing.* Portsmouth, NH: Heinemann, 1986.

Comer, James P. "As They Grow" section. "11 through 13: Looking Good." *Parents Magazine* April 1991: 168.

Hansen, Jane. *When Writers Read.* Portsmouth, NH: Heinemann, 1987.

Jacques, Brian. *Redwall.* New York: Avon, 1990.

Lane, Barry. *After THE END: Teaching and Learning Creative Revision.* Portsmouth, NH: Heinemann, 1993.

Lloyd-Jones, Richard, and Andrea A. Lunsford, eds. "Report of the Secondary Strand." *The English Coalition Conference: Democracy through Language.* Urbana, IL: NCTE, 1989.

Richter, Hans. *Friedrich.* New York: Scholastic, 1961.

Rief, Linda. *Seeking Diversity.* Portsmouth, NH: Heinemann, 1992.

Response
Donna Barnes

This chapter presents a realization that all teachers *must* come to: "Where once I would have felt guilty sitting on the rug alongside my students immersed in a book, I now acknowledge it is the basis of everything else I do." This is an extremely powerful realization—*"I now acknowledge it is the basis of everything else I do."*

Too often students *never* see anyone in their lives reading. Often the teacher is the only model of reading and writing that children have today. Few educators understand this. Recently, a local principal stated that when she sees a teacher reading silently, she knows it is that teacher's "down" time. According to her, modeling reading is not teaching. It is relaxing, not taxing like teaching physical education. Tony maintains that reading along with students is how you become versed in what the students are reading so you can communicate with them and recommend books to them as well as show them what it is to sit and read.

Tony examines reading expectations and writing expectations. Throughout this book everyone is struggling. Teachers know when something in the writing process does not work, and they try to do something to solve the problem. Many of the contributors glibly refer to UNH (University of New Hampshire, where Don Graves used to be a professor and where Jane Hansen is currently a professor) as if the world knew what that meant. Is this East Coast narrowness or does everyone know about UNH?

Some contributors educate themselves through books. It is amazing how much effect *In the Middle, Living Between the Lines*, and *After THE END* have had on language arts teachers.

Tony is also realizing that modeling is necessary in writing. It is as essential for a student to see an adult writing as it is to see an adult reading. Tony makes excuses about his not writing with the students. All teachers make or have made these same excuses. All teachers pay lip service to the need to write. It is not until the teacher sincerely and honestly writes and yes, brings pieces to final draft with their students, and yes, shares these pieces with the students, that students will believe and become active members of a writing workshop community.

Tony's concluding questions are thought provoking. He works hard to show the readers how he has built a better writing workshop through analyzing and thinking through his reading workshop beliefs, strategies, and routines. I can relate to this. Just thinking through the questions and recording them is helpful. And one of the best ways to put a teacher on the road to a solution to questions is to share questions and concerns with a trusted colleague.

7 The Other Stuff

Leslie A. Brown
University of New Hampshire, Durham

Contrary to a popular belief, teaching the basics is not at odds with process writing; instead, it is the final step in the process of discovering what you want to say and how you want to say it. "Can we legitimately call ourselves teachers of the writing process if we don't teach the last step in that process, editing the writing to conform to standard grammar and style?" asks Jane Harrigan in *Nuts and Bolts* (152).

As far back as I can remember, I hated diagramming sentences. As a student, I was caught in the upsweep of process writing, content before form, idea over structure. In his book *Write to Learn*, Donald M. Murray explains the writing process as a series of techniques or stages: collecting, focusing, ordering, drafting, and clarifying. Writing is a process of discovery with all of the starts and stops inherent in that search. Peter Elbow and Pat Belanoff add "thoughts about your topic when you were not actually writing, collecting material to use, talk with others, feedback, daydreaming, and false starts" to their definition of process writing in *A Community of Writers* (12–13). I engaged all of these methods in my student days. Pouring words onto the page, I was most comfortable freewriting, discovering what it was I had to say, and worrying about the other stuff later.

The problem is that now I have to read that kind of writing, unrefined. In the course I teach at the University of New Hampshire, Freshman Composition, I frequently get freeform writing masquerading as the final draft. Each fall I enter the classroom eager to meet the students and watch them grow and sometimes flourish as writers. I view my position as a vocation. My major frustration within the limits of a fifteen-week semester is that we have to spend considerable class time on editing and refining students' basic skills. The trouble with freeform writing is that it is hard to find the sparks of light in the quagmire of comma splices and tangled sentences. For example, one student wrote about a trip abroad: "The stop signs I noticed didn't have writing on them, they were red with a white strip, either did any other road sign have writing on them." Here her sentence camouflages what might have been a sharp image.

It is fair to say that most composition experts agree that the way we have taught grammar, as a separate entity, has not improved students' writing. Lloyd Jones proved this lack of conversion in *Research and Written Composition.* But there must be a happy medium between freewriting and clarity. To my mind, the function of grammar and mechanics (here I include punctuation, accepted spelling, sentence length and structure, syntax, and usage) is to clear the way for the original idea or the vivid image. This student's sentence, "While standing on the river bank, over looking lushes, Lake Merriam in sunny South Carolina, I reminisced over the past week's events and watched the glider-planes swooping down onto the lake, and jetting off into the sky," loses its focus and imagery in a fog of errors. Basically clear writing reflects clear thinking, not to mention the fact that it is easier to read. Donald M. Murray calls correct usage "the grammar of meaning. It clarifies. It is not the make-up or the hair style. It is essential to the discipline of thought."

Given the fact that the writing process is an evolving form, that each draft is more skillfully crafted than the previous one, there are many opportunities for the writer to refine sentence structure, to pick out the spelling errors, to choose an original phrase over a cliché. After all, how many of us can come up with a persuasive text on the first try? In a revised version, for example, one freshman decided to place a comma in his sentence for added emphasis and clarity: "Thunder would remain, pounding its large drum farther off in the distance as the rain packed up to leave."

Given, then, that some teaching of the basics is advisable, I am faced with another problem, the fact that my students come to college from widely varying backgrounds. The range can go from a student who cannot recognize a verb to a student who knows enough to have questions about style. An example of the former is the student who described Natalie Goldberg after having read *Writing Down the Bones:* "Natalie's thoughts are embedded within her, and meander to the surface over a long process . . . . There is no write solution to the reader, in digesting her ideas." An example of the latter is the student who began an essay on the Vietnam Memorial Wall with the following effective fragment: "Black, etched, hard, and cold."

An older student described his background in grammar as "very limited," while another freshman admitted, "I had some grammar in high school, but I don't remember much from it." The exception is the student who replied, "Grade school and high school is where I received the most background. I feel comfortable with what I know, and I accept that I do make mistakes." However, most students in Freshman Composition would agree with the student who said, "The last time I had grammar taught to me was freshman year in high school. It was a short lesson. The teacher didn't like teaching it, and we didn't like it either." Only a select few arrive in my classroom with a solid knowledge of the way the language works. Part of my job as a writing instructor is to decide when and how to address these gaps.

The challenge here is to fit in remedial grammar and mechanics without alienating the majority and boring the few. I have to search for ways to infuse students with enthusiasm about the discovery that is writing, while at the same time convincing them that they have an investment in learning accepted conventions. What passes for standard English in the students' eyes may not come across to the reader. For example, one student had a novel approach to an adverb in this sentence: "I was clueless, Eric suggested why don't we drive and we'll figure somewhere to go adventurely." And a student who disliked quotation marks wrote this: "Sitting patiently at the window seat looking outside we heard in the background large cheese."

Unconventional spelling is always a large presence in Freshman Composition. "Parents should be scene and not herd" came from an essay on coming to college, while another student described a pizza this way: "Every bight was filling." One young woman got confused between academics and politics: "So far most of my friendships have survived from everyone going to coolege." Another student began her essay with an almost-effective lead, "I finally mustard the courage to tell him." Ironically, one word that is often misspelled is *writing* itself ("My writhing hasn't improved this semester.").

One way to start addressing these problems is by convincing the students that you are on their side. Not many teachers delight in ferreting out misplaced modifiers such as the following: "His sleeping habits were truly erratic, crashing through the door no earlier than 3:00 am." In fact, at UNH we have heated debates in our staff meetings over the whole nasty issue of teaching grammar. "Why all this obsession with error analysis?" sniffed one teaching assistant, who reflected the opinion of many on the writing staff. "Teachers who are more concerned with errors in surface features rather than with issues of invention and revision are not teachers of writing, but of editing, at best, and of inferiority, at worst."

In response to the comment about obsession with error analysis, I can assure my colleagues that I do not make a hobby out of collecting and ridiculing the downside of student writing. In fact, the student samples cited throughout this chapter all emerged from the first few weeks of one semester ("The first couple of weeks in college was wierd."). Rather, my concern here is to admit that we have problems—large gaps of student knowledge—so that we can work together to develop solutions on all levels.

Most writing instructors find taking class time to go over the *lie/lay*s and the *to/too/two*s distasteful. However, the secret reason why we find teaching grammar so challenging is because many of us have forgotten the terms and labels that we learned in *Warriner's*. The art student who recently asked me with a grumble, "I mean, what is a gerund and why should we care?", could be speaking for the majority of the writing staff. We are rusty without our handbooks on hand and terrified that some brash student will ask us when to use "that" rather than "which" and our ignorance will rise to the surface right there in the middle of class.

What everyone agrees on is that teaching process writing is much more fun. Who wants to undangle participles or replace missed modifiers when we could be delving into focus, or audience, or more lovingly, voice, instead? The problem is that we cannot teach writing unless there is some agreement on the conventions of the language. This fragment is hard to follow: "Chicken salad sandwiches, and other foreign contraptions that I choose to pass bye." English teachers inherently know that clear writing works better, as in this wonderful student sample about fall in New England: "There wasn't the same explosion of fire engine red, burnt yellow, and honey-dipped bronze in the trees." The point is that it is not necessary to wallow in long grammatical terms in order to understand how to punctuate. So here, in the spirit of our staff discussions, are a few ideas for dealing with the gaps.

Some instructors at UNH elect to cover the basic grammatical problems in individual conferences. These teachers allow their freshmen to warm up for several weeks before they hold an editing conference. By this time, each student's recurring problems, be they the ubiquitous comma splice ("Some people hunt as a sport, others hunt to sell the body parts such as skins") or the *their/there* syndrome ("Their are three errers in the sentance"), have surfaced. During the editing conference, the instructor, side-by-side with the student, edits an entire section of the essay at hand. Bruce Ballenger, author of *The Curious Researcher,* calls this joint effort "the teachable moment."

Other instructors of English 401 have their students work together in small groups to correct the circled errors on their papers. Patricia Sullivan, current director of the UNH composition program, takes samples of errors from her students' papers, puts them all on one worksheet, and then has the students themselves analyze the problems.

In the case of the tangled sentence, writer Andrew Merton claims a reasonable success rate by teaching his students to write simple declarative sentences in the active voice. Presumably the student who wrote the following would benefit from Merton's advice: "This was a great feeling, of which is much harder to come by latter in life." Further on in his essay on a trip to Florida, the same student wrote, "Knowing this, my brother knew a day would come when he would have to make a pre-trip to Florida to set up a place to live and other commodities." Describing the Miami nightlife, he drew near his conclusion, "Quickly the few remaining spaces of open floor were taken up by a furry of drunk and intoxicated locals." Here the awkward constructions only add to the confusion.

So, we continue to grope for elusive solutions, bearing in mind that the chemistry of each class is different. The threat of a quiz that could work wonders in one class could just as well bomb in the next.

What are we left with? The belief that if we can make the material relevant to students, motivate them by showing that they do have a vested interest in clarity, then they will respond. Brock Dethier, longtime writing instructor at UNH, puts it this way: "Mostly I try to get them to see the logic and sense in grammar and punctuation, to get away from the feeling that they're being bossed around by arbitrary rules." Giving students the gift of an interest in presenting themselves well in this large and confusing world may be the key.

I begin with a few suggestions. Early on, I give them a checklist, at the top of which is the simple verb *proofread.* Many students, bleary-eyed early Monday morning, rip their essays from the printer and plop them on my desk without a second glance. Sometimes I offer ten minutes of time at the beginning of class for them to ask for my help in editing before they hand in their finished papers. One problem that I have run up against here is that students are unaware of what needs to be done and subsequently do not know what questions to ask me. This sentence, "I saw a flashlight shinning a womans' rear end," was repeatedly passed over during that class time.

Another approach is to copy a student essay for the entire class to read and then edit. Here I will follow up our discussion of content by asking the class if there are any grammatical problems. For example, the students will immediately see the confusion in the following sentence: "As I flipped my fingers through its crisp new pages a folded piece of paper caught my fingers." At the very least, someone will recognize that the sentence "doesn't flow" and will ask for a revision: "I believe this sentence is far from complete." Peer pressure and engaging the author to read his or her paper aloud to the class help immensely.

The next suggestion on my checklist is to buy a handbook. And use it. Favorite handbooks at UNH are the *St. Martin's,* because most of the examples are from actual student essays; *The Bedford Handbook for*

Writers, because it is the one required for English majors; and *A Pocket Style Manual,* because it is short, clear, and inexpensive. One way to familiarize students with the handbook is to arrange them in groups to write quiz questions based on the handbook. A week later they take a quiz made up of their own humorous or trick questions. An example of a quiz question would be, "Where does the comma go in the following sentence, 'While the students were drinking Jack Daniels appeared'?"

At times I will assign a section of the handbook for a student to read and prepare. For example, the woman who wrote this sentence, "We should of worked up a sweet with all of that work but there was a cool breeze blowing on that summer day," began by looking up commas before moving on to verb forms and spelling. Her job then was to find out what was wrong and why, and finally to correct each error I had marked.

Early in the semester I work to create a common vocabulary since, as Donald M. Murray has noted, "There is no consistency among teachers" concerning vocabulary and (often) rules. What I know as a "verb," for example, may be an "action word" to my students. Here is where I use the board to write and then explain writing terms like "focus" and the constant, pervasive grammatical errors that the class makes. Popular contenders are apostrophes in any context, the ubiquitous run-on, and the failure to punctuate at all. Recent examples of student samples are the following sentences:

> It was especially fabulous because there were no fathers to question us as to the who's, what's, where's, and when's of our evening.

> When I go to a concert I put on my black head banging leather boats stretch pants, a sexy shirt I also do my hair big.

> Acting and feeling like a real tourist we all had our cameras out and working.

Once these sentences are on the board, the students are much more likely to see the problems.

Recently a student wrote down a saying that his athletic older brother always tells him:

> Your the boss
> You know best.

I gave him a chance to correct himself, and he immediately changed the "Your" to "You're." The class piped in with other examples: "Your puppy is cute" and "You're beautiful." By involving the students with their own words and their own classmates, I believe they have more of an interest in clearing up the mistakes.

After we have settled on a common vocabulary, it is safe to have a little fun with the basics. One way is by making the students grammar experts and having them do the teaching. I begin by organizing the class into groups according to the problem and allowing them ten minutes of class time. Last spring the comma group made flash cards with sentences like the following to see who knew where the comma went: "I once was a puppy being loved and now I am a dog being beaten." The colon group presented bubblegum pops to students who knew the correct placement of colons and semicolons in this example: "My classes this semester are the following English 401 French 401 Underwater Basketweaving 512 and Co-ed Naked Pottery 014." The usage group presented a couple of regulars, "Jane told everyone to get their coat" and "I should of asked before I went."

The point here is to make incorporating grammar fun by using games, teams, and of course, rewards. In addition to M&Ms and Reese's Pieces, one group gave out coupons for university activities for correct answers or for improvements on sentences like the following student example: "I walked in behind of her and when I entered I felt every eye on me, I glanced over quickly every inquisitive face, not one familiar." Keeping grammar fun is a constant challenge, but the students do rise to the occasion.

On April Fool's Day, I gave the class a grammar quiz, consisting of a letter to them from me. In it I misspelled their names, used passive verbs, incorrect pronouns, the works. They were writing so furiously that no one saw the "Happy April Fool's Day" note at the bottom of the page until the quiz was done. At that point we noted how insulting it is to receive a letter with your name misspelled.

In addition to reviewing the rules with humorous examples ("I' dont know I'm board"), we do talk in class about how the language works. I tell students to trust their intuition and use common sense, especially in punctuation. Patricia Sullivan asks her students to think of punctuation marks in terms of road signs and signals, while Brock Dethier asks his students how much they want to stop the reader, using a period, for example, as a full stop. At UNH we advocate students reading their essays out loud to pick up the natural pauses and to see if the text sounds clear. One instructor even reads a paragraph out loud and hiccups at every inappropriate comma to make the point.

Motivating most students usually boils down to two factors: peer pressure and grades. I can lecture them on the benefits of clarity, pretend we are the staff of *The Washington Post,* feed them M&Ms for every correct response. What works best, though, is their knowing that the other students will read and comment on their essays during our weekly paper exchanges—and that ultimately their grades will plunge if all the grammatical errors obscure their meaning. Faced with their classmates and grades, students are less likely to come up with sentences like "Pro's writing is used for all intensive purposes" and "To each's own."

What is continually frustrating to so many of us in our craft is having to spend so much of our limited class time reviewing, and in all too many cases presenting for the first time, the conventions of the language. Naturally, we want to see the vast potential of students realized. We are pained to watch marvelous images and original ideas sink under the load of confusing punctuation and syntax. Time devoted to going over the basics is time lost to exploring leads, expanding paragraphs with the sparkle of specifics ("The only thing I missed about going to church was watching colors from the stained glass windows dancing on the floor."), pursuing and narrowing a topic, or even having the students themselves make up a writing assignment for everyone ("Write about an experience that changed you in a positive way."). A recent discovery of mine has been that reflective essays evaluating the students' own work produce prose that is insightful and elegant ("I have learned to take risks and follow my heart" and "I love to write about things that concern me and that I have a deep passion for"). Somehow this kind of personal writing does not seem as threatening to students.

All of these strategies bring us, finally, to the real world where they are eventually headed anyway. I enjoy going over with my students the kinds of writing they will do on the job—be it memo, report, or proposal—or at home, where it could be a short story or instructions to the plumber. And I point out that prospective employers are likely to deep-six application letters sprinkled with errors. After covering all the rules, I point out that I would not send in a manuscript without carefully proofreading it. Then I ask the students to do the same for me.

What are my conclusions about incorporating grammar into the writing process? To begin with, we have to start earlier. If students were taught the basics of recognized English throughout their early, middle, and high school years, my problems in Freshman Composition would be greatly reduced. There seems to be a pervasive attitude among students that grammar is not really that important. This student made a comment to that effect on his research paper: "I was so worried about wether the paper was gramitically correct that I didn't have much fun."

The process approach of starting young writers off by freewriting, having fun in a sense, has been a wonderful addition to the field of teaching composition. Early on students learn to love and not be threatened by their writing skills and potential. By the time they come to college, however, they do need the tools to write for all of their courses. Their power to communicate needs to be effective and well honed, so here is where fun has to (initially, at least) take a back seat.

Students have become accustomed to viewing the content of their essays as the higher form. It seems that English teachers, in their genuine enthusiasm for the creative aspects of the writing process, have not attended to that important final step, editing. Perhaps there is the sense that next year's teacher will handle the editing stage in the writing process. I don't know where it is lost. What I do know is that my students come to college unprepared. Teaching the editing stage of the writing process consistently throughout the elementary, middle, and high schools would insure that college students come to the university with a solid foundation. Until then, my colleagues and I will be forced to improvise, filling in these gaps the best we can.

At UNH we continue to make do. We use class time and conference time to address these problems. We use the board to write samples from the students' own papers for all the world to see. We engage the students to make up humorous examples and find the missing apostrophes. We discourage them from being careless and allow them time to ask questions and proofread their essays.

For a generation of students who are, as one student put it, "used to being entertained," we ask them to become the entertainers. At times and against their wills, we ask them to read, read, read. These students are bright and have good ideas, but all too often they do not possess the tools to best express their ideas. If they simply do not know the ground rules, how much can we fairly expect of them? As UNH English professor Thomas Carnicelli exclaimed to me recently, "At some point someone has got to try to introduce some rigor." We owe it to our students on all levels to teach them the skills they need to transform their rough drafts into striking prose.

I am not comfortable sending students off at the end of the semester if they cannot punctuate properly or consistently write coherent and effective sentences. If I am confused by the following sentence, "Without alcohol, their children have remained without it as well, indubitably leaving less cases of alcoholism in modern days, as some people become less strict in their religions," what meaning can the sociology instructor pull from it? That is the reality. That is what many writing instructors continue to struggle with. I would be the last one to propose that we return to the purgatory of memorizing *Warriner's*. What I do propose is that we, as a community of professionals dedicated to the process approach to writing, make the final steps, editing and then proofreading, a stronger part of the writing process.

Works Cited

Ballenger, Bruce. *The Curious Researcher.* Boston: Allyn and Bacon, 1994.

————. Personal interview. 3 Mar. 1994.

Carnicelli, Thomas. Personal interview. 25 Mar. 1994.

Connors, Robert. Personal interview. 22 Mar. 1994.

Connors, Robert J., and Andrea A. Lunsford. "Frequency of Formal Errors in Current College Writing, or Ma and Pa Kettle Do Research." *College Composition and Communication* 39 (1988): 395–409.

Dethier, Brock. Personal interview. 7 Mar. 1994.

Elbow, Peter, and Pat Belanoff. *A Community of Writers.* New York: Random, 1989.

Hacker, Diana. *The Bedford Handbook for Writers.* 3rd ed. Boston: St. Martin's, 1991.

————. *Rules for Writers.* 2nd ed. New York: St. Martin's, 1991.

Harrigan, Jane. Personal interview. 22 Mar. 1994.

Lester, Mark. *Grammar in the Classroom.* New York: Macmillan, 1990.

Lunsford, Andrea A., and Robert Connors. *The St. Martin's Handbook.* 2nd ed. New York: St. Martin's, 1992.

Merton, Andrew. Personal interview. 9 Mar. 1994.

Murray, Donald. Personal interview. 10 Mar. 1994.

————. *A Writer Teaches Writing: A Practical Method of Teaching Composition.* Boston: Houghton, 1968.

————. *Write to Learn.* 3rd ed. Fort Worth: Holt, 1990.

Newkirk, Thomas, ed. *Nuts and Bolts.* Portsmouth, NH: Heinemann, 1993.

————. Personal interview. 8 Mar. 1994.

Noguchi, Rei R. *Grammar and the Teaching of Writing.* Urbana: NCTE, 1991.

Shaughnessy, Mina P. *Errors and Expectations: A Guide for the Teacher of Basic Writing.* New York: Oxford UP, 1977.

Yount, John. Telephone interview. 23 Mar. 1994.

Response
Kay Morgan

This chapter will either make teachers laugh or cry. The samples of student errors will be all too familiar to us, regardless of what grade we teach. Teaching grammar is an area of teaching writing that has perplexed many of us since our earliest days as English teachers. In those days, now long past for some of us, we knew intuitively that teaching grammar as a separate subject was not how we wanted to do it nor, we suspected, the best way to do it. How to integrate it into the study of reading and writing, however, was not clear. We marked up student papers and wrote examples and definitions of terms on the blackboard, growing more convinced that kids ignored our written comments and had no understanding of how the terms on the blackboard connected with their writing. Now, years later, the issue remains, and students' lack of understanding has increased geometrically and to the point that, as a college teacher, Leslie is still facing the problems teachers faced twenty years ago with high school students.

The urgent problems in high school students' writing now focus on spelling, usage, and punctuation, areas that used to be addressed at the middle school level. Grammar factors into the equation when punctuation issues involve clauses and phrases, nouns in apposition, and other sticky points. Students respond, "Huh? What's a noun?"

Is the writing-process approach the villain? To some extent, it is. Who wants to discuss *its/it's* in a writing conference when substantive questions of content also present themselves? How can teachers justify teaching basics in a mini-lesson to all students, whether they need it or not? So, what happens to teaching grammar? It sinks slowly into oblivion.

The writing-process approach isn't solely responsible for the decline in teaching grammar. The teaching of English was synonymous with teaching grammar through the nineteenth century and into the early twentieth century. This was the golden age of rote memorization and the expectation that students would recite and declaim often, and suffer the corporal-punishment consequences if they recited poorly. In addition, many students studied Latin, which taught them more than they ever wanted to know about the structure of language.

We have mercifully moved beyond those days and into a type of education that focuses more on process and less on product; more on thinking and less on memorization of facts. Simultaneously, the media explosion and the effect of the primarily visual medium of television has drawn thousands of children away from the printed word and the chance to experience reading and writing as a primary way of learning. Not only has the media had a profound effect on the way students learn, it has also changed the language so that "different than" has become standard spoken English instead of "different from," "donut" has replaced "doughnut," and "would of" is about to replace "would've."

As English teachers, we will continue to struggle with the teaching of grammar and usage and probably feel less than adequate as we do so. Leslie's creative ways of dealing with the problem may work for many of us. An additional suggestion which has worked with ninth graders (still somewhat impressionable) and sometimes with tenth graders in Writing Workshop is to mark in the margin of their papers a code for the error in a particular line of the text: "sp." for spelling, "p." for punctuation, etc. Do *not* locate the error for the student. They must go through the paper, numbering each sentence in which an error occurs, and write the sentence again on a separate piece of paper numbered in the proper sequence. This activity follows the submission of "final" drafts, which have been through peer editing and self editing. The teacher is a resource for students in the correction process, as are the grammar books and handbooks on shelves in the back of the room. Does this work? It has variable success, as with most teaching techniques. Most students hate to do these corrections, so at the least, it motivates them to do a better job of editing *prior to* submission of the final draft, which is as it should be.

Perhaps there is still a place in the curriculum for diagramming sentences as a way for the visual learner to conceptualize the way the language works; perhaps memorizing parts of speech is to English teaching what memorizing times tables is to math teaching. Or has the latter gone by the wayside with the advent of calculators??? Bring on the M&Ms!

8 Picture This: Bridging the Gap between Reading and Writing with Picture Books

Franki Sibberson
Scottish Corners Elementary School, Dublin, Ohio

As a first-grade teacher moving to a fourth-grade position, I was very excited about the possibilities an intermediate classroom might hold. I had read everything by Nancie Atwell and Lucy Calkins and was certain that I could implement an individualized reading and writing program. I had a library full of the best novels for intermediate students and I had read as many of them as possible before school began. My goal was to build a community of learners in the classroom who would choose their own books for reading and their own topics for writing. There would be daily time for reading aloud, group sharing, and conferencing. The format of the day and the activities would not be very different from the format of the first-grade classroom. I would give intermediate students the same freedom to learn that I gave my first graders. The main difference would be in the literature they were reading.

The first year went smoothly, and the students were reading and writing like crazy. All of the students were reading great books such as *My Daniel* by Pam Conrad and *The Lion, the Witch, and the Wardrobe* by C. S. Lewis. However, their writing was not what I had expected. Most of their "stories" were simple ideas drawn out to chapter book length. Their writing went on and on, without having many of the qualities we talked about in literature. (There were simple plots, little character development, etc.) I read several stories about Frankenstein invading New York City and Nintendo heroes taking over the world. Steve's story began, "Dan, Scott, Charlie, Jim, and Steve went to play soccer against the Ninja Turtles." It seemed as if the students were competing to see how many classmates' names could be included in their stories. Although I knew that the children had great stories to tell, they did not tell them through writing. The relationship between students' reading and their writing was not evident. I realized that as a class, we did not have a large number of books with which we were all familiar. We could not really discuss character development or story structure as a class unless we responded to the five or six novels I had read aloud to them. Because it took so long to read a chapter book, I could not seem to find a way to ever get that large base of shared language that was so present in my first-grade classroom. I also realized that their models for writing should be on a different level than their models for reading.

I thought back to my years as a first-grade teacher and realized that the first graders' writing was very connected to their reading. Quite frequently, after reading a cumulative tale such as *Drummer Hoff* by Barbara Emberly, several students would create their own story with a similar structure. I reread Lucy Calkins's book *The Art of Teaching Writing* and found that these connections were evident in many primary classrooms. Calkins asks, "[C]ould it be that their new ability as readers, combined with a growing awareness of their own written products and their interest in the 'right way', means that they want their texts to resemble those they read?" (*New Edition* 75). This reading-writing connection that is so evident in young writers seemed to be missing from my classroom. Although I did not expect my students to write their own versions of books that they had read, I did want them to make strong connections between their reading and their writing.

I began to wonder if the inclusion of picture books in my program would make a difference in their writing. I started to research the idea, only to find that picture books were very rarely discussed after the primary grades. There was virtually no professional material pertaining to picture books with older students. I finally stumbled on a chapter in *Living Between the Lines* by Lucy Calkins and Shelley Harwayne that addressed this issue. The chapter described a "unit" on picture books with students of all ages. Calkins and Harwayne describe classrooms where picture books become the reading material for Reading Workshop as well as the focus for writing projects for a short time during the school year. After reading the chapter, I was certain that picture books were the answer. But I was not convinced that a short study of picture books would give me the results I was hoping for. I wanted more for my students than a "unit" on picture books. I wanted picture books to be an important part of my language arts program. By expanding on the ideas in *Living Between the Lines*, I began to envision ways that picture books could be used on a daily basis throughout the school year. I saw my classroom filled with picture books. I anticipated powerful class discussions over some of my own favorites. I pictured my fourth graders huddled together in small clusters throughout the classroom reading and laughing over picture books. Most important, I imagined students using picture books to influence their own writing. Because picture books were a familiar genre and possessed all of the qualities that make good literature, it seemed to make sense.

I drafted a proposal to the Martha Holden Jennings Foundation of Ohio and was awarded a grant to add a picture-book library to the classroom. With the money provided, I purchased the books that would become part of our classroom library. I chose books written for older children as well as books written for beginning readers, books that could be integrated across the curriculum, books for author studies, cumulative tales, nonfiction books, and different versions of the same story (see Recommended Works). I also asked each of my students to choose a special picture book that would be purchased with grant money to become part of the classroom library. The connecting thread in this variety of books was that they were all quality literature—literature that Shelley Harwayne says "makes a lasting impression on students' lives and on their writing" (3). They were good books that would be accessible to my students on a daily basis for classroom activities as well as for individual study. Although chapter books would still be the base of students' individual reading, I was prepared to make picture books a vital part of our language arts program throughout the year.

I met my first challenge on the opening day of school. Most of the students were very clear in communicating to me that they were beyond the baby books that they saw in the classroom. Josie asked why I still had my "first-grade books." Her voice was firm when she said, "Mrs. Sibberson, we learned to read chapter books in second grade. We don't need those picture books anymore." Picture books, of course, were for readers who were not able to read anything else, and these students could read "chapter books." My new fourth graders did not view picture books as literature, only as a stepping stone to "real books." So I spent the next few weeks sharing books with them that were written for older children—books which younger children would not yet understand. After reading books such as *The Stranger* by Chris Van Allsburg, *Trouble Dolls* by Jimmy Buffet, and *The Eleventh Hour* by Graeme Base, the students discovered these picture books were not "baby books" after all. Slowly, they fell in love with picture books all over again.

Creating an Interest in Picture Books

My journey with picture books was not short. I explored the world of picture books with my classes of fourth graders over a three-year period.

My first goal was for the students to feel comfortable with the picture-book genre. I wanted them to see how important picture books were before we started to learn from them. One of the first activities they participated in was a game called "What a Character!" This game gave everyone the opportunity to become familiar with many of the picture books in the classroom. I mounted one hundred picture-book characters on the wall and challenged the students to identify each one. It became a mini-research project trying to identify all of the characters. Our walls became a museum of the characters we would come to love throughout the school year. As students began to search for the characters in the books, the enthusiasm for picture books grew. "Look at this!" I heard as someone identified Glen Rounds's unique version of the lady who swallowed the fly. Then, as a small group of students identified Thomas from Robert Munsch's *Thomas' Snowsuit*, Scott yelled, "I'm keeping this book on my desk. This kid looks hilarious!" By the end of the second week, most students knew every character. As an added bonus, they had flipped through nearly all of the books looking for the 100 characters. Later, most students went back to all of those interesting picture books they had seen in their search!

Throughout the first quarter of school, we had fun with picture books. We used rhythm instruments to create sound effects, read picture books aloud to book buddies, recorded books on tape as storytellers do, shared books with parents, performed plays created with picture books, and read, and read, and read. By the end of the first quarter, the students were quite comfortable with picture books. They began to read all kinds of picture books, not only those written for older students. It was not long before they were revisiting "favorites" from their beginning years. Moriya began to read *Teeny Tiny* by Jill Bennett whenever she had the chance. I became accustomed to seeing her hug the book before returning it to the shelf. Cara began to point out the color changes in *The Napping House* by Audrey Wood, just as she had in first grade. Books such as *The Very Hungry Caterpillar* by Eric Carle and *Alexander and the Terrible, Horrible, No Good, Very Bad Day* by Judith Viorst began to come off the shelf for the first time during independent reading time. It was those favorites that took us even further along in our year with picture books.

Once the students had accepted picture books and could talk about them at a higher level, incredible things began to happen. Discussions went beyond whether or not they had enjoyed the book. Everyone, regardless of ability level, could look at what it was that made each book exceptional. They could disagree on the quality of shared picture books and they began to compare them. I recall a discussion after reading Patricia Polacco's *The Keeping Quilt,* when several students noticed the unique way that the author had shown the importance of the quilt in her life. She illustrated the book in mostly black and white pictures. The quilt, however, was in full color on each page. After listening to *The Ghost-Eye Tree* by Bill Martin Jr., Dan asked, "Do you think that Bill Martin used those short, choppy sentences to make us feel as scared as the kids in the book?" And, after reading *Tar Beach* by Faith Ringgold, Karen suggested that flying to freedom rather than flying off a roof was the real message in the book. Through reading, rereading, and discussion of picture books, the students began to look at literature in a different way. We finally had that base of language that was so important. Together we had shared at least one hundred books. One hundred books that we had in common! One hundred books that we could really look at to see why they were successful.

One of the things that occurred naturally in an author study of Cynthia Rylant's books was a discussion of structure. *The Relatives Came* is written in chronological order with an obvious beginning and ending. However, all of her books do not fit this typical structure. Students were curious as to why Rylant had decided to write *When I Was Young in the Mountains* in what Lucy Calkins calls "snapshot" structure (*Living* 144). Why had she not written about her experiences on the mountain in more of a narrative form? And why, in *Birthday Presents,* did she concentrate on only one day each year? Cynthia Rylant's books opened the students' eyes to the many structures of picture books. To their surprise, they found that some picture books fit two different structures interwoven to make the book complete. Anita Lobel's *Alison's Zinnia* was an alphabet book with a circular story structure, which we thought was a clever combination. And Shavonia made real-life connections to story structure when she came in one morning and said, "Mrs. Sibberson, I watched *The Flintstones* last night and it was a circle story! Fred got hit with a bowling bowl at the beginning of the show and at the end." For reference purposes, we made a chart in the room on which we listed some of the common structures found in picture books and the books we knew of which were examples of each structure. This would later help classroom authors when they were deciding on structures for their own writing.

The literary language in picture books was also a major focus of several of our discussions. Cumulative tales, books by Byrd Baylor, and poetic picture books all helped to introduce the students to the beautiful language that makes picture books so special. They found that each word seemed to be chosen carefully to fit the story. Whether the book had a rhyming text or not, they discovered that the language in some picture books had internal rhythm, even though the story was not written in verse. Each word had to fit the rhythm of the book like a puzzle in order for the book to make the reader feel as the author had intended. During each reading of *The Relatives Came*, everyone waited anxiously for the line that reads, "It was different going to sleep with all that new breathing in the house." We listened carefully for all the wordplay woven into *Agatha's Featherbed* by Carmen Agra Deedy, laughing at the way Deedy described a flock of geese as Agatha's "fine-feathered friends." And Cathi Hepworth's alphabet book *Antics,* in which the author uses words such as flamboyant and vigilant, helped us to appreciate an author's search for the best possible words. We began to keep lists of the words or phrases that we liked. We found that when we listened carefully, there were certain words which caught our attention in nearly every book. Not only the words but the pattern of language helped us bring more meaning to the story.

Illustrations also became a topic of many discussions. Jan Brett's books introduced the students to the idea that pictures often help tell the story. In several of Brett's books, one story is told in the text while another story is being told through her beautiful illustrations. A favorite was *Annie and the Wild Animals,* in which the reader is let in on a secret through the illustrations bordering each page. The illustrations in Byrd Baylor's book *I'm in Charge of Celebrations* sparked a controversy for the class. Although most of the children liked the book, they disagreed as to whether the pictures did the text justice. Many students felt that the illustrations needed to be more colorful, to stress the importance of the celebrations. And Moriya went back to her old favorite, *Teeny Tiny* by Jill Bennett, and found that the ghost appeared in all but two pictures. After careful study of the book, she determined that "the illustrations let the reader know that something really big is going to happen!" And it was fun to discover that the fox in *Rosie's Walk* by Pat Hutchins is never mentioned in the book's text.

Later, the students became fascinated by the number of books in our classroom about grandparents. We began to read the books to see how different authors approached the same topic. While some books like Aliki's *The Two of Them* tell of a long relationship between a grandchild and a grandfather, *Thundercake* by Patricia Polacco tells of one special memory that a child has about her grandmother. After reading *Grandpa's Face* by Eloise Greenfield, Dan commented that "the way the author described the grandfather's face made me feel like I really knew him." By looking at a variety of books about similar topics, students realized how many different ways there were to tell an effective story.

As we read more and more picture books, the students became interested in how the authors obtained the ideas for the picture books they had grown to love. We found that most picture books stemmed from incidents in the authors' lives. More recently published picture books tell the reader about this in the front of the book or in the "About the Author" section. Whether the picture book is a true-to-life account of someone's memory or an idea that came from an overheard conversation, each book has special meaning to the author because it was a part of his or her life. The students began to understand that authors write about the things they care about, which makes the reader care too. Readers and writers work together to give each story meaning. Courtney demonstrated this when she instantly fell in love with Judith Viorst's book, *Earrings*, about a girl who pleads with her parents to get her ears pierced. Courtney took the book home every night and read it to her mom. She told me that she wanted her mom to see what other girls were going through to get their ears pierced "and Judy Viorst said it way better than I could!" After several weeks of taking the book home, Courtney came to school with pierced ears!

The children's interest in picture books led them to wonder how others felt about this genre. They decided to conduct a survey at our school. They asked teachers and students to name their favorite picture book and to tell us why it was their favorite. Favorites varied, but our survey showed that, besides appreciating the books' beautiful illustrations, people love those books that bring back special memories for them. A favorite for many adults and children was *The Polar Express* by Chris Van Allsburg. It brought back many memories of Christmas and family to the readers surveyed. Another common favorite was Maurice Sendak's *Where the Wild Things Are*. One teacher responded that she was "a lot like Max as a kid. And my mom loved me in spite of it." Books that have meaning to the reader seem to be the ones that are remembered most. As authors, that was very important for us to know.

Picture books became an important tool for generating writing as well. As we began to read powerful picture books, students began to create very powerful writing. After reading *Mandy* by Barbara Booth as well as "The Picture" by Jeff Moss, Lindsay wrote the following piece in her notebook:

> As I run my fingers
> over top of
> my grandmother's hand
> I know she would never
> harm me by the
> softness and gentleness

of her hand. Gentle as a flower petal.
Soft as a cotton ball.
As I squeeze tighter and tighter
I can feel my grandmother's
hand shaking . . .
just a little.

And, following a read-aloud of *Faithful Elephants* by Yukio Tsuchiya, Christy wrote her own thoughts about war.

War

People kill.
People die.
Mothers, children, parents cry.
Fighting rages,
through the ages.
Guns fire.
Bullets go higher.
Bombs are dropped.
The dying is topped.
People fight,
for what is right.
Lives are given.
When it drops . . .
the dying stops.

Students had begun to see the power of picture books, as well as the power of their own writing.

The Reading-Writing Connection

Throughout the year, we continued to look at aspects that made picture books enjoyable. We used them as daily read-alouds and as part of integrated units of study. Finally, the students began to use the picture books as tools during writing workshop. At first, when they began to realize that their reading could enrich their own stories, they began to mimic favorite picture books. Instead of *When I Was Young in the Mountains,* Ron wrote *When I Lived in Charlotte, North Carolina.* Nancy wrote her own version of *Guess What?* by Mem Fox with her little sister as the focus of her story. The books were great! Students were beginning to look at what they had to say and then trying to find the best way to say it. Students had a pile of picture books on their desks to examine and analyze as they brought a piece of writing to a final draft. They began to see connections between what they were reading and what they wrote. As the year progressed, the students began to write their own books and stories using what they learned through picture books. Rather than merely mimicking a book that they enjoyed by changing the topic, they began to explore different ways to tell their stories.

As a class, we went back and looked at the books we were familiar with again and again. Each time we reread a book, we noticed another aspect that made it a quality piece of writing. As students began to notice things in professional authors' books, they also began to notice things in their own writing. At the beginning of the year, our classroom charts listed only books by "real," i.e., professional, authors. As the year progressed, our classroom authors' books were added to many of the lists. Naturally, we began to listen for great language in each other's writing. When Leslie began a piece, "Winters and winters ago," Travis jotted that phrase down on his own list of good beginnings. Later, when Travis reread his own writing, he discovered that he had several lines that he was particularly proud of because of the language he had used. His favorite line that showed up in two of his published pieces was, "I remember that teddy bear. He still lives packed up in boxes somewhere in the house." Travis had moved from looking for good language in picture books to being able to recognize it in his own writing.

When students in the class began to publish, Moriya told me that she really did not like to write. Knowing that she was expected to publish something, she wrote a poem about her dog, Lady, and "published" it in less than thirty minutes. I knew that Moriya would be a challenge, but I also knew she was a good writer. We began to brainstorm other ways that she could write about her dog. I encouraged her to look at several different picture books and hoped that one of them would inspire her to write more. After a considerable length of time, Moriya decided to write an alphabet book about Lady. She looked at many of the newly published alphabet books such as *Alphabet Soup* by Abbie Zabar and *Eight Hands Round* by Ann Paul and found that they were much more in-depth than the ones she remembered from her primary years. The ABC books were not merely one-word accounts. Moriya discovered that she could use the structure of an alphabet book to share some special moments she had had with her dog (Figure 1). It took her an entire quarter to complete *The A–Z Book of My Dog*, but it was well worth the time. The careful writing in the book conveyed Moriya's feelings about her special dog. Moriya is now a strong writer and rarely needs prompting. She realized through her first publication that the hard work was worth it.

Figure 1. Two Pages from *The A–Z Book of My Dog* by Moriya

Continued on next page

Figure 1 continued

One day before I was going to Israel, my dad and I put my zipper boots on my dog. She looked ridiculous!!

Esther worked on a piece about a trip that she had recently taken. She was concerned about all of the development that she had seen during her drive and felt that she should write about it. She read books about the environment such as *The Great Kapok Tree* by Lynne Cherry and decided that a description of what she had seen would allow the reader to share her concerns.

> Hill after hill, going up and down,
> Highs and lows.
> Pine tree after pine tree with green spikes.
> Leaves of every color you could imagine.
> And as the world moves on . . .
>
> the high and low hills turn into buildings,
> the colorful leaves turn into roads,
> and the spiky trees turn into telephone poles.
> One question was left.
> What if everything disappeared?

Satsuki, a very talented pianist, decided to write a picture book about her love of piano. After looking at the things she wanted to include in the book, she concluded that a book with a repeated phrase would best suit her needs. Her first draft repeated the phrase, "I love piano." When she completed this draft, she decided to look at other books with repeated phrases in them. Satsuki was not satisfied with her first repeated phrase because "in the other books I read, the repeated phrase was so good that you knew it was the most important part of the book. I want mine to be more like that." She experimented with several different phrases and finally ended up with "Piano, piano. I like it so much—the fingering, the hand positions, the chords, and such. Piano, piano, I like it so much." Satsuki's book readily became a class favorite. The hard work involved in making her words fit together just right helped her to create a popular publication.

Picture books became an important part of daily mini-lessons. The children were intrigued when an author could expand a single scene, character, or memory into an entire picture book. *My Great Aunt Arizona* by Gloria Houston and *Miss Rumphius* by Barbara Cooney became favorites when we discussed character development. *Roxaboxen* by Alice McLerran and *The Best Town in the World* by Byrd Baylor were commended for their vivid descriptions of special places. And after discussing the way Diane Siebert was able to give such a vivid description in *Train Song,* Mary realized that she could "stretch" her memory of a roller coaster ride to create the following piece.

Gemini

I felt the roller coaster creep up, click, clank, clackety, clack. It
    seemed it would stay
creeping up, but I didn't look down.
Then it shot down, my grip tightened and my stomach swam around
    on my insides.
The Gemini went so fast Life was a blur.
I could hear my mom screaming in my ear.
I gripped the bar and pressed my chest to it.
I felt my palms sweating as we raced down another hill.
The wind brushed against my face sharply.
My stomach churned and my spine hairs rose.
After a last turn, the roller coaster raced into finish leaving my
    stomach behind.
After I got my stomach back, I had to balance it out and unbuckle.
So there's my exciting but frightening ride on the Gemini.
And that's just the first time the Gemini ended.

Other mini-lessons focused on the structures of the books my students wrote. Matt shared his story about his dad. The story began in the
morning and ended at bedtime. When I asked Matt why he chose this
structure, he said that he thought most books were set up this way. He
went to look through our picture books only to find that we had very few
books that began in the morning and ended at night. This prompted long
discussions with the class about the focus of their writing. Students read
and reread picture books to find that most of the books that they loved
focused on one aspect of a relationship, a memory, or a story. Focusing
on one important aspect made the book more memorable. After much
deliberation, Matt went back and chose the part of his story that meant
the most to him. He rewrote his story, writing only about his bedtime
routine with his dad. Bedtime seemed to be a special time for Matt and
his father, and the relationship was better depicted in his second attempt.

After Matt's experience with focusing on the important part of his
story, many other students began to do the same. When Leslie wrote
about her dog, Gabby, she realized that a story about how she often says
good night to Gabby was more effective than telling everything she could
about her pet:

Good Night Gabby

Before I curl up in my warm bed, I have to say,
"Hello, my sweet puppy—move on over."
If that does not work, I have to say,
"My sweet puppy, *please* get off my pillow."
Then I gently put my hand under her black fur.

I lift. She growls.
Now I have a place to sleep.
As though I'm feeling guilty, I say,
"Gabby, I am sorry."
Then I pet her.
She licks my hand and face until I laugh aloud.
Good
night,
Gabby.

John used these same techniques when he wrote about his younger brother:

My Brother Chris

Small, 30 pounds, 3 years old,
Chris wakes up and comes in to watch TV.
Climbing silently into my bed
He wakes me up by turning
on the TV, with the control.
I pick him up and stuff
him under the blanket.
He laughs like mad.
The day goes by.
Chris goes to sleep.
Small, 30 pounds, 3 years old.
Chris wakes up and comes in to watch TV.

All of the writers in my classroom relied on picture books to help them at some point during the year. Charlie wanted to put his ideas about a good friend together but could not find a structure that pleased him. Then he read *Grandma's Scrapbook* by Josephine Nobisso. This author wrote the book in a structure Charlie had not considered, but one which was perfect for his writing style. Similarly, when Tyler did not know how to weave two vacations into one story, he decided to separate the stories in a manner similar to one used by Judy Blume in *The Pain and The Great One*. And, after Cara read *The Talking Eggs* by Robert San Souci, she realized she could tie fantasy into a real-life story about her most embarrassing moments.

At the end of the year, the children in this class were definitely better writers and better risk takers than they were at the beginning of their fourth-grade year. The use of picture books opened their eyes to many of the qualities common to all good literature. As the students began to publish their own picture books, like Satsuki's Piano book and Moriya's *The A–Z Book of My Dog*, they were able to realize that they could reach the qualities of good literature. They were able to express their responses to reading more openly and had more in common with each other, and thus were better able to assist each other in peer conferencing. Their conversations seemed more natural because they could really help each other with their writing. Since they had so many books in common, I quite often heard students talking during writing workshop, and literature was the basis of these conversations. Students recommended books for writers to read or a new structure to try. They cited several examples for the writer to study. Lindsey referred Heather to Amy Hest's book *The Ring and the Windowseat* when Heather could not find a way to weave together the past and the present in a book that she was writing. Irene commented that the language and the rhythm of Esther's book reminded her of Bill Martin Jr.'s *Chicka Chicka Boom Boom*. And when Lauren suggested that Cara try to write an alphabet book to tell her story, Cara knew she could research these books in just a few days. Students referred to picture books during conferencing, writing, reading, and during sharing time. We began to post charts around the room to help us keep track of the books that we knew might help us later. The chart titled "Books with Great Beginnings" included *Koala Lou* by Mem Fox and *July* by James Stevenson. Other charts listed books with great language, cumulative stories, and books with characters that we really got to know. As Nancy said, "If we've all read a book, we can help each other notice things, and if I've read a really good book that I think will help someone else with their story, I can share it with them." The picture books became a tool for the writers as well as for their peers who were responding to their writing.

Reflections

As my students and I looked back on our year with picture books, we could not imagine the classroom without them. Although they seemed like "baby books" at first, everyone agreed that they had become an important part of our year. Charlie recalled being hesitant about reading picture books during the first few weeks of school. Later he said (laughing), "I can't believe we didn't want to read them. They're so fun and they're so good!"

My students' writing is far from perfect, and my pursuit of the perfect solution continues. I am concerned that the use of picture books has limited my students to only wanting to write picture books. Although the qualities of good literature transferred to their writing of picture books, it did not transfer as clearly to their other writing. For instance, they were not very concerned about word choice in a letter about the environment. Ideally, I wanted the qualities of good writing evident in picture books to transfer to *all* of their writing, regardless of genre.

I do not believe that the transfer of much of my students' learning is complete. My hope is that it will become more evident in their own writing over the next several years. The inclusion of picture books deepened the students' appreciation for good literature and quality writing. I hope that somewhere down the road they will transfer their discoveries into all of their writing—not only their picture books. I am confident that they look at their writing as a much more meaningful part of their life because of picture books. I know they saw a strong connection between their reading and their writing.

Mem Fox discusses this issue of "transfer" in her book *Radical Reflections*. She writes about the power of reading aloud and the power of literature. She speculates that successful authors often know how to write with perfect rhythm, language, etc., because of the literature they read—possibly years ago (105–18). When Mem Fox addressed this issue at the 1994 Dublin Literacy Conference, she told the audience of her own experiences in writing. She credits several pieces of writing that truly affected her own. For example, after the publication of *Wilfred Gordon McDonald Partridge,* Fox realized that there were several similarities between the theme of her book and the theme of another book that she had loved years earlier. And in her autobiography, *Dear Mem Fox,* she tells of her amazement when she discovered that "the phrasing, and the when, the where, and the who in the first paragraph of *Possum Magic* mirrored exactly the opening verse of the Biblical story of Ruth, which I had learned by heart at drama school seventeen years before" (137–38). Fox's research supports my own theory that my students' experiences with picture books in fourth grade will live on in them as they continue their lives as writers.

Although many of the completed books that these students produced were fit for any children's bookstore, I worried about the time factor of writing picture books. Because the writing and illustrating of a picture book is a long-term process, the students were not going through the writing process as many times as they had in the past. Instead of publishing six to eight pieces of writing a year, they produced three or four. Subsequently, revising and editing were not occurring as many times during the year. I found that I needed to give more "assigned" writing outside of their personal writing so that they had the chance to edit and revise more often. I required them to publish letters, news articles, etc., throughout the year. Philosophically, I struggled with this decision, but found it to be the best solution with this class. I wanted all of their writing to be authentic and as self-directed as possible. However, I worried that they would not perfect the actual skills that I usually teach during the editing stages of the process. I know that the time they devoted to their personal writing was well spent. I did not want to sacrifice any of it, merely so they could go through the "process" more often.

The processes that I've seen these students use are far more impressive than some of the products. I was astounded to see the connections made between reading and writing when a student was attempting to perfect a piece. As a teacher, I was proud of every writer who wrote from life experiences. I was pleased with the pride they had in their picture books. However, without knowing how Satsuki came up with her final repeated phrase and without knowing that Moriya did not even like to write in September, our published books may seem like typical books that fourth graders write. Knowing that process gives more credibility to their work. During the 1991 Writing Institute at Columbia University, Lucy Calkins talked about our efforts in the writing classroom. She stressed the importance of helping the *writer* rather than merely perfecting the piece of *writing.* I felt that the processes my children went through to get to their products had changed the way they thought about their writing. In turn, the use of picture books had helped my students develop as writers. My fourth-grade classroom was much more like my first-grade classroom. The strong connection between reading and writing was evident. I felt good about what my students were doing in reading and writing, and they felt good about it too. We were able to have fun with picture books and to transfer that love of books to our writing. The students were more willing to take risks and to experiment with language. Many of them succeeded in writing what they consider a quality picture book. Others set goals for future writing projects. Lauren would like to write "one of those repeated phrase books where the repeated phrase is so good, it sticks in your head forever." I feel confident that some day Lauren will write that book.

I do not feel that my research with picture books is complete. Because I taught some of my students in both first and fourth grades, I was able to see how they connected their reading and writing at different levels. In first grade, most of the connections came in the form of imitation. As I read and reread certain books to my first graders, they imitated the form and wrote different versions of the stories they wrote. This seemed very natural for them. As they progressed through the fourth grade, I found that students began to pick and choose. They were able to find things that they liked in various picture books and use several authors' techniques to create their own pieces of writing. Some of my students went a step further and actually learned from different authors in order to create their own writing styles. At some point, students began to feel so comfortable with their own writing that they actually read good literature without "looking" for something to help them in their own writing. They had developed their own styles, and the reading-writing connection became more natural. I would like to watch this progression more closely over the next several years.

Since the time that I received the picture book grant, many more professional resources have become available on the topic. Ralph Fletcher's book *What a Writer Needs* is very valuable to me as I attempt to give students the tools they need to become more powerful writers. *After THE END* by Barry Lane is also helpful when I want specific ideas for using literature to make reading-writing connections during revision. Other recent resources include *Lasting Impressions* by Shelley Harwayne, *The Art of Teaching Writing; New Edition* by Lucy Calkins, and *Beyond Words* by Susan Benedict and Lenore Carlisle.

I am excited about the possibilities that picture books hold when used in intermediate classrooms. I was pleased with the growth that I saw in my own students and am certain that as I become familiar with more picture books and professional literature, I will be able to give students even more tools for writing. Picture books are a powerful genre in children's literature which can add authenticity to all writing workshops. I believe that we are at an exciting time in teaching students the writing process and that the inclusion of picture books can only enhance the process for students and teachers everywhere.

At the beginning of my study, I knew that the picture book genre was overlooked in most intermediate classrooms. However, it is the genre with which intermediate students are all most comfortable. Because of their familiarity with this genre, the children were able to identify the elements which make these stories effective. These literary components, common to all good literature, are more easily viewed in picture books. Additionally, due to their brevity, picture books can provide the necessary shared language experiences that chapter books cannot. The reading of a chapter book can take up to a month, while most picture books can be enjoyed in one sitting. Thus, picture books can be enjoyed daily to foster discussions pertaining to story structure, content, character development, form, use of language, and other literary techniques. The use of picture books allows all students to participate in higher-level discussions, regardless of individual reading level.

Through reading, rereading, and discussions of picture books, intermediate students can make discoveries that will transfer into their own writing. Because many fourth graders are reading at a much more sophisticated level than they are writing, it is difficult for them to make connections between reading and writing. In *Living Between the Lines,* Lucy Calkins states, "When young people write mostly half page narratives, but read mostly book-length novels, it takes a big act of imagination on everyone's part to regard their writing as similar to their reading" (138). The use of picture books can help bridge this gap between reading and writing for students at all ability levels.

Works Cited

Benedict, Susan, and Lenore Carlisle. *Beyond Words: Picture Books for Older Readers and Writers.* Portsmouth, NH: Heinemann, 1992.

Calkins, Lucy M. *The Art of Teaching Writing; New Edition.* Portsmouth, NH: Heinemann, 1994.

———. *The Art of Teaching Writing.* Portsmouth, NH: Heinemann, 1986.

Calkins, Lucy M., and Shelley Harwayne. *Living Between the Lines.* Portsmouth, NH: Heinemann, 1991.

Fletcher, Ralph. *What a Writer Needs.* Portsmouth, NH: Heinemann, 1993.

Fox, Mem. *Radical Reflections.* New York: Harcourt, 1993.

———. *Dear Mem Fox, I Have Read All Your Books, Even the Pathetic Ones.* New York: Harcourt, 1992.

Harwayne, Shelley. *Lasting Impressions: Weaving Literature into the Writing Workshop.* Portsmouth, NH: Heinemann, 1992.

Lane, Barry. *After THE END: Teaching and Learning Creative Revision.* Portsmouth, NH: Heinemann, 1993.

Recommended Works

Ackerman, Karen. *Song and Dance Man.* New York: Knopf, 1988.

Aliki. *The Two of Them.* New York: Greenwillow, 1979.

Bahr, Mary. *The Memory Box.* Morton Grove, IL: Whitman, 1992.

Base, Graeme. *The Eleventh Hour.* New York: Abrams, 1989.

Baylor, Byrd. *The Best Town in the World.* New York: Macmillan, 1983.

———. *I'm in Charge of Celebrations.* New York: Macmillan, 1986.

Bennett, Jill. *Teeny Tiny.* New York: Putnam, 1986.

Blos, Joan W. *Old Henry.* New York: Morrow, 1987.

Blume, Judy. *The Pain and the Great One.* New York: Dell, 1974.

Booth, Barbara. *Mandy.* New York: Lothrop, Lee and Shepard, 1991.

Brett, Jan. *Annie and the Wild Animals.* Boston: Houghton, 1985.

Brinckloe, Julie. *Fireflies!* New York: Macmillan, 1985.

Buffett, Jimmy, and Savannah Buffet. *Trouble Dolls.* San Diego: Harcourt, 1991.

Carle, Eric. *The Very Hungry Caterpillar.* New York: Putnam, 1981.

Cherry, Lynne. *The Great Kapok Tree.* New York: Harcourt, 1990.

Conrad, Pam. *My Daniel.* New York: Harper, 1989.

Cooney, Barbara. *Miss Rumphius.* NewYork: Viking, 1982 .

Deedy, Carmen Agra. *Agatha's Featherbed.* Atlanta, GA: Peachtree, 1991.

de Paola, Tommie. *Now One Foot, Now the Other.* New York: Putnam, 1980.

Ehlert, Lois. *Feathers for Lunch.* San Diego: Harcourt, 1990.

Emberly, Barbara. *Drummer Hoff.* Englewood Cliffs, NJ: Prentice Hall, 1967.

Fox, Mem. *Guess What.* New York: Harcourt, 1990.

———. *Koala Lou.* New York: Harcourt, 1988.

———. *Possum Magic.* New York: Harcourt, 1983.

———. *Sophie.* New York: Harcourt, 1994.

———. *Wilfred Gordon McDonald Partridge.* New York: Harcourt, 1985.

Greenfield, Eloise. *Grandpa's Face.* New York: Philomel, 1988.

Hepworth, Cathi. *Antics.* New York: Putnam, 1992.

Hest, Amy. *The Ring and the Window Seat.* NewYork: Scholastic, 1990.

Houston, Gloria. *My Great Aunt Arizona.* New York: HarperCollins, 1992.

Hutchins, Pat. *Rosie's Walk.* New York: Macmillan, 1986.

Lewis, C. S. *The Lion, the Witch, and the Wardrobe.* New York: Macmillan, 1950.

Lindbergh, Reeve. *Grandfather's Lovesong.* New York: Viking, 1993.

Lobel, Anita. *Alison's Zinnia.* New York: Greeenwillow, 1990.

MacDonald, Amy. *Rachel Fister's Blister.* Boston: Houghton, 1990.

MacLachlan, Patricia. *All the Places to Love.* New York: HarperCollins, 1994.

McLerran, Alice. *Roxaboxen.* New York: Lothrop, Lee and Shepard, 1991.

Martin, Bill. *The Ghost-Eye Tree.* New York: Holt, 1985.

Martin, Bill, and John Archambault. *Chicka Chicka Boom Boom.* New York: Simon and Schuster, 1991.

———. *Knots on a Counting Rope.* New York: Holt, 1987.

Moss, Jeff. "The Picture." *The Butterfly Jar.* New York: Bantam, 1989.

Moss, Thylias. *I Want to Be.* New York: Dial, 1994.

Munsch, Robert. *Thomas' Snowsuit.* Toronto: Annick, 1985.

Nobisso, Joseph. *Grandma's Scrapbook*. San Marcos, CA: Green Tiger, 1990.

Paul, Ann. *Eight Hands Round*. New York: HarperCollins, 1991.

Polacco, Patricia. *The Keeping Quilt*. New York: Simon and Schuster, 1988.

————. *Thunder Cake*. New York: Philomel, 1990.

Pomerantz, Charlotte. *The Chalk Doll*. New York: Lippincott, 1989.

Ringgold, Faith. *Tar Beach*. New York: Crown, 1991.

Rosen, Michael J., and Franz Brandenberg, eds. *Home: A Collaboration of Thirty Distinguished Authors and Illustrators of Children's Books to Aid the Homeless*. New York: HarperCollins, 1992.

Rounds, Glen. *I Know an Old Lady Who Swallowed a Fly*. New York: Holiday House, 1990.

Rylant, Cynthia. *Appalachia: The Voices of Sleeping Birds*. San Diego: Harcourt, 1991.

————. *Birthday Presents*. New York: Orchard, 1987.

————. *Miss Maggie*. New York: Dutton, 1983.

————. *The Relatives Came*. New York: Bradbury, 1985.

————. *When I Was Young in the Mountains*. New York: Dutton, 1982.

San Souci, Robert. *The Talking Eggs*. New York: Dial, 1989.

Scieszka, Jon. *The True Story of the Three Pigs*. New York: Viking, 1989.

Sendak, Maurice. *Where the Wild Things Are*. New York: Harper, 1963.

Siebert, Diane. *Heartland*. New York: Harper Trophy, 1989.

————. *Train Song*. New York: Thomas Y. Crowell, 1981.

Stevenson, James. *July*. New York: Greenwillow, 1990.

Tsuchiya, Yukio. *Faithful Elephants*. Boston: Houghton, 1988.

Van Allsburg, Chris. *The Stranger*. Boston: Houghton, 1986.

————. *The Polar Express*. Boston: Houghton, 1985.

Viorst, Judith. *Earring!* New York: Atheneum, 1990.

————. *Alexander and the Terrible, Horrible, No Good, Very Bad Day*. New York: Atheneum, 1972.

Williams, Vera B. *"More, more, more," said the baby: Three Love Stories*. New York: Greenwillow, 1990.

Wood, Audrey. *The Napping House*. New York: Harcourt, 1984.

————. *Silly Sally*. New York: Harcourt, 1992.

Zabar, Abbie. *Alphabet Soup*. New York: Stewart, Taboria, and Chang, 1990.

Zolotow, Charlotte. *The Moon Was the Best*. New York: Greenwillow, 1993.

————. *This Quiet Lady*. New York: Greenwillow, 1992.

Response

Donna Barnes

Teachers will learn so much from this chapter. They may want to reread it and reread it. Teachers of older children will find themselves wanting to use picture books with their students. Franki shows stamina by sticking to her belief that the examination of picture books will help a student's writing improve. She was able to weather the spoken and unspoken attitude of "that's too babyish" and convince her students that picture books are often more difficult to read than chapter books. In many instances they are written for adults to read aloud to their children.

Franki's description of her first quarter was most impressive. She relaxed and took her time to slowly enjoy reading and rereading these picture books. Often in school and in life everything is too hurried. Students and teachers read something once and hurry off to the next event. This fourth-grade teacher shows how she read and reread and talked. Reading and rereading these books must transfer to the students rereading their writing also.

Franki's students' writing shows over and over the powerful effect picture-book reading had on them. Satsuki's repeated line works very well. "Piano, piano, I like it so much—the fingering, the hand positions, the chords and such. Piano, piano, I like it so much."

Franki was concerned that the use of picture books limits students to only writing picture books. She needs to remember that there has been an explosion in the field of children's literature. There are historical fiction books, science fiction books, poetry books, nonfiction books, etc. Surely she integrates all of these into her curriculum already. If her students can take a picture book approach to a science, social studies, or math topic, they will be able to transfer their skill from personal narrative to content writing.

9 No Talking during Nuclear Attack: An Introduction to Peer Conferencing

Karen Weinhold

Practically immune by now to the urgency of the blatting, we slowly slid from our seats to our practiced positions under our desks as the emergency bell warning of imminent nuclear attack resounded in the hallways. In a crouched position, head tucked between our knees, arms and legs pulled in from the aisles where the teacher patrolled, we sent each other secret, coded messages, stifled giggles, and failed to take in the dire consequences of talking during nuclear attack!

We had so many things to talk about:

"Is Skippy taking Ellen to the dance Friday night?"

"I thought they broke up before school yesterday."

"They did, but then they made up at Kelleher's after practice. He even paid for her shake. I was there."

"Girls, be quiet, or you'll be staying with me after school!" (This was back in the days when the teacher could just keep a student on the same day he or she misbehaved, without having to send a written notice home, wait for it to be signed, be assured that it was convenient for the miscreant to be picked up on that day and that it didn't interfere with an orthodontist appointment; dance, music or skating lessons; baby-sitting; or custody balance.)

Thus detained, we often were punished by having to produce writing assignments such as "The Importance of Silence during Simulated Nuclear Attack" or the less thought-provoking "I Will Not Talk during Civil Defense Exercises," written one hundred and fifty times, legibly, until fingers cramped in agony. To this day I cannot understand why the teacher—our leader, savior, guide—remained erect, a moving, talking target throughout the drill, while our silence had to be automatic and total.

Silence dominated my education. The only good mouth was a closed one. Never speak until your raised hand has been recognized by the teacher. Almost all of the after-school "time" I had to do was for unnecessary talking. When I began my own teaching career, I was determined never to humiliate students the way I had been just for talking at inappropriate moments:

> Miss Mullen, would you like to share with the rest of the class what was so important to say to Miss Dupont that it couldn't wait 'til after school? Come, come now . . . I think I heard the name Skippy, and Ellen, and something broken up? Please tell us. We can hardly bear the suspense. Is it because one of you is interested in this Skippy person? If it was important enough for you to disrupt my lesson, certainly the whole class needs to be informed.

I might have lasted a week before I broke my own resolution:

> Susan, I know you and Jeff are a hot item, but could you please keep the personal stuff for after class . . . or share it with all of us so we can go on with the lesson? Thank you.

I couldn't believe the words that fell out of my mouth—and continued to fall for the next twelve years. Clearly I could understand now how I'd been the bane of many of my teachers, and how the low conduct marks they gave me had truly been justified. Talking had no place in their—or my—classroom. And then, in the summer of 1981, I went to a three-week writing institute at the University of New Hampshire, and everything changed.

"Conversation is the laboratory and workshop of the student." They told me Emerson said that. "Organisms change and grow with interaction in the environment. Challenges cause this growth. No challenge, no growth. This is not a passive model," informed Jane Kearns, my instructor. "The writing process combines freedom with discipline." Sure, and the discipline required was all mine! How to completely shift gears, from the wondrous, desirable ideal of the silent classroom to the promoted cacophony they touted? Did I really want to do this? I thought about the amount of time I spent struggling to maintain silence in my adolescents' classroom. I thought about what I was experiencing in the morning during the first week of the institute as I wrote and wrote and wrote, knowing I'd have a peer's willing ear to conference with each day. Those first meetings were painful:

> *Her:* "I can't believe you lived through that and can now write about it."
>
> *Me:* "Yeah."
>
> *Her:* "Isn't it hard to have to remember all that stuff you'd probably rather forget?"
>
> *Me:* "Yeah."

> *Her:* "Do you think you could show more of what you were think-
> ing and feeling when the doctors gave you the odds?"
>
> *Me:* "Yeah."

Although my monosyllabic responses didn't exactly demonstrate
it, I was, in fact, breaking through years of educationally nurtured silence. This writing encouraged—no, exhorted—me to bring my real life
into the classroom, and use my own experience as the basis for my
writing. (WHAT??? No more, "A Day in the Life of an Eraser" or "The Value
of Being a Good Listener"?) Not only that, but now I could talk about
what I'd written with someone whose sole intent wasn't to bleed all over
my paper, conducting postmortem dissections that could only lead to the
dead-ended mortuary of the trash can? Did I really want this for my
classroom? I decided I did. Over the next decade I tried. I became a
believer, convincing myself that what was happening in my classroom
was the best thing since artificial sweeteners.

At first, I was the only one in my K–8 school experimenting with
"writing process." I dabbled. I cast out, then quickly reeled in. I could go
three days with this "loosey-goosey" circus atmosphere, then I'd panic.
How could I legitimately write in the day's plans, "Students will confer
with partners using first drafts of fear pieces, looking for strengths which
already exist," when I knew that what was going on during these pairings
was all too reminiscent of the Skippy/Ellen exchanges of my own youth?
Often UNH sent visitors to see how we were implementing this writing-
process approach in our classrooms. Don Graves spent an entire day. I
trailed him like a puppy as he modeled peer conferencing for my students:

> "Shep, that roast beef sandwich must have been delicious if you
> were as starved as you've said."
>
> "Yeah."
>
> "Could you tell me more about it? What did the roast beef look
> like?"
>
> "Like meat."
>
> "Was it rare? medium? well-done? Did it have a lot of fat? or was it
> lean, all trimmed up? Was it thick or thin? juicy or dry? Did the
> sandwich have mayo? mustard? salt? pepper? Tell me about the
> bread . . . ."
>
> "Oh, I get it. Well, the meat was red and juicy, and when I took
> that first bite, I forgot all about how scared and hungry I'd
> been, and I just let the juice run down my chin, and that's
> when I saw my Mom crying, so I grabbed a napkin real quick,
> but that wasn't what she was crying about . . . ."

Two minutes, and Shep was writing as if possessed, and Professor Graves was halfway through another conference. Those sitting nearby eavesdropping had also picked up their pencils and were madly scribbling.

Tom Newkirk visited, and sat down beside my most reluctant writer without even being cued:

> "Having some trouble getting started, Matt?"
>
> "Yeah, I've got nothing to write about."
>
> "I see you're wearing a Giants shirt—they your team?"
>
> "Yeah."
>
> "How come?"
>
> "Dunno."
>
> "You like football?"
>
> "Yeah."
>
> "You play?"
>
> "Yeah."
>
> "Tell me about your most frightening moment on the field."
>
> "Well, there was this gigundo dude—I bet he was like as big as Kong, man, even if he was only in eighth grade, and I was supposed to be blockin', and . . . ."

And Matt wrote for the next two days about the fear in the pit of his stomach as he faced that defensive lineman. I tried to get the students who had experienced some success with conferencing to model for the others. On the whole, the class was disbelieving, though they were quite adept at pretending otherwise. Whatever this new stuff was that caused their teacher to make them sit together and talk during class, they certainly didn't want to do anything to stop it.

Then Shep and Matt met as a pair to confer with these great first drafts. All Matt had to offer was that maybe if he ate red meat he, too, could inspire fear on the football field, and Shep confessed that he'd always wanted to play football, but he knew he was too much of a wimp. End of conference—on to last night's Giants-Bills encounter. The visitors left, and I was alone in that din, and I couldn't get comfortable with it.

So I spread my net and talked to my colleagues about the talking. Their skepticism was tangible, but they kindly, silently let me spout. Soon peer conferences were "in" everywhere: workshops, conferences, journals, lectures, and even *videotapes* abounded. In moments of complete honesty, which I tried to avoid at all cost, I did admit to myself that I was rescheduling my forty-five-minute periods so as to have little time for the charming children to converse, but my plan book continued to say it was happening just about daily. My conferences with them individually were unproductive because I had to keep putting out fires among the pairs scattered around my room. I knew it wasn't working, but by now I had become a proselytizer, and chewing and swallowing my own words, even with the tenderizing effect of my nearest and dearest colleagues' understanding, was hardly appealing. After many years of vacillating, of attending just one more workshop, taking one more course, reading one more book, I have decided to come clean.

The anecdotes that follow are my confession that I am dissatisfied with peer conferencing's effectiveness in all of the many, many ways I've tried to use it. So why not just abandon it entirely? Golf. If I'm quite lucky, once in every 18 or 27 or 36 holes I hit that sweet, soaring, exhilarating ball that makes all the frustrations of the game worthwhile . . . and keeps me coming back, over and over again, hoping to repeat. I try to remember just how I gripped the club, the exact stance, the rhythm of the swing, the position of the ball, the surge and force of the follow-through: to wit, every facet that produced that great lofting shot.

Every once in a very great while I have been witness to a successful, productive peer conference, one in which serendipity occurs, a question is asked, a nuance grasped, a character's motivation understood—and dynamic writing sparks fly:

> *Steve:* "Why did you have the son take his father's fishing hat when he ran away?"
>
> *Rene:* "It's supposed to be a symbol—but I guess it isn't very good if you didn't get it. Too subtle, huh?"
>
> *Steve:* "Oh, no, I do get it—it shows that he understood what was most important to his father, while the father is clueless about what's important to him, right? What a great touch! Do you think you could put a more obvious hint or clue in before he actually leaves, just to be sure we get it?"
>
> *Rene:* "No way—it'd give the whole thing away . . . unless . . . oh, yes, I know exactly what I'll do. How about if I have him get in an argument with his father early on because he knocked the hat on the floor and left it there? Then the father lectures him on how it isn't just a hat, etc. What do you think? Oh, this is going to make it so much better. Go shove Josh off the computer, will ya?"

After an exchange such as this, I do what I do after that golf shot: run through all facets of it in my mind. I go over the dialogue, body language, introductory mini-lesson, location of the pair—anything which might give a clue to lead to some repetition, some consistency. To date, nothing. Nada.

I've become an agnostic, and I am searching for a belief system— and I now know that I am not alone. Behind closed doors, secretly, in whispers, dozens of you have shared your doubts, misgivings, and failures. You have sought strategies and solutions. We know that writing process works, but not all parts of it work for each of us. I know what I don't want, yet I haven't been able to figure out how to get what I envision. If any of you secretly yearn for the old days, when "talking during nuclear attack" was a sure way to have censure rain down upon your head, when silence was indeed golden and the teacher had some modicum—or pretense—of control in terms of the in-house conversations, read on. Released from the threat of nuclear attack, maybe we can learn by releasing our own silences.

Talk about Talkin'

> *"Only at the beginning of adolescence do children direct their principal attention to works of their peers"*
> —Howard Gardner, *The Arts and Human Development*

"Did you read Ian's story yet?" probed bug-eyed Jim. "It's awesome— six guys get diced in the first two pages. You can almost smell the blood!"

"Not yet," admitted Mike. "But Daina wrote a story about first love and she almost has 'em doin' it!" he giggled.

> *"Adolescents have a lot to cope with in the space of a few years, adjusting to a new and changing body, figuring out who they are in comparison and contrast with others . . . becoming competent enough at some task to derive a genuine sense of self-confidence"*
> —Seminar for Parents on Adolescent Sexuality

> *"The other self develops confidence through the experience of being heard in small and large group workshops"*
> —Donald Murray, *"Teaching the Other Self"*

"Watch out—here she comes—quick, ask me one of those pushing questions she wants," demanded Shannon. "Oh, hi, Mrs. W., Bridget was just giving me some feedback on my lead. It's too flat and doesn't grab the reader's attention. No, we weren't talking about the dance Friday night! I told you, we were talking about my lead. OK, OK, I'll show you my revision by the end of the period. Hey, Ryan's lookin' for ya."

And so it goes . . . . My instructors in the writing process program at the University of New Hampshire (including Lucy Calkins, Don Graves, Tom Newkirk, Tom Romano, Paula Fleming, and Jane Kearns) repeated this tenet, a cornerstone of the process of writing: students learn best from directed conversation with each other about their writing. I heard it over and over again, so I tried it, over and over again: pairs, triples, quads . . . closely monitored, totally independent, semi-attended to—you name it, I tried it.

The sides of my cheeks resembled raw hamburger one quarter as I practiced sitting silently to the side of the dialoguing dynamic duo. As long as I was nearby, their talk straddled the socio-academic; however, they soon discovered it was just a matter of time until I'd move on again—they were absolutely certain they could out-wait me. One day I determinedly met with Clara and Ed for forty-three of the forty-eight minutes. Somehow they sent a coded message to another pair who nagged for my attention until it would have been certifiable neglect to ignore them any longer.

Two professors from the education department of the University of New Hampshire (John Carney and Grant Cioffi) "borrowed" my classes to field-test a six-week critical thinking skills unit on the elderly. I watched in amazement as they placed portable tape recorders in the center of each group of three students, explaining that since there were only the two of them they couldn't possibly spend an equal amount of time with each of the eight groups, and they were afraid they might miss something valuable in the discussion. What a clever ruse, I thought. So, the next time we met in small groups for sharing, I, too, carefully orchestrated the recording of their every word. Eavesdropping five minutes into the exercise I heard Clint whisper, "C'mon. She's never gonna listen to all of these tapes—she'd be bored out of her gourd. Besides, she has to work at the library tonight. I heard her tell Tim she'd get him that espionage book he's been trying to find. And the revised drafts are due tomorrow—so it's simply impossible!" And he was 100 percent correct!

> *"The relation in adolescence to other humans, which was all important in the first years of life, once again moves center stage"*
>
> —Howard Gardner, *Artful Scribbles*

OK, I'll buy that, I thought. Maybe if I create the pairings, now that I know their assets and liabilities and allegiances a bit, maybe if I plot the partnerships so that they complement each other, this will work.

"How can I expect any help from her?" Jon griped, pointing accusingly in Kate's direction. "She's never even seen a hockey game."

"All Lisa ever writes about is mushy, gushy stuff, and the guys are always jerks," Dwayne complained. "Can't I be with Jessica? She knows me better, and I don't have to be so careful not to hurt her feelings."

That sounded like a reasonable request to me, until I covertly heard Jessica's and Dwayne's "sensitive" exchange: "If you invite Ann you'll have to ask Kelly too—and then no one will want to come to your party cuz she's such a loser."

Shadowing another two, I learned the scores of the previous night's basketball and football games and then heard a debate about whether or not a brain continues to function in a decapitated head (and even if it did, kinda like the chicken who runs around the yard spurting blood from its open neck wound, speculation was rampant about the duration of this brain's activity, until three sets of couples were involved surreptitiously in this dilemma). Next I witnessed the development of a composite excuse for the unfinished social studies project due the next period and the creation of a pseudo-revision product to show me how helpful to each other they had been! Sure, they could collaborate together.

We modeled writing conferences that worked (carefully orchestrated by me and Dunkin' Donuts before school); we used the overhead projector to practice how to have a successful peer writing encounter (anyone observing witnessed focused, productive examples of profitable exchanges); on request, we even sent pairs to demonstrate for other classes (were those teachers struggling with peer conferencing too?). But none of it was sustained. I felt like a subversive in my own field, a CIA agent in my own classroom. The minute I disengaged from a duo, moved out of their immediate aura, I knew exactly where the conversation was headed:

> "OK, she's with Stacy and Caroline. Now tell me what happened after Briana met that cute guy from Exeter in the mall. Is he going to call her this weekend? Will she go out with him?"

or

> "Derek said to tell you that Chad's going to be the goalie in tomorrow's playoff, so if Stacy really likes him, she should come. Briana's mother has room in her van."

or

> "Look out, she's headed this way. Quick—what did you tell her you were trying to get for a reaction from your reader when the guy practices by cutting the chicken's head off?"

I was unsettled. Frenetic. I gave it up. I put it back in. I wrote about how to create collaborative pairs in your writing process classroom, and tore it up. I never told anyone that it didn't quite work for me; I just assumed that I didn't quite "get" it. I could talk about the pitfalls to avoid, but I never said that I found any way to make it work. And then I met my own personal Waterloo.

During the 1990–91 school year I held the position of teacher-in-residence for the education department of the University of New Hampshire. I traveled to many schools to observe graduate students doing their teaching internships. Everywhere I went I focused on the conferencing techniques and strategies being used, at all grade levels, readiness through grade 12. I was appalled by what I saw. Rarely did a discussion stay on topic for more than a minute; huge blocks of "empty" time emerged. Teachers intent on modeling responses for specific groups lost contact with students on the periphery. These students thus learned to quickly move to the outer reaches of the direction the teacher was taking, adapting with great acuity to this method of hiding.

Even among the most experienced teachers, reaching 50 to 60 percent was the best I ever saw anyone accomplish, like the gold medal of conferencing Olympics! Some teachers kept detailed records, noting students' status in indecipherable cryptic, and using a flow chart that would boggle the founders of TQM. Others were more random, scattering themselves thinly among the most demanding or most conspicuously indolent. Even when a carefully charted routine for visiting with each student existed, days went by during which students were "on their own"—which translated into "free."

I almost never saw even the most diligent pupil choose to initiate a conference and then set about performing the revising operations suggested by the encounter. Those who sustained the oral interchange eventually shut down on the follow-through. Many had mastered elaborate sign language; faces and bodies contorted into lengthy secret telephonings across classrooms.

Dedicated, determined teachers flailed themselves daily; they worked exhaustively at implementing this facet of the process, reading the research, flocking to workshops, yet not admitting to colleagues how they couldn't get a handle on this whole peer conferencing thing. What these observations did for me was to remove some of the isolation and guilt I'd been feeling about my own inability to make it all work as I'd heard it described by the process proponents. However, I was not in a position to tell these cooperating teachers that I had observed how conferencing wasn't working in their classrooms! Such a comment, no matter how tactfully cloaked, would have seriously impaired my effectiveness as intern-evaluator. I would have been resented and distrusted.

Eager as these teachers were to share their expertise, guidance, and children with my novices, they were very wary of the intruder's opinion and assessment of their programs and methodologies. It had taken months of delicate interweavings and subtle machinations to create an atmosphere of trust and parity among us; I was not about to throw it all away by pointing out to them that this was not working.

Slowly the internship students and I began to hedge our post-observation collaborative conferences with slender intrusions of probing, doubting questions. Tentatively, hesitantly, we began to share our concerns, but it was well into spring before full-blown confession surfaced, and the year was over for the interns and me in May, leaving us all adrift. I now knew that it wasn't just for me that peer conferencing wasn't working, and I also had to face the fact that I was helping these beginning teachers to continue a practice I could see wasn't working for them either. Was this blasphemy? Did I want them to witness our increasing skepticism, participate in our defection, at a time when they most needed solid curriculum practices?

Politically, I deemed it unwise to crusade now, especially since it had been a one-year position only and I had no further influence on either the interns or their cooperating teachers. UNH had been good to me, and I had no solid research to back up my findings. I still doubted my own years of experience enough to fall back into silence. I bid them all a fond farewell and retreated to the safety and hypocrisy of my classroom once again.

What a disturbing interim it had been! How could I reconcile all of this? First there was the practice and theory proffered by the researchers and experts in the field, for whom I had so much respect; after all, they had completely altered both my philosophy and practice in my writing classroom. Then there was what I now know to be true after a decade or more of trying—peer conferencing in the many, many ways I explored it did not work for me. Whether it was because I just could not effectively teach directed student exchange or because it was a flawed practice seemed immaterial at this point. I had been unable to potty-train my own children using M&Ms (I ate the candy before it could serve as reward!); I had been unable to teach them as teenagers how to drive because my own panic at sideswiping mailboxes, telephone poles, and curbs had permeated the car; I read to my youngest from birth through high school, and he still won't pick up a book.

I had accepted all these apparent failures and moved to alternative measures without being burdened by guilt, shame, and responsibility, yet I couldn't seem to do the same in my classroom. I could tell another parent, "Well, that certainly didn't work for me; I gained ten pounds and ended up with twice as much laundry because of the extra training pants," but had no such candor about the obvious failure of my peers' writing collaborations—why?

And now I'm back in my seventh- and eighth-grade reading/writing classroom, faced with the same dilemma I had when I left: how to get peer conferencing to work for me the way the orthodoxy says it should and will if properly crafted. I continue to peruse the literature, run to workshops and conferences, observe, question, and practice—but deep in my instinctive teaching self I sense failure. It is not a successful, productive component of my program. I asked Michael, a writer who needed feedback, to write how he felt about peer conferencing and its effectiveness. Of course, I expected a paean, and was quite surprised when he turned in the following:

> The most important part of writing process is the peer conference, in my opinion. If it works well, a conference can be an excellent way to get feedback from the group any author is most interested in: the readers. Conferences help most in the revision stage, and most students find them useful. However, the system is far from perfect. One difficulty I have encountered routinely has been finding an effective partner. It's often the most difficult to find "good" conferencer when you most need one—that is, with your best writing. Here's a typical day's example of conference hunting.
>
> You've just finished an action-packed sci-fi murder mystery. You're really excited about it, but you have some questions. You're also wondering if there are too many plot twists and shoot-outs. You scrawl that final period and start looking around the room. You need a conference! Scanning the room, you see Jake is free.
>
> "Hey, wanna conference?"
>
> "Sure."
>
> The two of you settle down on the cushions as you begin to read, "The shuttle raced through space." You look up as you finish. Jake's eyes are locked in space. This is not a good sign.
>
> "So," you ask cautiously, "what do you think of it?"
>
> "OK. Well, pretty good."
>
> "Any suggestions?"
>
> "No. It was cool. You see the World Cup last night?"
>
> You pursue this line of questioning a little further.
>
> "Just one thing I could change?"
>
> "Well, I guess you wanna use less big words."
>
> This is clearly a lost cause. After a few more minutes of futile probing, you give up. He did suggest fewer adjectives, but that's not a recommendation I usually take. You need a few good words here and there to keep things interesting. Not a great start, but you decide to try again. Seeing Mac's pen stagnant, you make your move. He doesn't mind conferencing,

so once again you settle in among the cushions. As you read, he appears attentive. This might just work out . . .

"So, what do you think?"

"I thought it was pretty cool. The laser thing was cool."

"Any suggestions?"

"More shooting, man!"

This is clearly going nowhere. You end your discussion with Rambo as quickly and tactfully as possible. You have just experienced what I call a "shoot 'em up" conference. Most of my stories involve violence, but the combat is always critical to the character development or the plot. In a "shoot 'em up" your partner eats up the action but misses the reasons behind it. One of the most intense and powerful stories I have done involved a marine sniper, who upon seeing a horrific product of war through his scope, finds himself unable to complete his mission of assassination. Violence and its effect on the soul is the theme of the story. After one conference on the story, my partner told me that it was good, but the sniper should have killed more people. The point had been missed.

You look around again. This is getting old, but you still might find someone. You see that Meghan's free, so you ask her to confer. She listens all through the story, even gasping at the end. You can't help but think that this one might turn out okay.

"So, how was it?"

"Great! I liked it a lot!"

"Any suggestions, stuff I can do to make it better?"

"No, it was great! Maybe a little less gunfire, but it was like, really cool."

One or two conferences like that, where the person thinks it's perfect, can be encouraging, but four or five get old fast. You're just about to ask someone else for a conference when you hear the teacher's voice: "That's the class. On to social studies!"

Let's look at what we have for input after forty-five minutes of conferencing:

—less big words

—more shooting

—less shooting

You've already ruled out the first one, and the other two contradict one another. Not much to go on!

These are only a few of the common pitfalls young authors often face in the conferencing system. Finding a good partner can be difficult because reading comprehension and writing skills in a typical class vary greatly, making it easy to go over one kid's head while hitting another around the kneecaps.

A good partner will tell you specifically what he/she liked and didn't like, and ask questions to get the ol' creative juices flowing. Then he/she makes some suggestions, not demands, for improving the piece. After awhile you start to figure out whom you can conference with, and seek out these people.

When they work, conferences can turn a mediocre story into a masterpiece. Two heads are better than one, and good conferences channel that kind of input while still allowing the author the freedom he/she needs to develop the story.

In its totality, I think writing process is a great way to teach writing. I love to write, and I do it in some of my spare time. If I had learned to write in the old traditional way, I doubt I would enjoy it as much as I do now. Process lets me create many pieces each term, allowing me to experiment with many different styles and genres, and then develop the ones I like. It allows me the freedom to create, and to me, that is the most important skill of all.

I feel inadequate and incompetent, and I deplore feeling this way. I am working as hard and as fast as I can; I am structured, organized, and vigilant—but I know they are "getting away with murder" and not benefiting from their exchanges.

They know how to model an ideal conference. They can talk or write their way through a correct (on the surface) performance, but their writing is not improving as a result of it. I know their writing can improve through conferencing because I am often awed by the difference a single meeting with the teacher can produce. Over and over again this year I have been able to practice enough restraint to allow a student to talk through a problem before jumping in with a suggestion or solution. (Of course I've had to usurp homeroom, study hall, and lunch time to fit in many of these conferences.) Each successful exchange has helped reinforce my belief in the tool of conferencing. But I am only one person in five classes of twenty-thirty students. Logistics clearly show that with this ratio we'd be lucky to get completely through two pieces in the course of a year. That just won't do. It's a conundrum!

So, I need to either throw in the towel and just plain give up on peer conferencing (with which I've been struggling for over ten years!), or I need to find practitioners who have made them a viable part of their curriculum. I'm a doubting Thomas, so I need tactile proof, not just rhetoric, that adolescents can learn from each other during a conversation about their writing that does not necessitate my hovering and minute maintenance. I'd like to sleep, conscience-free, recreating in my dreams dialogues such as those I've seen replicated in print:

> "Melissa, could you tell me more about your main character? Is she intentionally mean, or has something happened that makes her that way? I mean, I really care about what happens to her, but I know I'd feel differently if I had more background information about her."
>
> "Sure, Jan, I can do that. What if I filled in by saying that when she was eight she was kidnapped by aliens, taken to their space ship where they put her through all kinds of tests, and now she just freaks whenever anybody connected with doctors or hospitals or the medical profession comes near her. That's why she used her

Ginsu knife to decapitate that nurse on the bus as the unsuspecting RN leaned across to administer CPR to her seatmate who passed out . . . ."

"Sounds like a great plan to me. Now tell me more about what she saw and felt as she severed the nurse's head. Did you do any research yet to find out if the head still works after it's cut off?"

Working conferences . . . heaven.

Works Cited

Gardner, Howard. *Artful Scribbles: The Significance of Children's Drawings.* New York: Basic, 1980.

————. *The Arts and Human Development.* New York: Wiley, 1973.

Murray, Donald M. "Teaching the Other Self: The Writer's First Reader." *College Composition and Communication* 33 (1982): 140–47.

Seminar for Parents on Adolescent Sexuality. Newton, MA: Education Development Center, 1978.

Response
Kay Morgan

Teachers have often shared Karen's frustration with peer conferences. Too many conferences seem to be just an opportunity for teenagers to chat. High school kids are quick to jump at the chance to share gossip, to talk about who's going out with whom and about the upcoming party on Friday night.

This may only be a way of rationalizing the extra "talk" that goes on in conferences, but it seems that even when an adult conference group gets together, they spend quite a lot of time catching up on each other's lives, sharing news of themselves and their children. It seems that individuals need to reconnect on some level as friends and confidants before they can risk sharing their writing. When students are asked to confer, perhaps with a partner they don't know well, a certain amount of pre-conference socializing may be necessary before the real work of the conference can proceed.

James Britton suggests that "talk" is critical to adolescents establishing relationships with others as well as to their pursuit of ideas (*Language of Learning.* Middlesex, England: Penguin, 1972. 37). According to Dan-ling Fu, it is probably the means by which students investigate and organize new fields of interest (*My Trouble Is My English: Asian Students and the American Dream.* Portsmouth, NH: Boynton/Cook, 1995). This may suggest that even the extra conversation that occurs in conferences has some merit. Fu states that "conversations are essential steps to our writing; stimulating our thinking, organizing our thoughts, and searching for words in our writing." Neither Britton nor Fu probably regard discussion of the weekend activities as the kind of "talk" they have in mind, but it is possible that the pre-conference conversation might spark some writing ideas. The problem is to move students beyond "talking" and into "conferring."

Accepting the reality that a certain amount of extraneous talk will occur, strategies to try to help students move beyond "talk" and focus on the conference task include the following:

1. Partners read each others' drafts silently, and write a response which they return along with the draft at the end of the conference.

2. In an oral conference, each partner writes at the end what he or she learned from the conference. Collect the "I learned" statements along with the drafts.

3. Model conferences frequently.

4. Ask students to model conferences for their peers.

In some classes, however, teachers may virtually eliminate the oral peer conference, because of the kids' inability to focus on the conference task.

Karen's student, Michael, raises some interesting points regarding conferences that only add to concerns about spending a lot of time during Writing Workshop in peer conferences. He has such a hard time finding anyone to respond to him in a helpful way that it is surprising he persisted in the effort.

Would he receive better feedback if he asked his conference partner to focus on more specific points? Probably not. He would still get the comment, "More shooting" from Mac and "Less shooting" from Meghan. He has also had the experience of having his peers completely miss the point of his story; doesn't that make him feel even less inclined to pursue peer conferences? Does he ever reach the point where he decides to confer with the teacher and skip the peer conference step in the process?

If he ever did find a good conference partner, he would continue to return to that person. What happens to the people who are not good conference partners? Do they ever have successful conferences about their own work? In other words, is there a good conference partner "out there" for each person, no matter how weak he or she may be as a conference partner to someone else?

What can teachers do to help train students to be better at peer conferences? Is it a skill that can be taught? Modeling a conference isn't enough; should teachers have specific questions that the conferee needs to respond to, and limit the conference to those questions?

Michael's final point, that conferences can turn a mediocre piece into a masterpiece, is intriguing. It reveals his belief in the value of a conference; at the same time he has certainly had his share of bad conferences. If he remains optimistic after his history with peer conferences, then teachers should continue to set aside time in their classrooms for conferences.

Is it necessary to have peer conferences remain as a part of the writing process? The answer is yes. Feedback from their peers is a powerful motivating force for teenagers and for all writers. A question a teacher would have asked a student elicits a much stronger response when posed by a classmate, and revision occurs more often in response to suggestions from classmates.

Finally, peer conferences are one more way to create the student-centered classroom. The teacher is relieved of being the dominant voice pointing out the flaws in a piece or asking the right questions, because students take on this responsibility.

Teachers need to answer the question of the relevance of peer conferences in the writing process in their own classrooms. Like all aspects of the process, the theory behind the peer conference is sound. If the actual implementation makes the teacher uncomfortable or raises the noise/frustration level to unacceptable levels, then other activities may provide acceptable alternatives. Dialogue journals or response logs kept by a conference partnership might, for example, lead to more significant feedback for certain students.

10 There Is Never Enough Time!

Donna Barnes

Donald Graves says, "Your own demonstration of literacy through writing and reading sets the tone for your students' inquiry and reflection" (16).

Lucy Calkins says, "If we keep notebooks ourselves and move from those notebooks into larger writing projects, then we can anticipate and respond to the predictable problems that will emerge" (52).

Nancie Atwell tells us, "Children need to know adults who write. We need to write, share our writing with our students, and demonstrate what experienced writers do in the process of composing, letting our students see our own drafts in all their messiness and tentativeness" (18).

Tom Romano maintains, "I must and can show my students I write. Above all, I can make sure students in every one of my classes actually see me writing a number of times" (48).

Jane Hansen says, "The writing teacher finds time to write and share with her class. This gives her credibility as a writer with her students—and with herself" (7).

Donald Graves further says, "If children are to cross that threshold and demonstrate a higher quality of literate engagement than we have seen before, teachers' literacy will have to change as well. Teachers . . . are themselves insatiable learners. By demonstrating how they learn to their children, they encourage the children to learn in the same way . . . . They listen, read, and write in order to understand the world around them—for themselves . . . . Although as teachers your professional lives are centered on the children, you first need to read, write, listen and learn for yourself" (123).

I know and I believe all of these things. I want to read and to write. I *need* to read and to write. BUT the realities of my life are always in the way. Life interferes with my desire to read and write.

BECAUSE

to do for the house:

do food shopping
pick up cleaning
walk the dogs

wash the floor
pick up Cait at 4:30
do the laundry
pay the bills
cook dinner
iron something to wear
wash the dishes
make a cake for tomorrow
run

to do for school:

correct graphs
staff meeting 7:45
conference with Barlow's—noon
finish report cards
see Principal about Nick
do budget
curriculum meeting—3:00
call guest speaker
team meeting 10:40
see Bob about Math project
put personal portfolio together
plan next unit

to do for me:

thank you note to Paula
wrap gift for Cait
read *The Giver*
write MCELA grant
reread Calkins
write this chapter
recommendation for Beth
write in notebook
read the paper
call Diane
send package to John
get a new shirt
buy card for Franko
read the mail

HELP!   HELP!   HELP!   HELP!   HELP!   HELP!   HELP!

There Is Never Enough Time!

There's no time—no time to read, no time to write, no time to clean the house, to cook a fancy meal, to run, to walk, to pay the bills, to correct papers, to plan a new curriculum, to do research, to go shopping, to plant a garden, to paint the house, to do anything fun or not so much fun. There is no time to do anything whether it is in my personal life, my professional life, or my life in school.

Do I read? Do I write? For pleasure or professionally—does it matter? I have no time, I am too busy, I am too tired. This has been my theme song for years. I used to think it was because I was a wife, mother, and teacher with all those added roles of chef, custodian, chauffeur, gardener, friend, confidant, shopper, painter, dog catcher, doctor, vet, etc. Now I know I have no corner on the market for being overwhelmed, busy, and tired. We all wear many hats; we all have numerous roles we play. Everyone needs to eat, so we're all cooks of a fashion. We all need to exercise; so we are all runners or tennis players or volleyball players or walkers. We all need to have clean clothes, houses, desks, and yards, so we are all custodians, accountants, and gardeners.

We are all teachers; therefore, we all must do research to keep up with new ideas and new publications in our field. To be credible language arts teachers, we all *must* read and write *both* in the classroom and outside the classroom. As teachers we all need to plan lessons and activities, correct papers, develop budgets, be members of schoolwide committees, meet with parents, meet with teachers, meet with administrators, and make out grade cards. Even with this list, I have probably forgotten something. What can we do? What can I do? What *do* I do?

This year I began teaching in a new multi-age pilot program. I moved from being a second-grade teacher to being an upper-elementary teacher with mixed ages of children. It is the only multi-age class in the district; it is new, it is fun, and it is time-consuming. It absorbs me. Because the multi-age is so overwhelming and because I was so busy, so tired, or so preoccupied, I forgot to go to a fiftieth birthday breakfast in my honor. It was 10:15 on Saturday morning, February 8th. I was not even dressed, but I was dusting a shelf in the kitchen on which my daughter had written "dust me." I glanced up at the wall calendar: "Saturday, February 8, BREAKFAST—8:30—UNION BLUFF." Yikes!!! I forgot my own party. At that moment in utter horror I grabbed the nearest pen and wrote:

50 Reasons I Forgot

I was tired.
I looked ugly.
My hair was too long.
There was snow on the driveway.
The Olympics were beginning.
The cat threw up.
I was worried about the class.
I needed to read USM papers.

The house was a mess.
I had nothing to wear.
I was stressed about parents.
I had no money.
I needed to shave my legs.
The car needed gas.
The dog ran away.
I had to work.
The car had 95,000 miles.
There was no heat.
The driveway was too steep.
My eyesight was failing.
The Democratic candidates were crying.
My stars were not aligned.
It was too cold.
I had bills to pay.
I had to do report cards.
I had to make out lesson plans.
I was too stressed.
The medicine was gone.
The washing machine broke.
The cellar was flooding.
The guinea pig died.
My son was on the phone.
My husband wouldn't let me.
I had to go shopping.
I was too hungry.
I was too fat.
I was too old.
I was too gray.
The tuition was due.
I had a headache.
I was nervous.
I was worried about life.
I was worried about death.
I was worried about the town.
The world was changing.
"OLDIE" was published.
Dan Quayle had my same birthday.
I was reading George Bush's lips.
Too many things to think about.
I forgot!!!!!!

Writing the poem helped assuage my guilt at the moment; it consumed me and was my first response to a panic situation. There were still, however, the people at the restaurant. I sent them all a copy of the poem as an apology. One person who received it commented, "Writing it up probably took longer than going to breakfast!" Actually, she was wrong.

It really took no time at all, I enjoyed doing it, and felt much better after I wrote it.

I wonder if we all have these feelings of being overwhelmed, of having so much to do that we spin in circles achieving nothing? When does the point come when we calm down and become sane again? We do all get renewed energy. When does it come: after a good night's sleep, after a time away from the daily routine, after an escape weekend, after a heartfelt journal entry?

I recently spent a weekend away and returned renewed and energized for a good solid amount of time. My mother always told me, "A change is as good as a rest." I think she was right; do mothers know best?

My writer's notebook (see *Living Between the Lines*, Chapters 4 and 5) has lately been a source of rejuvenation for me. When life becomes overwhelming, I write and it helps. Weeks after the forgotten birthday party, when I became rational, I was able to see solutions to my original list poem, "50 Reasons I Forgot." This response poem is called "50 Ways to Remember":

50 Reasons I Forgot	**50 Ways to Remember**
I was tired.	Go to bed earlier.
I looked ugly.	Don't look in the mirror.
My hair was too long.	Get a haircut.
There was snow on the driveway.	Shovel it.
The Olympics were beginning.	Tape the Olympics.
The cat threw up.	Get rid of the cat.
I was worried about the class.	Don't worry. Be happy.
I needed to read USM papers.	Don't assign them.
The house was a mess.	Hire a cleaning person.
I had nothing to wear.	Borrow your daughter's.
I was stressed about parents.	Go run.
I had no money.	Return some bottles.
I needed to shave my legs.	Wear pants.
The car needed gas.	Ride your bike.
The dog ran away.	Let her run loose.
I had to work.	Quit.
The car had 95,000 miles.	Buy a new car.
There was no heat.	Make a fire.
The driveway was too steep.	Make a tunnel.
My eyesight was failing.	Get glasses.

The Democratic candidates were crying.	Switch parties.
My stars were not aligned.	Read your horoscope.
It was too cold.	Put on a sweater.
I had bills to pay.	Forget them.
I had to do report cards.	Let the kids do them.
I had to make out lesson plans.	Let your partner do them.
I was too stressed.	Go to the movies.
The medicine was gone.	Take an aspirin.
The washing machine broke.	Don't do the laundry.
The cellar was flooding.	Leave the house.
The guinea pig died.	Cry.
My son was on the phone.	Let him leave a message.
My husband wouldn't let me.	Go anyway.
I had to go shopping.	Why?
I was too hungry.	Eat.
I was too fat.	Exercise.
I was too old.	Momentary insanity.
I was too gray.	Get a rinse.
The tuition was due.	Have him pay himself.
I had a headache.	Take an aspirin.
I was nervous.	Go run.
I was worried about life.	Watch the soaps.
I was worried about death.	Watch the news.
I was worried about the town.	Don't.
The world was changing.	For the better.
"OLDIE" was published.	Don't read it.
Dan Quayle had my same birthday.	So does Betty Friedan.
I was reading George Bush's lips.	Read a good book instead.
Too many things to think about.	Sing.
I forgot.	Remember.

How to keep a rational point of view will always be a goal; but as teachers, all our lives are roller coasters of busy times and calm times. There will always be times when everything feels like it is closing in and we become overwhelmed. We can't always go away for a runaway weekend when life becomes a merry-go-round—too bad. But we can grab a pen; sometimes it helps.

Simultaneously our professional life knocks at the door. As busy people there is no time to read or to write BUT as language arts teachers we must read and we must write to be credible to the students. We must read and we must write to continually feel and understand the process we ask our students to go through daily. We must read and write daily to be readers and writers. We must read and write daily in the classroom to be models for the students. Sure!

Recently, a friend of mine who is a sixth-grade language arts teacher was sharing her portfolio with me. She made it during the year as her class made their own portfolios. I was struck by how little personal writing she had included. At the very moment that I was pondering this and fumbling for some diplomatic words to express my concern, she blurted out, "I have no time in my life to write. So I write poems." I do too! I write list poems like the birthday one. Poetry is my genre these days. There is an economy of language that fits into my economy of time.

"Why Can't I Write?", a poem that was published in the April 1991 *Language Arts*, was written partly in school. It was written during our language arts block in a moment of frustration. It is not a list poem—or maybe it is. As my school secretary says, "It's short and jumpy and full of short sentences." Of course, she would write it differently, but it fit well into my state of being harried most of the time.

Why Can't I Write?

Why can't I write?
Because   Mrs. Barnes, can I start over? I messed
                            up, and I can't erase the whole thing.

Why can't I write?
Because   Mrs. Barnes, can I read this to you?
                            Mrs. Barnes, do I throw this in the garbage
                            when I'm done?
                            Mrs. Barnes, what is this word?
                            Mrs. Barnes, I don't want to write about
                            Texas anymore. I want to write about my
                            grammy and grampy and my aunt and my
                            cousins,
                            and I want to call it "Unexpected Guests."
                            Is that okay? and
                            Mrs. Barnes, can I read this to someone else?
Why can't I write?

Why can't I write?
Because   Mom, what's for supper? I'm starving!
Why can't I write?
Because   Mom, is my jeans skirt clean? I need it
                            NOW.

Mom, I've got softball practice at 5:00.
Will you drive me? and
Mom, Ben doesn't love me anymore, and I'm
just going to die.
Mom, I made the play, and I'm on my way to
Broadway, and
Mom, when are you going to wash this floor?
My feet are sticking.
Mom, I need a book for English tomorrow.
What should I read?

Why can't I write?

Why can't I write?
Because

Honey, are you going to walk the dog today?
I've got a meeting.

Why can't I write?
Because

Put deodorant on the list for the next time
you go shopping, okay?
Honey, have you seen my gray slacks? I can't
find them anywhere.
Do you have any white buttons for my blue
shirt? Two of them just disintegrated.
Where did you put *U.S. News*?
Honey, did you call the plumber yet? The
basement is still flooding.
Honey, we have to go to the Johnson's on
Sunday. I know you don't want to; but we,
yes WE, have to go.

Why can't I write?

Why can't I write?
Because

I have to answer the phone.
"Hello."

Why can't I write?
Because

Mom, I just got a bill from the financial
aid office. My loan was reduced, and YOU
owe the college $2,000 more!
Mom, my stereo broke. What should I do?
I'm hungry.
I got a B in Economics.
Can I come home for the weekend?
Will you pick me up? Don't come before 6:00.
I have to write a paper.

But, why can't I write?????

Bill Teale commented in the introduction of *Language Arts* (272)
that the poem "provides an insightful analysis of the problems classroom
teachers run into in attempting to take on the role of writer in addition to
all the other tasks in their lives." I ask myself, don't teachers who teach

writing HAVE to be writers? How can you teach—and I hate that term, *teach*; I don't teach; I help children learn—so how can I help children learn to write unless I know how to write? How can I know how to write without writing? I would not dream of coaching someone in tennis unless I knew how to play tennis and, I might add, play tennis well. The same goes for writing. I cannot hope to guide children in writing without being a writer.

Sometimes I feel I write best when I am most harried. Isn't that a contradiction? My principal left me a note after she saw "Why Can't I Write?" in *Language Arts* asking, "Did you REALLY write this in school?" Yes, I really did begin it in school, but I finished it at home, or rather away from school.

I have no place where I can write. I want a studio, a room (as Virginia Woolf would say) to call my own. I have no place where I can be alone for long, sustained periods of time. At home, the minute I sit, the very minute, someone comes and talks to me. It's probably because I seldom sit. Can you listen and write at the same time? I can't. If I read the paper, people talk to me. Then they wonder why I don't know what I read. Can you listen and read at the same time? I can't. If I sit and watch television, someone asks me if I am sick. The only place I am ever alone is in my car driving back and forth to school.

Naturally, I finished "Why Can't I Write?" while driving back and forth to school. I have a notebook sitting on the passenger seat of the car. I'm not sure that is the solution to finding the time and place to write. For me there are no solutions but rather evolutions—changes. With time, with families growing up, with myself growing older and perhaps wiser, with continued questioning of why I do what I do, I can change things.

At this point I can safely say I am writing more but not enough:

Why Am I Writing More?

Why am I writing more?
Because . . .

I want to.
I like to.
I need to make the time to be legitimate as a Language Arts teacher.

Why am I writing more?
Because

Things have changed.
Mrs. Barnes is not the only one in charge.
Mrs. Barnes, I know what to do.
Mrs. Barnes, I know we are all teachers here.
Mrs. Barnes, I know who can help me.

Mrs. Barnes, I know I need to reread
everything I write.
Mrs. Barnes, I know where and with whom I
can read.

Why am I writing more?

Why am I writing more?
Because . . .   Mom, I've grown older and more mature.
Why am I writing more?
Because   Mom, I know my shirt is in the laundry and
I don't want it ironed.
I have my license now and I can drive
myself.
But, may I have the car?
Mom, boyfriends are old-fashioned.
Mom, I can wash the floor myself.
I'm in high school now and all my books are
assigned and that's sad!

Why am I writing more?

Why am I writing more?
Because . . .   We both saw "Thelma and Louise" and
learned
from it.

Why am I writing more?
Because   The dog runs herself.
Honey, I'll do the shopping sometimes, or
at least make the list.
Honey, I know you don't sew and I do.
U.S. News goes to the first person who gets
home and it's neither of us.
The plumber comes on a regular basis.
Honey, I won't tell you to go to the
Johnson's
I'll ask you.

Why am I writing more?

Why am I writing more?
Because . . .   Mom, I'm not a first year student anymore.
Why am I writing more?
Because   Mom, college is great!
Mom, I'd rather be in Cambridge than at
home.
Mom, I went to a U2 concert.
Mom, I have a major field of concentration.
I still write papers.
I'm still hungry all the time.
But, I don't want to come home for the
weekend.
And I have a summer job. HERE!!!

So, now I can write more!!!!!

It's not enough writing, because I go for long stretches without writing anything, but when I can and do write on a daily basis, I feel great! "Why Am I Writing More?" also shows me that something else has happened. I have stepped out of the "take charge" mode. I moved away from "I am the boss" or "I am in charge of everyone's health and welfare" and into a we, us, together mode. I have changed as well as circumstances have changed. Some changes come with age and time; some come from colleagues and reading.

Ah-ha, reading—I need to read for pleasure, for myself. I need to read for school. I need to read all those young adult novels that I never read when I took Children's Literature or that have been published since I took the course. I need to read all the new literature about reading and writing and thinking. I need to find the time, or rather take the time, to read Linda Rief's new book or Nancie Atwell's new book, or the new literature on portfolios.

I don't take the time or make the time often enough. Yet when I do force myself to read, it opens my eyes to new possibilities. I read *Living Between the Lines* and could not put it down. It inspired me to read *Girl from Yamhill* and *Little by Little* and *Hey, World Here I Am*. *Living Between the Lines* made me STOP. It made me rethink everything I was and am doing. It helped me to ask my students to also stop their harried, busy ways and reflect.

My school life parallels my personal life and my professional life, and I suspect it is the same with many teachers. Just as there is no time in my life to read, write, cook, clean, etc.; there is no time in school where there are sustained, uninterrupted periods of time. Donald Graves referred to it as the "cha-cha-cha curriculum" (Summer Institute, UNH, 1988). I call it the "blippy school day in a Nintendo lifestyle."

Sarah recently wrote to me in her Reading Journal and said,

> Dear Mrs. Barnes,
> Hi, how are you? I'm fine. I'm reading *A Blossom Promise*. It's by Betsy Byars. I'm on page 60 because I haven't gotten to read much for the past week. So I'm not any farther than before . . . .

I was horrified; we read every day! Why hasn't Sarah "gotten to read much for the past week?" I asked her to explain more. She wrote:

> When I sit down to write, I can't just write. It takes me awhile to get started. We also get lots of interruptions, which makes it harder to read and write. We only have 35 minutes to write and if you think of it, that's not much. And only 35 minutes to read too. I think one day have writing for an hour and ten minutes and then reading for an hour and ten minutes. I also like the idea of reading

conference one week and writing conference and letter the next week and so on. Also, maybe a shorter circle time because it takes us awhile to get into writing. Also there is too much going on so I can't think.

—Sarah

Maybe Sarah is right. Maybe too much is going on; maybe there are too many interruptions. Maybe thirty-five minutes is not enough time to really get into writing or reading. I began to think seriously about why there is no time to read and write in school. I always think better if I write about it, so in school during writing time I began to list why there is not time to read and write. Aaron, Justin, and Tracy helped complete the list during a writing conference:

50 Reasons Why There Is No Time to Read and Write in School

The room is too hot.
The room is too cold.
The room is too crowded.
The room is too messy.
The room is too loud.
The room is too quiet.
The P.A. system is calling for Josh.
The Geography Bee is Friday.
The Spelling Bee is Wednesday.
The Power Company will hold a special program.
Circle time goes over.
There is a special sex ed program.
Barbara Bloom is speaking on editing.
The P.A. system is calling for Mary.
The Principal has an important message.
The guinea pig died.
Staci's dog died.
Melissa is moving.
The calendar says Monday but it will be Wednesday's schedule.
Assessment tests will be all week.
The NAEP Test is all day Friday.
There will be an I.Q. test on Thursday.
Brent is whining.
The filmstrip projector broke.
Aaron broke the ruler.
There is too much work.
Flute or clarinet or sax will have a lesson.
Chorus will hold a special meeting.
Friendship group is meeting.
Playground beautification is meeting.
There is no paper.
It's Valentine's Day.
The P.A. system is calling Audrey.

No one is on task.
We have to go to the bathroom but we are in a trailer.
The newspaper just came out.
The book order arrived.
Eben's feelings were hurt.
Kristin is crying.
Charlie threw up.
There is a message from Mr. G. Math group needs to meet in the morning.
The mapping group needs an all day work session.
Darcey lost her lunch ticket.
The computer won't print.
A bird flew in the window.
The pencil sharpener fell off the wall.
Art and gym never end.
Ryan is absent and needs work.
There is no heat in the school.

The scary thing about this is that it is true. Some of these things like "room too hot, cold, or messy" can be changed, but some are beyond our control, such as an ongoing sex ed program, assessment tests, and schoolwide programs. There is the dilemma, the struggle, to find long periods of uninterrupted time. Uninterrupted time is essential for reading process and writing process to occur in any meaningful way, as Sarah explained earlier. It is an ongoing problem in public schools today.

I keep changing the daily schedule, looking for the stretches of time. It is like continually moving the furniture in a room, searching for the best way to make the room feel bigger. Here the search is for the best daily schedule. Tracy said, "Maybe if the day was a little bit longer we'd have more time. We don't have time to read and write because we have too much to do in one day like Math, Thematic Unit, and our Specials." How do we get more time?

There's a new schedule on Monday. It will be the third one this year. I think it will work—Language Arts will be two hours long, 1:00–3:00.

This year I have learned how to enlist the students' help. I just asked them to make a Learning Log entry—to write about why there is no time in school and what we could do about it. I now know that students have powerful insights. I also realize if the students grapple with the problem—if they understand the problem—then they can also explore solutions. When they invest their time and their energy, they are committed to a successful solution. Often all our heads together are better than just one head.

Another significant help for me in dealing with my "blippy" school day is discovering a couple of colleagues, co-workers, who believe as I do. I have two teachers with whom I can talk, who know what I mean and don't think that I'm crazy.

In fact, the three of us have formed a support group. We meet each Wednesday morning at 7:30 for breakfast and sharing. One week we share writing that we have in progress. The following week we share a book together. Currently, we are reading *After THE END: Teaching and Learning Creative Revision* by Barry Lane. Earlier this year we read Shelley Harwayne's *Lasting Impressions*.

Of course, getting to school at 7:30 a.m. is a royal pain for me. First of all, I am not a morning person, so I hate to scurry around in the early morning. Second, to get to school by 7:30, I need to leave the house by 7:00. That means before I leave I need to feed the dogs, put them out, feed the cats, make my lunch, put the trash out (wouldn't you know that Wednesday is trash day), put the recycling bin out, take a shower, dress, move cars around, and on and on. That means I ought to get up at 5:00 a.m., but I don't.

The 7:30 meeting is well worth the hassle. After meeting and sharing and talking and exploring ideas for reading or writing for myself or for my students, I am energized. My battery is charged and I am ready.

Years ago in a telephone conversation, Jane Hansen told me that a person cannot work in a vacuum. I was pleading to be accepted into the University of New Hampshire Summer Institute. Jane said that it is best to have another teacher or an administrator attend the institute with you. I argued with her, begged, pleaded, and was accepted. But I now know she was absolutely right. When the PA system interrupts for the seventeenth time of the day, it is far easier to explore solutions with a friend.

This has been a story about the need to read and write personally and professionally at home and at school on a daily basis. For teachers who play any number of roles in their busy lives it is often difficult to follow the advice of the leaders in the field. We all—teachers and students—need to slow down and get our priorities straight.

I just hired a cleaning woman for one day a week. It has taken me close to twenty years to say no to dusting and vacuuming, but I did it. I just finished reading my fifth book this week, *Nothing but the Truth* by Avi. It feels good and I need to do more!

I am learning how to say no to the world and yes to myself. I am learning to do this at home as well as at school. I have moved from I to we and can trust both at home and at school that together we can achieve much more than anyone alone ever will. And I've done it by writing and by reading—but not enough!

Works Cited

Atwell, Nancie. *In the Middle*. Portsmouth, NH: Heinemann, 1987.

Barnes, Donna d'E. "Why Can't I Write?" *Language Arts* 68 (1991): 301–02.

Calkins, Lucy M. *Living Between the Lines*. Portsmouth, NH: Heinemann, 1991.

Cleary, Beverly. *A Girl from Yamhill*. New York: Morrow, 1988.

Graves, Donald. *Discover Your Own Literacy*. Portsmouth, NH: Heinemann, 1990.

Hansen, Jane. *When Writers Read*. Portsmouth, NH: Heinemann, 1987.

Harwayne, Shelley. *Lasting Impressions*. Portsmouth, NH: Heinemann, 1992.

Lane, Barry. *After THE END: Teaching and Learning Creative Revision*. Portsmouth, NH: Heinemann, 1993.

Little, Jean. *Little by Little: A Writer's Education*. New York: Viking, 1987.

———. *Hey World, Here I Am!* New York: Harper, 1986.

MacLachlan, Patricia. *Baby*. New York: Delacorte Press, 1993.

Romano, Tom. *Clearing the Way: Working with Teenage Writers*. Portsmouth, NH: Heinemann, 1987.

Response
Karen Weinhold

The frenetic pace of this piece leaves me breathless. Even though teachers do almost all the same things as Donna, they never list them that way, and I may even be too tired now from the sheer volume of activities in which we all engage daily to even write this response! How can teachers profess to believe that in order to improve writing it is necessary to write when they rarely (as in almost *never*) write during the school year? This is one of the things the three editors have never shared at our writing support group meetings, and I am already experiencing a sense of relief merely from confessing.

Donna's epiphany that the shift to a more collaborative functioning freed up some time for her own writing can give all teachers hope. In many aspects of the curricula teachers have given up producing recipes and turned much of the decision making over to the students. Metacognition heightens dramatically when choice and reflection are encouraged.

So why can't teachers realize that this shifting of focus and control might work for writing time as well? There seem to be certain things that our profession just doesn't readily grasp. Should Donna worry about having an accident while she's attending to her writer's notebook on the passenger seat? Should she try using a tape recorder?

Only at the onset of each new piece in the classroom, after topic searching has been resolved, do I actually get some sustained writing time for myself.

I have begun some of my favorite pieces this way—too bad I've never finished any of them. Perhaps I should write a list poem of titles and leads.

Thank you, Donna, for candidly sharing the inability to find the time to write. Somehow it helps to know that all teachers are not alone. However, they need constant reinforcement to practice the classroom modeling that they all tout so loudly. We all need a "clean, well-lighted place" (quiet would be nice too!), but it's time to face the reality that teachers will never write again if they wait to find one.

11 A Touch of Madness: Keeping Faith as Workshoppers

Bill Boerst
Jamestown High School
Jamestown, New York

In the apparent chaos of a busy school schedule, workshopping teachers must sometimes stagger weakly down the hall marveling at the neat rows, the steady drone of authoritative teachers' voices steadily filling vessels, the well-oiled clockwork of a traditional school day. They envy. They wish. They doubt. I do.

Which is as it should be. In spite of their feistiness, teachers who use workshop approaches don't have all the answers. Never did. Never will. But just so we don't lose the drive of commitment, it might pay to do something therapeutic at the end of each year by looking at what has happened in our classes.

I use Nancie Atwell's *In the Middle* as my model. Three consecutive days each week we have writing workshop in the forty-two-minute periods; during the other two days we have reading workshop. On a given writing workshop day, we follow a routine of mini-lesson followed by time to write and confer (53–148). I provide students ownership (choice of mode or genre and topic), time (approximately thirty minutes of each slot in the three days devoted to individual writing), and opportunities for response (conferring, authors' days, outlets for going public).

Some colleagues may find fault with allowing students self-determination by carefully structuring an environment which gives them room to explore. But how valuable is coercion? At best, it creates a clone or a puppet, a teacher-pleaser. This phenomenon has little to do with learning; it has more to do with vessel-filling, a philosophy of education which contains far too many flaws for this seasoned instructor (Cayley 7–9). At worst, coercion creates the opposite of a teacher-pleaser—a rebel, one who learns to seek failure as reward. This phenomenon threatens to disrupt our school systems. When we debate coercion vs. non-coercion, we must consider this truism: people usually learn (i.e., internalize) what they want to learn; they rarely learn what they don't want.

A Good Year

Anne began with a prose piece that looked ahead to college after high school graduation. Then she collaborated on an allegedly true "bigfoot adventure" with a storyteller friend. One of her outstandingly candid works was a personal narrative about her night in jail. She had it published in our classroom literary magazine under a pen name. Her short story "My Lost Friend" was a tale of teenage suicide. Then she wrote a love poem followed by an essay describing what it was like to be living in her boyfriend's parents' home. Her last four pieces were all poems. One was a moving tribute to her absent father. The others were heartrending accounts of a breakup with her boyfriend. Anne was learning to use writing as a reflection of her life and a reflection on it. Without the consistency of writing three days a week, her rich tapestry of work would not have been created.

After one attempt at a broad personal essay and unsuccessful forays into short-story writing, Karl became a poet during the rest of the year. He began with long, rambling fantasy pieces but gradually trimmed down to more regular stanzaic organization. Here is his account of how he developed his poem "Life Reeks of Pond Scum":

> I had my typewriter in my lap as I sat on the floor of my room. I was trying to come up with some off-the-wall idea for a poem when my cat began his shrills. As I looked at him, I began to think of all the things in this world that stink.
>
> I just began typing about them, not knowing where they would lead. I included such things as pollution, parents, and personal hygiene. Some I exaggerated like "I hate my parents" and "My face has broken out." I typed and typed, not even thinking about what I was doing. It was just fun whether it came out right or not.
>
> In the end, ironically, I never included so much as a syllable about my cat. I finally read the finished product, laughed, glanced at the clock (which was 4:30 a.m.) and again glanced at my cat. Again, I thought of how much I hated him, and how life sucked, and just thought of the scum in the bottom of a pond. I didn't know why. Finally after 20 minutes of brainstraining, I entitled my work "Life Reeks of Pond Scum."

Karl found his writing roots by having the freedom to experiment. He wrote because he had time and space for writing. At year's end he was attempting a chapter book which he intended to continue during the summer.

Unlike Karl, who appeared unencumbered by language limitations, Eric had major problems with mechanics and usage, particularly spelling. My goal was not to have him improve these areas so much as to have him surmount his obstacles and write regardless. All the drillwork in the world would make little difference in his language control, but his experience with language might change his outlook. The editing aspect of workshops, with its emphasis on small, manageable areas of improvement, helped make his struggle possible. Initially he was taciturn and rebellious. His attitude announced, "I can't write, so I won't." But he wrote. He began with an account of a trip he had found boring. Then he seemed to pursue himself through a series of fantasies. He made up his own obituary for the year 2001, followed by his own wedding announcement for the year 1999. Meanwhile he was collaborating on a survey and attempting his first experiment in poetry. A highlight of his year was an acrostic cluster, in which he attempted to create a poem for each individual in his English class. While he didn't finish this project, the poems he completed were witty and accurate portrayals. Moreover, Eric's mini-lesson for his own class, as well as another, resulted in a fellow student's pursuing the same goal. In his mini-lesson Eric explained to classmates his acrostic cluster, really a genre he had created. He used the overhead to illustrate, showing some of the poems. Eric rounded out the year with a comedic monologue about flying in a plane. He left my class seeing himself as a writer despite certain language deficiencies.

I could go on. I could talk about Brenda, who wrote consistently high-quality material centered around her own life. I could mention Jason, who finally realized in the last marking period that he had something to offer the world of reading and writing. I could praise Nea, who, after failing one marking period, had a poem published in the international magazine *Skipping Stones*. I could cite Client, who kept writing through a drug rehabilitation and three subsequent hospital stays for emotional problems. In fact, he went public with one of his pieces at a local poetry reading. These successes occurred not because I am a super teacher, but simply because I structured the learning atmosphere to promote love of relevant reading and writing experiences. In other words, I provided ownership, time, and opportunities for response.

Without workshops, how much of what I recounted above could have been realized? During the year I was frustrated at not being able to predict such progress from apparent chaos. Instead, I had to feel my way along, trusting in the experience. I recalled Anterrabae, the imaginary friend in Hannah Green's *I Never Promised You a Rose Garden,* admonishing Deborah about the sane life, "That rind is cracking your teeth—

why not spit it out at last?" She replied, "I can't stop chewing now, even if I don't seem to be getting anything much" (242). Some days I would be elated by the growth in a particular writer; at other times I would wonder whether I was helping or hindering development.

On the Edge

For an endeavor so rooted in the empirical craft of writing (we prefer hands-on to hands-off), it is interesting that workshopping can carry overtones of evangelism. When I am discussing process approaches with a colleague or student, part of me sometimes pulls away and observes. It has a good laugh at the rise and fall of my indefatigable voice, its crusty, enthusiastic edge, frantic gestures clawing air. While at these times I am no Elmer Gantry, no Father Tom of Michael Dorris's *A Yellow Raft in Blue Water*, I nevertheless "doth protest too much." I watch myself assuming the role of defensive justifier once again. ("Why can't you just enjoy life?" my wife often asks, forgetting I already am.)

Part of this edge comes from doing battle in department meetings to defend alternative teaching styles. Part of it is lodged in the uncertainty of being different and an accompanying need to rehearse (not unlike the rehearsal part of writing). But a major component must be the simple desire to share good news. (You too can be saved, Brother.) It's just plain old-fashioned enthusiasm. What's wrong with it, unless we notice people driven back a step or two or tiptoeing by our doors or taking the other hall? I rarely see such sparks over gerunds or direct objects. (Although I somehow vaguely remember getting fired up about those, too. Maybe I *am* mad.)

Life on the edge is precarious, but it helps to know that the strange is not so strange. Consider this advice from Zorba the Greek: "You have everything but one thing—madness. A man needs a little madness or else—he never dares" (quoted in John-Roger and McWilliams 457). George Sheehan once said, "If you want to win anything—a race, yourself, your life—you have to go a little berserk" (426). Cynthia Heimel echoed that observation: "When in doubt, make a fool of yourself. There is a . . . thin line between being creative and acting like the most gigantic idiot on earth" (372). That dash of madness might be just what we need to prevail.

What, after all, is normal? Normal is everything the same. It is everyone doing the same thing probably in the same way, possibly at the same time. Who decides normal? A school faculty. We should examine what happens when change visits normal. Boundaries move. Rules are altered, and people who tend to play by rules become uncomfortable. Their only recourse is to force a return to rules, which they interpret as maintaining standards. Thus, you get remarks like "Some people are not using the prescribed spelling lists" or "Some people have been changing the departmental final exam." One classic statement I will never forget was "You wouldn't buy a coat if it didn't have straight seams, would you?" (as if one learned straight seams by not having crooked ones). Instead of a classroom reflecting the force of a leader's personality (or better yet the force of twenty-two students' personalities), you get cloning. I prefer to call it droning. Or drowning.

Change in school is not simple. As an institution, the school exists to preserve ritual. If that ritual is worth preserving, there is no problem. Then you have a celebration of what exists—a mutual pat on the back. But what if change seems advisable?

One of the most cumbersome machines to move is a public institution. Maybe that is because even the words—PUBLIC INSTITUTION—are awe-inspiring, so that what we think we have hold of is something like the Pledge of Allegiance or the Gettysburg Address, when in fact we are dealing with an age-old means of self-preservation.

Having sat in many, many faculty meetings, I can state that their main purpose is usually to keep things as they have been or to justify their existence. The most respected individuals, those with the most seniority and therefore authority, are those that over the years have either blended in with the system or changed it to suit their own natures. The reasoning goes like this: we've spent considerable time developing *our* pattern; why abandon it now? Research findings matter little. There is a monolith to maintain.

Confronted with PUBLIC INSTITUTION, what can the beleaguered teacher do to create space enough for meaningful change? I would suggest procedures I have used or seen used successfully. The first is negotiation. When you need room to fly, approach the teachers most directly affected by your proposal. Call it a pilot project if you wish. But get clearance for two years in which to try an alternative. These days, when public education is being called sharply to task, teacher groups are increasingly willing to allow flirtation with alternatives.

When the two years are up and accountability rears its head, go back to those meetings loaded with research data—both your own action projects and data from established literature. If possible, take with you two or three friends from a support group as backup. Given more than one carcass, scavengers become less certain. If matters get testy, it would be sensible to ask for the other side's data; otherwise keep the tone polite. I have been amazed at how school veterans are quick to demand research findings on the new but rarely apply the same measuring devices to the old.

A New Wave

The struggle might not remain quiet. As with those supersonic deer alerts on cars, the nonroar may be crystal clear to a target audience. What happens when the schools and the real world outside schools clash? In his book *The Broken Cord*, Michael Dorris describes a conflict between academia and the world outside. In schools, "there is no enduring place for the frantic, the desperate, the hysterical." Students learn "to be wary, to withhold their fervor." What results is schools preoccupied with trivia at the expense of important considerations (139–41). Researchers Britton and Applebee have documented that this is the problem at the root of language misteaching in public schools (Fulwiler 6–7, 48–52).

Our dilemma may be like that of the Lakota Sioux Indians, who go beyond tolerating alcohol abuse in the tribe, even pressuring tribe members to drink. One who chooses not to drink is ostracized. Abstinence is equated to being a white person (Medicine 133–58). One could picture a member of a particular school or department who for reasons of conscience decides not to follow the majority, only to find he has lost the support and indeed the companionship of his colleagues. This is what now happens in many public schools.

What can be done to get schools more involved, more expressive, more at the cutting edge? According to Brazilian educator Paulo Freire, individual autonomy must be achieved through cognitive breakthroughs via language (Fulwiler 7–8). But liberation is threatening. Once we have unleashed individual autonomy, there is no going back. We will be riding a new wave, one long advocated by Frank Smith.

A New Order

When Nancie Atwell advocated ownership, time, and response in reading/writing, she upset the status quo. Taken generally, these tools seem noble. Specifically applied, they empower students with language, and not just with language facility, but with language itself. They imply that an individual can grapple with the power of language and grow from that encounter. There may or may not be an intermediary; but there will be growth and self-realization.

I vividly recall one student who was learning writing through workshop procedures. Doing what he had learned, he wrote a highly critical letter to a local school board concerning his particular confrontation with a principal. The letter was organized and well-supported as well as caustic. Because of his letter, this student received further discipline. For what it was worth, I made certain I complimented him on his risk-taking and writing craftsmanship. I have often wished I could have done more to support him. Here was a case in point—a clash between empowerment and ritual.

We are not talking about steady-as-she-goes growth here. We are talking about idiosyncratic leaps: the eureka factor. We are talking about empowerment. With empowerment, the hierarchy builds from the bottom up, not the other way around. Teachers who are used to passing morsels out in a timed sequence will have to do some serious rethinking.

Let us look more specifically at each of the Atwell requisites. First, ownership. The concept here is that a student must shape her destiny in the classroom. For a teacher to shape it is ludicrous because real readers and writers do not tolerate tyranny. If we want our students to become true readers and writers, we shape the classroom experience to offer genuine choice. But then what happens to the power of the teacher, or of the teaching establishment? It must be compromised to give students opportunities for growth. The teacher is now a cooperative learner and an exemplary model as well as a leader. Also a patient observer.

In addition to owning their goals and activities, Atwell says students should have time to shape and develop their destinies. If reading and writing are important, then these activities should be carried out during class time as well as outside school. Here is where process supersedes product: how we do it matters more than what we do. The underlying assumption is that each learner is capable of using her time and analyzing that time use. Once again, the learner has control. Teachers may encourage, model, and nudge; the learner shapes destiny. For many of us teachers, rooted in manipulation techniques, such autonomy appears to fly in the face of order. That is only because one ritual is being replaced by another less neatly packaged.

The last—and perhaps most misinterpreted—tenet is opportunity for response. Learners must be free to seek response to their concerns, not in terms of letter or number grades so much as constructive opinions. Response is gained through various types of mini-lessons, conferences, displays, printed publications, group shares, authors' days, learning journals, book spotlights, and arts performances. Whether the audience is one or twenty-seven matters less than that there is at least one sympathetic ear or eye. Audience is a genuine consideration for real readers and writers. What perhaps threatens us teachers most is the possibility that readers and writers will seek audiences beyond our reach. Yet that is the very behavior we should applaud, for bouncing work off others is the way language users develop. Not everything can be measured by the teacher; not everything needs to be measured.

Threat to the establishment? Most certainly. Channels of communication open up, and the keys are thrown away. Yet the procedure is not chaotic. Messy, maybe, but not without an order of its own. It is structure for freedom. It is Freire's cognitive breakthrough via language.

Then There Are Others

I cannot lie. We have failures in workshops. At the end of the year, Jerry still had no completed works in his permanent writing folder. Four days before the end of school, the principal, at wits' end over his constant insubordination, expelled him because he threw French fries in the cafeteria. Jose, on his second tour through English 9, managed to get one piece into final form. More a talker than a writer, he even failed during the year to use a breakthrough technique I offered called scribing. The one piece he completed was an interesting cross between a memoir of another person and an autobiographical incident. His setting was a white-water raft excursion. Jose went to the final exam teetering between pass and fail. Once again his fate in English would be a big question mark. Mark, also on a second tour, was quite similar to Jose. (They were inseparable friends.) A talker, not a writer, he defied my every attempt to get him rolling. Yet he was popular among his peers, with an endless supply of amusing observations and anecdotes to perform.

The Need to Fail

Some failure must be built into the system. As Donald Murray says, "Literature is the distillate of enormous failure" (106). William Faulkner describes this type of failure as a road to success: "Get it down. Take chances. It may be bad, but it's the only way you can do anything really good" (quoted in Murray 235). Marian Mohr is more blunt: "Think of garbage as compost" (1).

Danielle was a teacher-pleaser who tried diligently all year to write. She began with no concept of how to arrive at her own topics. Once she had learned some search methods, she plugged away at her one chosen genre, poetry. During the entire year she had trouble moving beyond obvious themes and forms. But she continued trying because she had the room to try. I suppose I could have looked at her lack of growth between

> You come to my room at night
> when the moon is shining bright.
> You tell me to be very quiet
> and not turn on a light.
> (December)

and

> The reasons we broke up
> are very plain to see.
> Whenever we had a fight,
> I blamed you and you blamed me.
> (June)

as failure. Instead, I decided that this was Danielle at a certain stage in her writing life. In spite of my conferences and mini-lessons, she had experienced a year of triteness without breaking away. The hope remained that next year would be different. There was no need to judge. Chatting with her two years later, I learned that Danielle still cherished our writing experiences and wished she could have them again.

Kay progressed all year until she reached the last marking period. Then, as she admitted in a dialog-journal letter, she fell apart as a reader and writer:

> I'm sorry I haven't been on the ball lately, but I have a severe case of senioritis.

Her writing in the last marking period supported that confession. It consisted mainly of hastily assembled acrostic poems. Of her three stated goals (to go public, to try different kinds of poems, to try writing another children's book), she barely attempted any one. Yet viewed against three other productive marking periods, this lapse did not seem momentous. Kay was failing within the confines of growth. She was living proof that writing is idiosyncratic.

Cory was similar to Kay except that what stopped him was the discovery of a book centered on his problem of stuttering. Once he focused on this book, his other reading and writing went to the back burner. I viewed this apparent failure as a success: he was merging his life concerns with his reading/writing concerns. He stated it this way in a dialog-journal letter:

> I have had a hard time fourth marking period putting my work into final form. I just haven't been motivated fully. Which is really no excuse . . . . I have found a book that really interests me. That's why I have had such a hard time finding a book until now. Because I really don't like reading books that don't interest me . . . .

> I have really enjoyed writing in my dialog journal. That's been a real uplift on days when I'm down. I use it to talk about more than the book I'm reading. Or use it to talk about something that's on my mind. I don't know if that's okay or not. But it's been nice.

When a system builds in room for a certain amount of failure (I call this failure without failing), it will encourage risk taking, which can lead to individual growth. Walter Pater calls this using disgust to build perfection.

Doing What We Say

Perhaps the ultimate sign that things are okay is what happens in our own writing. I like to tell my teacher interns, "If you ask students to do something, you must be willing to try it too." That advice is good for me as well. My poem "Note from Underdog," an attempt to capture the polar extremes of teenage ideals and withdrawal, was struggling toward realization from some hasty notes I had scribbled last summer. In the fall I conferred with two students about it because I had doubts about dialect forms I was using. Emboldened, I read it to my writers' group. Out of that came a decision to change plural *parents* to the singular *parent* as more in keeping with the changing nature of the family in these times. Then I submitted it to an Illinois literary journal.

Another poem, "Geriatric Studies," based on increasing forgetfulness my wife and I notice in our parents, seemed stopped because I couldn't decide which of two forms was preferable. I bounced both versions off my writers' group because it had been their suggestions that prompted the two versions. At last I chose one that seemed better and sent it on to *Mature Years* magazine. The rejection from its editors explained that I had exceeded the sixteen-line limit. A new decision now was whether to cut lines or search for another market.

In my much more philosophical poem, almost a broad personal essay, "Existential Knowledge," I feared to let loose because I didn't want to face ridicule. I still have not shared it with the writers' group, but I sent a copy to one member asking whether she thought it was really a poem. At this writing I am waiting to hear from her. I want to know the truth at the same time that I dread learning it. This testimony reminds me that I am a writer, yet so many barriers shake the conviction. As I begin to revise a certain line, the dog must be let out or the car's oil changed. Students' important needs crowd out my best intentions.

About the time I feel burned out, as if nothing will ever again flow from pen to paper, I wake up at 3:30 a.m., the nearly complete text of this article bloating my brain and burning my fingertips. So I go downstairs to call myself a writer once again. Madness is back, and I welcome it like an old friend.

Works Cited

Atwell, Nancie. *In the Middle: Writing, Reading, and Learning with Adolescents*. Portsmouth, NH: Boynton/Cook, 1987.

Cayley, David. *Ivan Illich in Conversation*. Concord, Ontario: Anansi, 1992.

Dorris, Michael. *The Broken Cord*. New York: HarperCollins, 1989.

Fulwiler, Toby. *Teaching with Writing*. Upper Montclair, NJ: Boynton/Cook, 1987.

Green, Hannah. *I Never Promised You a Rose Garden*. New York: NAL, 1964.

John-Roger, and Peter McWilliams. *Do It!: Let's Get Off Our Butts*. Los Angeles: Prelude Press, 1991.

Medicine, Beatrice A. "An Ethnography of Drinking and Sobriety among the Lakota Sioux." Diss. University of Wisconsin-Madison, 1983.

Mohr, Marian M. *Revision: The Rhythm of Meaning*. Upper Montclair, NJ: Boynton/Cook, 1984.

Murray, Donald. *A Writer Teaches Writing: A Practical Method of Teaching Composition*. 2nd ed. Boston: Houghton, 1985.

Smith, Frank. *Insult to Intelligence*. Portsmouth, NH: Heinemann, 1988.

———. *Joining the Literacy Club*. Portsmouth, NH: Heinemann, 1988.

Response
Karen Weinhold

Over a three-week period during the summer, teachers are reborn as writing-process teachers on the UNH campus in Durham, New Hampshire. School districts pay for their conversion, and the university grants graduate credits and sends them back to their classrooms. Although teachers bond with similar zealots at the university, they are alone in their classrooms and in their buildings when the bell opens school in September. Their faith may last two days; then the ground beneath their feet shifts and reverberates from their trembling.

Teachers are terrified of failure. For fifteen years I had taught "English," traditionally and rigorously. My reputation balanced on words like "strict," "fair," "thorough," "hard-working," and "funny." Why was I throwing it all away? First I closed my doors, then my windows. I sat on my rank book because it contained no grades, only coded symbols of drafting progress and problems. The students were befuddled by the activities because most of the writing took place in the class, and doing more than a rough and final draft was novel. Whenever anyone came to observe, I simply created an instant writing lesson in which *everyone* participated. This so intimidated the observer that none ever returned for a second dose, and each wrote glowing reports of the industry of the adolescents. My terror remained unabated.

I began to dabble. Moments of panic brought on grammar drills. By March I was a total wreck, swinging recklessly between tradition and process, my writing program in chaos, my professional self-esteem disintegrating daily. I had no one to talk to, to share my worries and concerns with, to explore failure with.

Reading Bill's piece brought all those awful feelings of doubt, instability, and inadequacy crashing back; perhaps they've been niggling just below the surface all along! The difference is, he's brought them out in the open, thrown them on the table in the sunlight for observation and assessment. Can teachers truly evaluate aspects of their failures? Are teachers secure enough now with this concept of process to examine candidly its strengths and weaknesses and *not* blame these problems on their inability to implement the orthodoxies of the writing gurus? Is it acceptable to admit that, although they espouse the process approach to the teaching of writing, they have reservations about some of its ramifications and have adapted the tenets to fit their own style and intuitive educational beliefs?

If there are more teachers who feel as Bill does at the end of his piece— optimistic, bolstered by the progress his failures have achieved—then we all should feel a surge of encouragement, a renewal of faith in what we've been trying to do and what we hope will happen in writing classes this year. And, just maybe, we'll be able to discuss some of this struggle with colleagues and administration, finding relief in the simple sharing of the burden. After all, it's what just reading about this "madness" has done for me—spelled relief! Thank you, Bill. We may teach different grade levels, different ages, and in different settings, but we face the same dilemmas. Now let's talk about them!

Afterword

This book shares stories from language arts teachers across the grades. Stories of struggles come from primary grade teachers, middle school teachers, high school teachers, and even a college professor. These shared stories come from men and women and from novices and veterans.

The struggles and doubts expressed here are similar ones regardless of the grade a person teaches. We can identify with Leslie Brown, a college professor, wringing her hands over the improper use of *its* and *it's;* we can identify as well with Michelle Toch, a first-grade teacher, cringing at the words "I'm ready to publish this!" We think you, the reader, will also be able to identify with many of these struggles. We hope our contributors' reflections and probings will help you reach solutions or new directions with your own struggles.

We invite you to join our forum to share your struggles with us. Tell us your thoughts, feelings, anxieties, and doubts about the writing process as you use it in your classroom. But also share with us your attempted solutions and new discoveries. We agree with Ruth Charney, who says in *Teaching Children to Care: Management in the Responsive Classroom* (Greenwich, MA: Northeast Foundation for Children, 1992. 258), " . . . the single most important factor in the preservation of a good teacher is the courage to admit failure, rather than to deny it in order to feel like a 'good teacher.'" There is no better way to improve our teaching than by communicating honestly with each other. If you choose to share with us, please send your thoughts to:

Barnes, Morgan, Weinhold, Editors
Writing Process Revisited
c/o National Council of Teachers of English
1111 W. Kenyon Road
Urbana, Illinois 61801-1096

Please share this invitation with your colleagues. We want to offer practical strategies and insights to teachers for coping with the realities they face as they use the process approach regularly. We hope that future teachers will be the resistant voice leading to probing, searching, and articulating about teaching writing.

Index

Editors

Donna Barnes has a varied background which includes teaching grades 2 and 5, grades 7 and 8 social studies, as well as a multi-age grades 4, 5, and 6 in North Berwick, Maine. She has been a lecturer for the University of Southern Maine in Language Arts Methods and the Teaching of Writing. Besides book reviews, Donna's poem "Why Can't I Write?" appeared in *Language Arts* (April 1991), and she was a presenter at the Canadian Council of Teachers of English Annual Conference.

Katherine Morgan teaches English at Oyster River High School in Durham, New Hampshire. In addition to her teaching responsibilities, which include Writing Workshop and Advanced Writing, she chairs the Senior Project Committee, a pilot program encouraging interdisciplinary work by seniors. Her writing credits include a children's story in *Cricket* magazine (Nov. 1988); a teacher resource book for limited English speaking students, *Survival Vocabulary Stories: Learning Words in Context* (J. Weston Walch, 1990); and a collection of her great-grandmother and great- great-grandmother's letters, *My Ever Dear Daughter, My Own Dear Mother* (U of Iowa P, 1996).

Karen Weinhold has spent more than twenty-five years in English classrooms, teaching grade 5 through graduate school, including a year with preservice teachers as the teacher-in-residence in the Education Department at the University of New Hampshire. Nancie Atwell chose Karen's piece, "Empowering Students through Reading and Writing Process," to conclude *Workshop I*. In 1989, Karen presented at NCTE's Annual Convention in Baltimore, and she has conducted several local, state, and university workshops in reading and writing. Karen presently is a member of the seven/eight team in North Hampton, New Hampshire.

Contributors

Tony Beaumier is a sixth-grade language arts teacher at the York Middle School in York, Maine. He helped create writing programs for both his school and the American School of Guatemala. Tony has previously published "A Shakespeare Festival for the Middle Grades" in *English Journal* (April 1993), and is currently working on a book, *Celebrating Shakespeare in the Middle Grades*. He has also presented workshops on his Shakespearean festival for middle grades.

Kate Belavitch has taught self-contained second-grade and sixth-, seventh-, and eighth-grade grammar, writing, and computers in Manhattan. She is a graduate of the master's program in reading and writing at the University of New Hampshire. Presently she is working as an adult literacy tutor and raising two preschoolers. She and her family live in New Hampshire.

Bill Boerst has been a teacher of English since the early sixties, covering grades 7 through 12, and ranging from New York and Philadelphia to Liberia, West Africa. With Tom Romano he was a teacher and writing coach in Writing Process Seminar at ERIC 2—Chautauqua-Cattaraugus BOCES, as well as a founding member of Chautauqua Area Writers. Bill has presented at several local and state conferences, and has published extensively, including essays in *English Journal, Language Arts,* and *Ideas Plus, Book Two.*

Leslie A. Brown is currently an instructor of composition at the University of New Hampshire. She has fifteen years of experience teaching writing, in all genres and at all levels. She worked twelve years as freelance writer of feature articles, profiles, and reviews, and six years as lifestyles columnist for *Portsmouth Magazine. Learning* (Nov./Dec. 1993) carried her article about illustrating along with writing process.

Robert K. Griffith has presented at numerous state, university, national, and international workshops and conferences, including the National Middle School Conference in 1985 and NCTE's Spring Conference in 1986, as well as the Canadian "Springboards '91." He has published articles in the International Reading Association's *Journal of Reading* and been an adjunct faculty member for the University of Southern Maine in methods courses in teaching writing and language arts in the elementary school. He co-developed and taught a multi-age program for grades 4–6 and a literature-based reading program at the middle school level. Bob is currently an elementary curriculum and instructional specialist in Newburyport, Massachusetts.

Franki Sibberson has presented numerous workshops at both local and state levels. She was the recipient of the Martha Holden Jennings Grant for picture books in the classroom, and in 1997 was named Ohio Outstanding English Language Arts Educator by the Ohio Council of Teachers of English Language Arts. She has taught graduate workshops at Ashland University, and she is the past chairperson and a present committee member for the Dublin Literary Conference in Dublin, Ohio. In the spring of 1995 she conducted a workshop entitled "Students and Teachers Create Their Own Portfolios." Franki has taught grades 1, 4, and 3-4 multi-age, and she presently teaches first grade.

Michelle Toch teaches first graders in Carlisle, Massachusetts, how to use Lucy Calkins's idea of writing notebooks. At the University of New Hampshire, Michelle studied with writer/educator Donald Graves, and his influence can be found in her work with her first graders.